高等学校
GAODENG XUEXIAO JIANZHULEI JIAOCAI

FIDIC条款
解析与案例

舒　畅■主编

FIDIC TIAOKUAN
JIEXI YU ANLI

重庆大学出版社

内容提要

　　本书通过详细讲解 FIDIC 1999 版红皮书施工合同理论条款,使学生全面掌握合同的实践应用及注意事项。逐条讲解是为了让学生学习记忆,熟悉对每一个小条款的运用方式,是掌握合同管理知识和进行工程管理的最佳实践应用。

　　本书在条款分析前有合同系列介绍,目的是在学习合同条款之前,先了解相关必要的知识和背景。条款分析后,还附有总结性概括,包括工程师角色在条款中的定义,索赔条款的总结,反索赔条款的总结,承包商责任和权力的对应条款和内容,合同定义的专业术语的列表,几个重要事件序列,以及小知识点的补充。

　　本书可作为工程管理和土木工程等专业本科、研究生教材使用,也可作为相关专业从业人员自学或培训使用。

图书在版编目(CIP)数据

FIDIC 条款解析与案例/舒畅主编.—重庆:重庆
大学出版社,2015.5(2021.7 重印)
高等学校建筑类教材
ISBN 978-7-5624-8762-3

Ⅰ.①F… Ⅱ.①舒… Ⅲ.①建筑工程—经济合同—
案例—中国—高等学校—教材 Ⅳ.①D923.65②TU723.1

中国版本图书馆 CIP 数据核字(2014)第 306595 号

FIDIC 条款解析与案例
主 编 舒 畅
策划编辑:林青山
责任编辑:桂晓澜 版式设计:桂晓澜
责任校对:邹 忌 责任印制:赵 晟
*
重庆大学出版社出版发行
出版人:饶帮华
社址:重庆市沙坪坝区大学城西路 21 号
邮编:401331
电话:(023)88617190 88617185(中小学)
传真:(023)88617186 88617166
网址:http://www.cqup.com.cn
邮箱:fxk@cqup.com.cn(营销中心)
全国新华书店经销
POD:重庆新生代彩印技术有限公司
*
开本:787mm×1092mm 1/16 印张:11.75 字数:271千
2015 年 5 月第 1 版 2021 年 7 月第 2 次印刷
ISBN 978-7-5624-8762-3 定价:38.00 元

前言

　　本书是为了适应云南省工程管理建设需要,培养具有工程的基础理论与专业知识,具有较强的工程实践能力的应用型高层次人才,以及适应国家的双语课程建设的需要,强化工程教育国际化意识而编写的。FIDIC 在国内外都有大量的研究和学术专著,但是适应本科教学的教材很少。希望此书为本科、研究生,初级或中级及以上专业人才,在工程管理的核心课程合同管理学习方面提供一个学习的范本。

　　本书的出版得到了云南省省级双语示范课程的课题基金的支持。云南省计划在 2012 年至 2015 年期间,每年立项建设 10 门双语教学示范课程。本课程的教学理念在于"双语化,精品化,经典代表,树立典范"。工程教育观念国际化就是要将云南省高等工程人才培养的改革和发展置于东盟和世界经济发展的大背景之中,从国际化的视野对工程人才培养的总体素质进行考查。FIDIC 合同条款是将最新的国外管理理念带进国内市场的最好的课程范例,也是对学生进行国际化培养方案实施的最重要的课程基础之一。

　　FIDIC 合同条款解析是典型的外资合同管理类课程,需要外资合同条款理论和工程管理实践课的背景。FIDIC 合同被称为土木工程合同的"圣经"、国际工程建筑业的通行惯例,是建筑业公认的工程施工、合同管理、项目管理和索赔的"最佳实践"。FIDIC 合同涵盖的合同事项极其完备,囊括了工程实施过程中可能出现的所有情形,内容全面,条款周密,措辞精确,脉络清晰,逻辑性强,在国际工程界备受推崇,是各种工程合同范本,是企业参与各种工程合同谈判、条款制定与修改最具参考价值的样板和指南,也是项目管理的必备工具。

　　掌握 FIDIC 合同条款,是每一个项目管理与合同管理者的必修课。对于企业参与国内外建设工程的市场竞争,提升项目管理水平,借鉴和吸收有利条款,规避合同风险和损失,切实维护自身权益具有重大意义。

本教材结合了 FIDIC 合同条款知识、工程管理专业知识和英语,对学生的全面发展有很大的帮助,是工程管理核心课程的重要参考教材。教材目的是帮助学生在 FIDIC 合同条款知识的基础上,掌握案例分析运用能力和用英语学习的能力。全书分为三大部分:第一部分是前言介绍(第 1 章至第 5 章),包括了 FIDIC 组织介绍、合同的演变和发展历史、产生的背景和前提、合同的特点、合同的语言特色、合同系列介绍;第二部分(第 6 章)是 FIDIC 红皮书的条款释义,大量的讨论问题,是作者在教学中总结出来的,针对法律、合同的理解和应用,能力要求很高。这种方法为学生所欢迎,可以帮助他们更深入地了解知识。为了适应国内的文化和知识背景,大量的案例都是选自于国内的。本章都是选用小的案例,针对条款单独进行解释,目的是帮助学生理解条款的运用;第三部分是附加知识部分(附录 1 到附录 6),是对第二部分知识的总结和小知识点的补充。

双语教材的建设,要避免成为英语专业式的语言教材,而应为教学目标服务,并使枯燥的学习过程成为多元化的思维、逻辑的建设和方法的学习过程。本教材除了结构上划分为三大部分以外,知识上又分为语言目标、知识目标、思维目标和文化目标四个层面。

(1)语言目标:双语教学使学生逐步掌握各专业的术语以及独特的语言结构与表达方式。例如,FIDIC 合同条款本身的结构就安排了前面 2～3 节课全部为合同术语的讲解,是个很好的典范。FIDIC 合同的语言没有太深奥或生僻的单词,但是句子冗长,结构复杂,未经专业训练过的学生阅读有困难,所以要经常拿典型句子放在大屏幕上进行解构分析;但是长句的目的是使表达的意思严谨,这是英语语言的一种特殊语言结构,也是合同语言的魅力,其他课程很难学到。这是 FIDIC 合同条款很适合作双语课的一个原因,应该帮助学生掌握这种语言结构。另外,还要能听懂该专业的外语授课,读懂该专业的外文教学资料,能使用外语就该专业的问题进行口头(课堂讨论)交流与书面(小论文)交流。

(2)知识目标:双语教学的知识目标应高于语言目标。专业是实施双语教学最直接、最有效的载体,获取专业知识是双语教学最为重要的目标。例如,原版全英文教材应该成为学生的主要教材,但是为了避免有阅读困难的学生产生学习障碍,应该再配备对应的中文版条款,还有相关的著作和文献阅读作为辅导材料,目的是让学生学会在实际项目和谈判中运用这些条款。

(3)思维目标:设立双语课的一个主要目标就是因为西方的思维跟东方的不一样,中国的思维侧重于描述和记录,而西方思维侧重于思辨和逻辑。作为理工科的学生,优秀的逻辑思维能力是非常重要的。FIDIC 合同条款中充满了这种逻辑的艺术,层层递推,严密推理,彼此互为证明。例如,在指定分包商一节中,先介绍了指定分包商的指派方式,与一般分包商的区别之一就在于指定方不一样。而后,又提出合同另一方是否有权拒绝这种指派,这样就引出了本门课初始时介绍的 FIDIC 的宗旨,在被证明后,条款又提出这样的另一方观点,原指派方是否有权否定,引出合同对于双方权利抗衡和平衡的巧妙设置,最后补充了相应的补救条款,圆满解决了这一问题。这种细微逻辑的训练,是管理中,尤其是合同管理的重要教学方法。

(4)文化目标:这种文化目标在法律和经济类的双语课中会尤其突出。例如,中介公司服务制度就会涉及中介服务对象的唯一性和排他性。如果想让学生深入了解这种制度的起源,就必须了解西方的文化背景。所以,双语课往往会涉及对西方文化的介绍和中西文化的对比。

本书由昆明理工大学舒畅老师完成,在编写过程中,大量的专家、同行提出过宝贵的意见,云南省双语示范课课题组、校方、学院和系教研组提供了大力支持。编写过程也参考了大量的文献资料,并促成了教学案例库的建设,对此表示莫大的感谢。

由于作者经验有限,书中难免有不足和有待改善的地方,也希望读者多多提出宝贵的意见。

编 者
2015 年 3 月

Contents

Chapter 1　FIDIC introduction

I　Introduction of FIDIC history

FIDIC is indeed a short form of French name "Fédération Internationale des Ingénieurs-Conseils".

FIDIC is founded in 1913. At the inception stage, there are only three members associations from the European countries including France and Belgium.

In 1949, the British Civil Engineering Association joined and hosted the FIDIC seminar in London, which was described by historians as the birth of the contemporary FIDIC. In 1959, the USA, South Africa, Australia and Canada all came in, thus did the FIDIC break the limit of regional boundaries and became a real international organization. Its headquarter is located in Geneva, Switzerland.

In 1996, China also joined and became its member. Today, its members and associations came from 97 countries, spreading all over the world, representing more than 1 million of professionals and most of the private practice consulting engineers in the world.

II　FIDIC Objectives

(1) Be the recognised international authority on issues relating to consulting engineering best practice.

(2) Actively promote high standards of ethics and integrity among all stakeholders involved in the development of infrastructure worldwide.

(3) Maintain and enhance FIDIC's representation of the consulting engineering industry worldwide.

(4) Enhance the image of consulting engineering.

(5) Promote and assist the worldwide development of viable consulting engineering industries.

(6) Promote and enhance the leading position of FIDIC's Forms of Contract.

(7) Improve and develop FIDIC's training and publishing activities.

(8) To promote and encourage the development of young professionals in the consulting engineering industry.

III Types of Members

(1) Member Association

A national association which is the largest association of firms providing technology-based intellectual consulting services for the built and natural environment in a country.

(2) Affiliate Member

Any association, organisation, firm or groups of firms which is based in a country having or not having a Member Association, and which supports the objectives of the Federation. This membership category is aimed at commercial organizations which aim to maintain a close contact with FIDIC and to support the federation's activities.

(3) Associate Member

Any individual, organisation, association, firm or groups of firms which is based in a country not having a Member Association, and which has a major part of its activity in the engineering consulting industry. This membership category is aimed at organizations that aim to become a FIDIC national Member Association.

IV FIDIC publications

FIDIC, in the furtherance of its goals, publishes international standard forms of contracts for works and for clients, consultants, sub-consultants, joint ventures and representatives, together with related materials such as standard pre-qualification forms.

FIDIC also publishes business practice documents such as policy statements, position papers, guidelines, training manuals and training resource kits in the areas of management systems (quality management, risk management, business integrity management, environment management, sustainability) and business processes (consultant selection, quality based selection, tendering, procurement, insurance, liability, technology transfer, capacity building).

V FIDIC Vision

Enabling the development of a sustainable world as the recognised global voice for the consulting engineering industry.

VI FIDIC Mission

To work closely with our stakeholders to improve the business climate in which we operate and enable our members to contribute to making the world a better place to live in, now and in the future.

VII FIDIC Values

(1) Quality

Quality has been one of FIDIC's fundamental principles ever since its establishment in 1913. Quality is important both in the work undertaken by consulting engineers and in the way that they are selected, and it is very difficult to achieve the first of these if the second is not also implemented.

(2) Integrity

The issue of integrity has always been important but has become even more so of late given the increased legislation in the UK and other countries and the anti-corruption procedures implemented by multinational development banks. FIDIC has responded to the changes by introducing its own updated integrity management system and has also drafted a government procurement integrity management system. It is essential that all integrity systems that are introduced are at least as comprehensive as those drafted by the federation.

(3) Sustainability

Addressing sustainability is, of course, crucial to the survival of mankind. The problem is that in many parts of the world the issue is ill-defined or misunderstood.

Many people are totally confused by the range and variability of sustainability assessment tools available. FIDIC is therefore preparing a publication on this issue and this in turn will, it is hoped, lead to much more consistency between the tools being used (or abused) in different part of the world.

Note

1. FIDIC's fast progress and it's quick expansion of its members in recent years.
2. FIDIC's multiobjective.
3. FIDIC's three types of members.

Coursework

1. Thesis about 200 words, under the title of "How do you value integrity in your study or work"?
2. How will vision and mission of the organization affect your valuation and choice?

Chapter 2　FIDIC contract evolvement

In 1945, the Institution of Civil Engineer, with the joint efforts of the Federation of civil engineering contractor, unified various civil engineering contract forms which were adopted by different countries before the World War II and promulgated a standard form which was widely recognized afterwards.

This standard form package is named as the General Conditions of Contract and Forms of Tender, Agreement and bond for use in connection with works of civil engineering Construction, and abbreviated as ICE Form.

In January of 1950, after the agreement of ACE (in London) who joined recently, ICE form was promulgated again after some amendment. It's reprinted in the march of 1951(3rd edition), January of 1955(4th edition), 1969(with some supplement) , June of 1973 (5th edition) and 1991 after repeated modifications.

Many professional associations imitated the ICE form and after some adjustifications, published their own contract conditions adapted to their national or regional legislation system. ACE associated with the British architecture export group to work on contract files that could be used elsewhere other than the U. K. , as approved by ICE and in urgent need of the international construction industry. This contract file is called the Overseas (Civil) Conditions of Contract with the short name of ACE form and was published in August of 1956. ACE form varies slightly with ICE form as to formation and main text content, and was constituted by standard tendering letter, appendix to tendering latter, and contract agreement sample. In order to be distinguished from ICE, its cover was printed in blue color. The ACE format is the first international standard conditions of contract for works of civil engineering construction, and it's divided into two parts, the first part includes 68 clauses, called the general condition, the second part is the particular conditions of contract, including the explanation to the first part and some new terms for selection.

Short after that, FIDIC worked with FIEC and published the construction contract conditions for the civil engineering in August of 1957 (1st edition) (CONS), often called FIDIC conditions, which is based on the formation of ACE. This FIDIC condition also consists of two parts.

After the recognition and approval of the FAWPC (International Federation of Asian and Western Pacific Contractor's Associations, Philippine, Rizal) in July of 1969, the 2nd edition was republished. The supplementary part of the 2nd edition which is called dredging and filling engineering particular conditions, becomes the 3rd part of the contract conditions later on. In 1973, it's reprinted after the recognition and approval of the AGCA (Associated General Contractors of America, Washington) and FIIC (Inter-American Federation for the Construction Industry, Panama).

There had been a big controversy about the 5th edition of the ICE form published in June of 1973, yielding a chance for further amendment on FIDIC conditions. The 5th edition deviated from the civil engineering conventions embodied in the 4th edition in some important aspects, and was criticized for being ambiguous in language and structure. While it enlightened the editors of the FIDIC conditions and thus contributed to the publication of the 3rd edition in July of 1977. [1]

Although not publicly acknowledged, the CONS dealt properly with the potential conflicts caused by different legislative systems. Many projects conducted world widely proved the success of its 2nd edition and 3rd edition, especially the later, with the evidence of the escalated economic growth in the Middle East and Far East countries in the 70s and 80s of the 21th century. The third edition was translated into German and Spanish. While when coming into the late 80s, arbitration cases multiplied and the 3rd edition started to gain public criticism. [2]

Thus the 3rd edition was critically examined by some lawyers sentence by sentence who are good at big term explanation, and the 4th edition was published in September of 1987. FIDIC conditions initially were drafted for international projects while later on were found out to be adapted to domestic projects as well, thus the word of "International" was removed from the 4th edition.

The second part of particular conditions of the 4th edition was expanded and published as a sole volume, and its clause number corresponds to the general parts and they together constitute the contract conditions specifying the rights and obligation of each party.

In 1988, after some editorial amendments aiming to clarify the real intention rather than altering meaning of the clauses, the CONS were republished.

Of the 1992's reprint, further amendment concerned only with punctuation and alteration of characters like "and", "or".

In November of 1996, FIDIC published the "1992 Fourth Edition Revised Reprint supplement to Contract Conditions for civil engineering construction in 1987", providing convenience for readers in three controversial aspects: dispute resolution, payment, and prevention of delay of issuing payment certificate.

The above publications have been recognized and approved by AGCA (Associated General Contractors of America, Washington), FIIC (Inter-American Federation for the Construction Industry, Panama) and IFAWPCA(International Federation of Asian and Western Pacific Contractor's Associations, Philippine, Rizal) and recommended as standard contract conditions to the International Association of Dredging Companies, international organizations like the World Bank, so on.

中文参考

[1] 1973 年 6 月出版的 ICE 合同条件第 5 版引起了很大争议,为进一步修改 FIDIC 条件提供了契机。ICE 合同条件第 5 版在一些重大方面偏离了其第 4 版所遵循的土木工程传统惯例。有人批评其编写风格、语言,认为思路不清晰。但它为 FIDIC 条款的编写者提供了修改思

路。于是，由 FIDIC 和欧洲国际建筑联合会（FIEC）联合编写 Federation Internationale Europeenne de la Construction（巴黎）于1977年7月出版了第3版。

[2] 到了20世纪80年代后期，导致仲裁的争议数目逐渐多起来，进而对红皮书第3版的批评也表面化了。有些律师精于词语解释，对红皮书的每一条、每一款都像过筛子似的细细地挑剔了一番。

Chapter 3   Advantages of FIDIC contracts

I   Background of FIDIC contracts

As a case has proved in 1999 in China, Three Georges Project Development Corporation sent bidding invitation to 6 qualified companies from different countries like the USA, France and Britain, with people possessing different levels of management and different languages, thus a standardized contract form recognized world widely is wanted.

In the majority of the cases, the contracting parties will react favorably to such a standardized form of contract, which should lessen the likelihood of unsatisfactory performance, increased costs and disputes. If the Contract is to be based on standard conditions of contract, tenders should not need to make financial provision for unfamiliar contract conditions. The widespread use of standard conditions also facilitates the training of personnel in contract management, reducing the need for them having to work with ever-changing contract conditions.

II   Distinguished advantages of FIDIC contract

(1) Clear conception with good logic, fair risk division between contractor and employer without ambiguous expressions.

(2) Specify the responsibilities and obligations of employer and contractor, and engineer respectively in case of too many claims during the implementation of contract.

(3) Since FIDIC contracts originated from ICE contract, to a great extent it's in resemble with the standard contract form in countries or regions where ICE is preferred. And this makes a wide adaptability of the FIDIC contract.

i. e. World Bank is the biggest investment and finance institute of civil engineering projects worldwide. And it clearly state that FIDIC contract is preferred in projects which World Band get involved in.

III   Highlights for the FIDIC contract conditions

(1) FIDIC contract conditions are drafted with reference to the British domestic contracts.

(2) the concept of FIDIC contract is rooted in British Common Law system.

(3) the wording is based on the principle of British law.

(4) the concept of FIDIC conditions of contract is established on the base by appointing a mutually trusted engineer as to project design and construction supervision.

(5) compensation concept is established on the basis of temporary B. Q. for final measurement and payment.

(6) division of rights of obligations is about risk sharing.

IV Book structure

Book consists of 3 parts：

(1) General Condition (一般条款), the part which is intended to be incorporated into each contract and remins as the main target of our course. The conditions of contract comprise the "General Conditions" and "Particular Conditions", which includes amendments and additions to such General Conditions.

(2) Guidance for the Preparation of the Particular Conditions (特殊条款编写指南), referred as "GPPC", which commences by proposing suitable wording to incorporate the appropriate General Conditions into a Contract, and which concludes with annexed example forms of securities.

(3) "the sample forms" including Forms of Letter of Tender, Contract Agreement and Dispute Adjudication Agreement, etc.

Regroup the 20 clauses in to 4 parts：

Part I : specification of respective role of Employer, Engineer and Contractor

Part II : is to clarify the obligations and liabilities

Part III : about terms in emergency cases

Part IV : covering risk issues

Note

①List out the advantages and highlights of FIDIC contract respectively.

②Conceive the basic structure of the book and describe it in your own words.

③Good contracts distinct by its risk devision, how do FIDIC contracts vary from the domestic contracts at this point?

Chapter 4　The characteristics of FIDIC contract language

(1) Interestingly, a census used to be made by the University of Reading about the language characteristics of the "Red Book" and the data collected from 38 countries showed that 71% of the interviewees credited it with the advantage of "easily to understand" followed by another contradicting comment of "incomprehensible".

(2) When reading the contract conditions, you may go through a lot of formal phrases like "notwithstanding" and technical terms like "force majeure". Because FIDIC contract originates from ICE, thus bearing the distinct features of British English and law language. Be that as it may, British English and law have always retained as some of the best ways to study English, and FIDIC contract conditions for university students and readers with similar background to learn international contract traditions.

For example: Notwithstanding any other provision of this Clause, if any event or circumstance outside the control of the Parties (including, but not limited to, Force Majeure) arises which makes it impossible or unlawful for either or both Parties to fulfil its or their contractual obligations or which, under the law governing the Contract, entitles the Parties to be released from further performance of the Contract, then upon notice by either Party to the other Party of such event or circumstance.

(3) Long sentence structure, which probably turns out to be the barrier for most of foreign language readers, especially Chinese readers with their reading. As shown by the selected sentence from the text "Notwithstanding any other provision of this clause, if any event or circumstances outside the control of the parties (including, but not limited to, Force Majeure) arises which makes it possible or unlawful...", the average length of the sentence is 17 words.

For example: Within 42 days after the Contractor became aware (or should have become aware) of the event or circumstance giving rise to the claim, or within such other period as may be proposed by the Contractor and approved by the Engineer, the Contractor shall send to the Engineer a fully detailed claim which includes full supporting particulars of the basis of the claim and of the extension of time and/or additional payment claimed. If the event or circumstance giving rise to the claim has a continuing effect. (20.1)

(4) Aiming to provide high quality contract form ever since its birth, FIDIC has shared no efforts in refining its language in pursuit of accuracy and authentic wording in case of discrepancy.

(5) You may notice that some words and expressions are identified by the use of Capital Initial

Letters. Therefore, the General Conditions, the Particular Conditions and the standardized forms should all use capital initial letters for words and expressions which are intended to have defined meanings.

For example, "Base Day" means the date 28 days prior to the latest date for submission of the Tender, "Day" means a calendar day and "year" means 365 days and some defined words like Contract, Employer, Engineer and so on.

"Engineer" means the person appointed by the Employer to act as the Engineer for the purposes of the Contract and named in the Appendix to Tender, or other person appointed from time to time by the Employer and noted to the Contractor under Sub-Clause 3.4 [Replacement of the Engineer].

"Contractor's Equipment" means all apparatus, machinery, vehicles and the remedying of any defects. However, Contractor Equipment excludes Temporary Works, Employer's Equipment (if any), Plant, Materials and any other things intended to form or forming part of the Pavement work.

"Plant" means the apparatus, machinery and vehicles intended to form or forming part of the Permanent Works.

Note

FIDIC 合同几本书的共同语言特点是:①语篇模式相同或相似;②条块分隔,层次分明;③标题导阅,一目了然;④附录随后,展示详情;⑤定义条款,界定重点;⑥内容完整,无一遗漏。

Chapter 5　FIDIC contract series

The rainbow series you heard of refer to the old conditions of FIDIC contracts. In 1999, FIDIC published the first editions of four new standard forms of contracts.

I　The most popular three books

The first three books were initially published as Test Edition in 1998, and the many reactions to them were renewed before the First Edition were published in 1999.

(1) For Construction-abbreviated as "CONS", which are recommended for building engineering works designed by the Employer by its representatives, the Engineer. Under the usual arrangement for this type of contract, the Contractor the works in accordance with a design provided by the Employer. However, the works may include some elements of Contractor-design civil mechanical, electrical or construction works.

The Old CONS

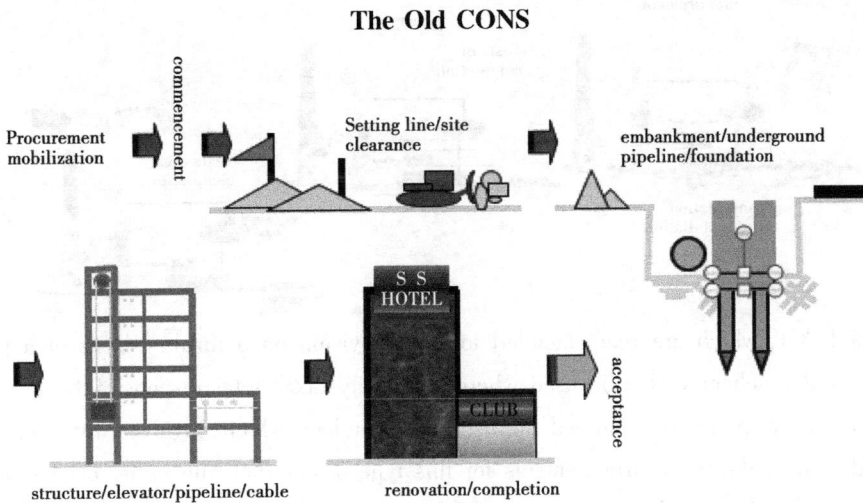

The New CONS

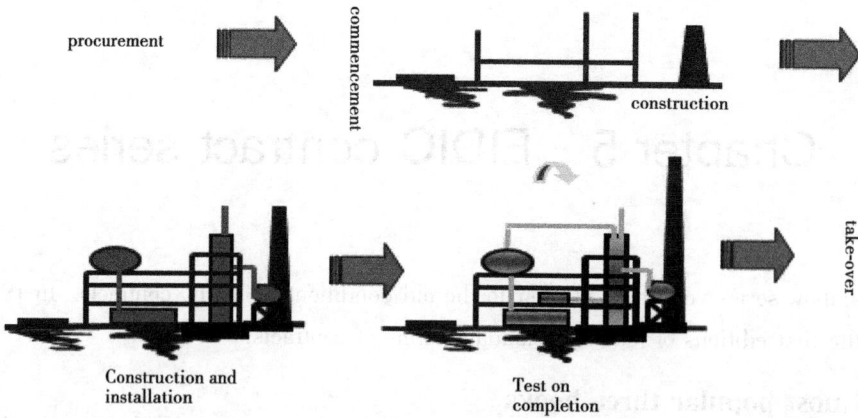

(2) For P&DB, which are recommended for the provision of electrical or mechanical plant, and for the design and execution of building or engineering works. Under the usual arrangements for this type of contract, the Contractor design and provides in accordance with the Employer's requirements, plant, or other works, which may include any combination of civil, mechanical, electrical or construction works.

New P&DB

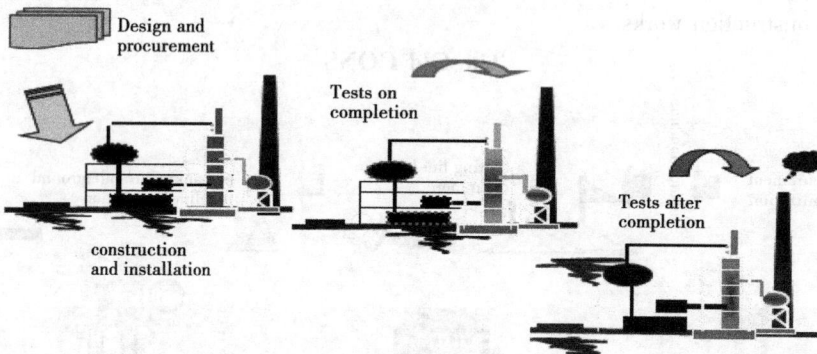

(3) For EPCT, which are recommended for the provision on a turnkey basis of a process or power plant, and which may also be used where one entity takes total responsibility for the design and execution of a privately financial infrastructure project which involves little on no work underground. Under the usual arrangements for this type of contract, the entity carries our all the Engineering, Procurement and Construction (EPC), providing a fully-equipped facility, ready for operation at the turn of the key.

(4) For Short Form of Contract, which is recommended for relatively simple or repetitive work, or for work of short duration or of small capital value.

II Selection of Book

(1) If the price for the contract is relatively small (say under US $500 000) or the construction time is short (say less than 6 months), or the work involved is relatively simple or repetitive 9 a good

New EPCT

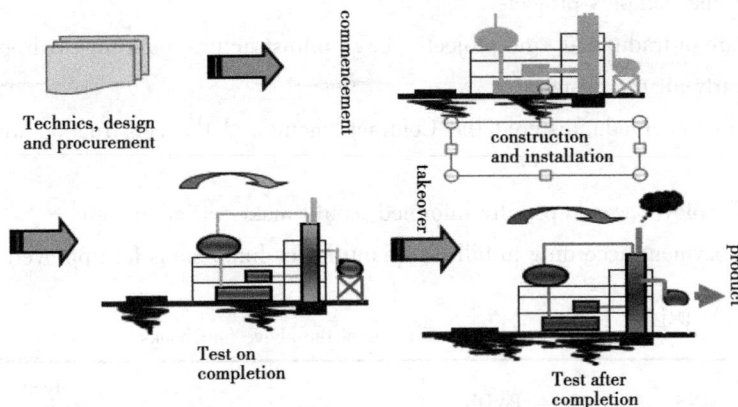

example might be dredging work (疏浚工程), then the Short Form of Contract will be considered, irrespective of whether the design is provided by the Employer or the Contractor, and of whether the project involves construction, electrical, mechanical, or other engineering work.

(2) If in traditional project, like electrical and mechanical works, including erection on site, the Contractor did majority of the design, so that the plant met the outline or performance specification prepared by the Employer. The Engineer (or Employer's representative) administered the Contract, monitored the construction work and certified payment, and payment was paid on lump sum basis, then choose P&DB.

(3) If it's a Privately Financed Project of the Building-Operate-Transfer (BOT) or similar type, and the Concessionaire (特许权所有人) probably requires to have a contract with the construction Contractor, i. e. an EPC (Engineering Procurement Construct) Contract, where the Contractor takes total responsibility for the design and construction.

If it is a Process Plant or a Power Plant where the Employer wishes the Contractor to take total responsibility for the design and construction, and hand it over ready to operate "at the turn of key", without an "Engineer" being involved.

If it's an infrastructure project (i. e. road, rail work, bridge, water or sewage treatment plant, transmission line, even dam or hydropower plant) where the Employer wishes to implement the project on a Fixed-Price Turnkey Basis, which is synonymous to conditions of:

①the Employer wishes the Contractor to take responsibility for the design and construction, without an "Engineer" being involved.

②the Employer wishes to higher degree of certainty that the agreed contrat price and time will not be exceeded.

③the Employer does not wish to be involved in the day-to-day project of the work, provided the end result meets the performance criteria he has specified.

④the Employer is willing to pay more for the construction of his project in return for the Contract bearing the extra risks associated with enhanced certainty of final price and time.

If it's a Building Project, where the preceding requirements are also what the Employer wishes here, then choose EPCT.

（4）If only the following requirements have been met.

①For large and complex projects.

②Projects are of traditional kind projects（e. g. infrastructure, building, hydropower, etc. ）, the Employer did nearly all the design.

③and the Engineer administered the Contract, monitored the construction work and certified payment.

④and the Employer was kept fully informed, could make variations, etc.

⑤and with payment according to bills of quantities or lump sums for approved work done, then choose CONS.

Table structure difference of the above four books

Code	CONS	P&DB	Silvery book	Green book
1	General provisions（14）	√	√	1. General provisions（6）
2	The Employer（5）	√	√	2. The Employer（4）
3	The engineer（5）	√	Employer's administrat or（5）	3. employer's representative（2）
4	The contractor（24）	√	√	4. The contractor（4）
5	The nominated subcontractor（4）	design（8）	design（8）	5. contractor's design（2）
6	Staff and labor（11）	√	√	6. employer's liabilities（1）
7	Equipment, materials and workmanship（8）	√	√	
8	Commencement, delays and Suspension.（12）	√	√	
9	Test on completion（4）	√	√	7. completion time（4）
10	Employer's take-over（4）	√	√	8. take-over（2）
11	Defects liabilities（11）	√	√	9. remedy defects（2）
12	Measurement and valuation（4）	Tests after completion（4）	Tests after completion（4）	
13	Variation and adjustment（8）	√	√	10. Variation and adjustment（5）
14	The contract price（15）	√	√	11. The contract price（8）
15	Termination by employer（5）	√	√	12. breach of contract（4）

continued

Code	CONS	P&DB	Silvery book	Green book
16	Suspension and termination by contractor (4)	√	√	
17	Risk and responsibilities (6)	√	√	13. Risk and responsibilities (2)
18	insurance(4)	√	√	14. insurance(3)
19	Force mejeure(7)	√	√	
20	Claims, disputes and arbitration(8)	√	√	15. disputes resultion(3)

Of the Federation Internationale des Ingenieurs-Conseils (FIDIC) standard form contracts, the Red Book (build only), Silver Book (design and build/EPC (engineering, procurement and construction) turnkey), Yellow Book (design and build/electrical and mechanical) and Green Book (small value, short form contracts) as mentioned above are most broadly understood.

III   The other colors of FIDIC

Following these four principal standard forms, FIDIC produced another four contracts: the White Book (consultancy services); Blue Book (dredging and reclamation works); Gold Book (design, build and operate projects); and Pink Book (the Multilateral Development Bank edition). These more specific standard forms are less common and generally less well understood than the earlier, established forms. The aim of this book is to give a brief introduction and some general ideas about these different colors.

White Book

The Model Services Agreement (fourth edition 2006) or "White Book" can cover general consultancy services including feasibility study as well as design and construction administration and project management. It is suitable where proposals for such services are invited on either an international or domestic basis.

While the White Book addresses the typical issues in a consultancy agreement, it is generally weighed more in favor of the consultant and contains issues which can expose an unwary employer to unnecessary risk.

Blue Book

The Form of Contract for Dredging and Reclamation Works (first edition 2006) or "Blue Book" is similar to the FIDIC Short Form of Contract (the Green Book) and for this reason it is sometimes called the "Blue-Green Book".

The most obvious difference between the two is the Blue Book's inclusion of provisions relating to dredging and reclamation work and ancillary construction. The particular nature of dredging work means the Blue Book separates dredging from other works and removes any obligation on the contractor to remedy any dredging work defects after completion, as stated in the taking-over certificate.

Gold Book

The FIDIC Conditions of Contract for Design, Build and Operate (DBO) Projects (first edition 2008) or "Gold Book" was produced in response to the growing need for a document to combine design-build obligations with a long-term concession arrangement. Previously, employers amended existing FIDIC forms, commonly the Yellow Book, adding maintenance and operation provisions. This created inconsistent market precedents, prolonged negotiations and increased expenditure.

The Gold Book's approach is to award a single contract to a single contracting authority, such as a consortium or joint venture, so as to optimize the co-ordination of innovation, quality and performance. This single-contract approach was intended to incentivize contractors to focus on the whole-life costs of the facility-the rationale being that if the contractor is responsible for long-term operation it is in his interest to design and build a quality plant with low operation and maintenance costs.

The Gold Book, therefore, combines design and construction with long-term operation and maintenance.

Pink Book

The FIDIC MDB (Multilateral Development Bank) Harmonised Edition (2005) or "Pink Book" was published in response to the regular amending of the Fidic General Conditions, by the world's banking community.

The amendments made were often standard and repeated leading to inefficiencies at the procurement stage. Different multilateral development banks (MDBs) used varying amendments creating uncertainties for the documents' users. The Pink Book simplifies the use of the Fidic contract for MDBs, their borrowers and others involved with project procurement, such as consulting engineers, contractors and contract lawyers.

Based on the Red Book (1999 edition), the Pink Book is only applicable when the project is MDB-financed and the contract is one for building and engineering works designed by the employer. The Pink Book was prepared and agreed by the heads of procurement of various notable MDBs and will likely be the common form going forward.

Chapter 6　Contract provision interpretaion and cases

1　General Provisions

1.1　Definition

※ **Discussion**：Why shall these phrases and terms be defined prior to the beginning of contract conditions?

On one hand, contracts identified as legal documents are to confine the rights and obligations of both parties, abiding by the principle of accuracy and strictness. On the other hand, civil engineering projects usually go through complex procedure, which have to be administrated through the instrument of contract. It's highly laudable thing for all the people to work together towards a common goal, while problems of coordination may arise in different situations, especially when interest of different parties are concerned, not to mention under such circumstances as complex as international projects.

For example, Contractor is entitled to claim for "Cost" under certain circumstances as specified in the contract, and lacking of definition will cause great difficulties to reach common understanding on its calculation method.

1.1.1　The Contract

1.1.1.1　Contract

The "Contract" hereto is the sum-up of all contract documents which means the Contract Agreement(合同协议书), the Letter of Acceptance(中标函), the Letter of Tender(投标函), these Conditions(本合同条件), the Specification(规范), the Drawings(图纸), the Schedules(资料表), and the further documents (if any) which are listed in the Contract Agreement or in the Letter of Acceptance.

Different from the domestically-used contracts, FIDIC requires all contract documents complied to be a "contract package", including the Letter of Acceptance and Letter of Tender.

Sub-clause of "Contract" lists the documents which together comprise the Contract in the same sequence as the order specified in Sub-clause 1.5 of Priority of Documents. Any letter of Acceptance or Contract Agreement will typically contain a list of documents which comprise the Contract, and any such priority over Sub-clause "Contract".

※ **Discussion**：How to determine whether a contract file can be incorporated into a contract package?

Subject to its "legal effectiveness"（法律效力）

A stamped file can't be regarded as effective contract file before delivery achieved. Legal proofs are needed on completion of tasks like fax record（传真记录）, sign on receipt certificate（签收凭证）, courier receipt（快递收据）, etc.

1.1.1.2　Contract Agreement

※ **Discussion**：Is Contract Agreement necessary to be included in Contract files?

Even if the applicable law does not necessitate a Contract Agreement, the later if often considered advisable, in order to record what constitutes the Contract under CONS.（不一定,但是通常建议有。）

※ **Sample form**

Contract Agreement

THIS AGREEMENT made the ＿＿＿＿ day of ＿＿＿＿ 20 ＿＿＿＿ between ＿＿＿＿ of ＿＿＿＿（hereinafter called "the Employer"）of the one part and ＿＿＿＿ of ＿＿＿＿（hereinafter called "the Contractor"）of the other part.

WHEREAS the Employer is desirous that certain Works should be executed by the Contractor, viz., and has accepted a Bid by the Contractor for the execution and completion of such Works and the remedying of any defects therein.

NOW THIS AGREEMENT WITNESSETH as follows：

1. In this Agreement, words and expressions shall have the same meanings as are respectively assigned to them in the Conditions of Contract hereinafter referred to.

2. The following documents shall be deemed to form and be read and construed as part of this Agreement, and the priority of the documents shall be as follows：

（a）the Letter of Acceptance；

（b）the said Bid and Appendix to Bid；

（c）the Conditions of Contract（Part II）；

（d）the Conditions of Contract（Part I）；

（e）the Specifications；

（f）the Drawings；

（g）the Priced Bill of Quantities；

（h）and other documents, as listed in the Appendix to Bid.

3. In consideration of the payments to be made by the Employer to the Contractor as hereinafter mentioned, *the Contractor hereby covenants with the Employer to execute and complete the Works and remedy any defects therein in conformity in all respects with the provisions of the Contract.*

4. The Employer hereby covenants to pay the Contractor in consideration of the execution and completion of the Works and the remedying of defects therein the Contract Price or such other sum as may become payable under the provisions of the Contract at the times and in the manner prescribed by the Contract.

IN WITNESS where of the parties hereto have caused this Agreement to be executed the day and year first before written.

The Common Seal of _____ was hereunto affixed in the presence of: _____ or _____ Signed, sealed, and delivered by the said _____

in the presence of: _____

1.1.1.3   Letter of Acceptance

Letter of Acceptance is the document which would typically have brought the Contract into effect. Under CONS, the Contract typically becomes legal biding when the Contractor receives the letter of Acceptance, as stated in CONS 1. 6: The parties shall enter into a Contract Agreement within 28 days after the Contractor received the letter of Acceptance, unless they agree otherwise.

During the process of tendering, 4 ~ 5 times of tendering clarifications or more will be executed and correspondingly, many letters addressed as "letter of acceptance" will be issued.

※ **Highlight**: this letter of an acceptance is the acceptance to that corresponding letter of tender rather than any others. [1]

"We accept the offer contained in your Letter of Tender dated _____ to (design), execute and complete the above-named Works and remedy any defects therein, for the Accepted Contract Amount of _____ Unless and until a formal Agreement is prepared and executed..."

※ **Discussion**: the letter of acceptance verse notice of the Employer to the Contractor "site is ready". [2]

Letter of Acceptance can be defined as formal acceptance in reply to the Letter of Tender from Employer to Contractor and comes into effect only when bearing signature. More than which, it also includes the negotiations on issues like the clarification and confirmation to the ambiguous part and correction of mistakes, which are attached as memoranda with signatures of both parties.

However, CONS allows for the possibility that there may be no such Letter of Acceptance. For example, the Parties may sing a Contract Agreement which brings the Contract into effect, but without a "A Letter of Acceptance", the signing date of which will be the reference for the Letter of Acceptance, and the Accepted Contract Amount must be defined in the Contract Agreement. [3]

1.1.1.4   Letter of Tender

In the "Letter of Tender", the tenderer offers to enter into a legally-binding contract. [4]

It's called a "Letter of Tender", so as to differentiate it from the overall package of documents called the "Tender". "Tender" comprises two parts, one is the core called the "Letter of Tender", the other includes all kind of schedules to be filled in by tenderer and tender securities.

"Letter of Tender" is not a lengthy document, but is important under CONS because when the Letter of Tender is accepted in the letter of Acceptance, these two letters will typically create a legally-bidding Contract. [5]

※ **Sample form**

Form of Letter of Bid

Name of Contract: *

To: * [insert name of Employer]

Gentlemen:

1. *In accordance with the Conditions of Contract, Specification, Drawings, and Bill of Quantities and Addenda Nos. [insert Addenda Nos.] for the execution of the above – named Works we, the undersigned, offer to construct and install such Works and remedy any defects therein in conformity with the Conditions of Contract, Specifications, Drawings, Bill of Quantities, and Addenda for the sum of [insert amounts in numbers and words] [as specified in the Appendix to Bid or such other sums as may be ascertained in accordance with the conditions].*

2. *We acknowledge that the Appendix forms part of our Bid.*

3. *We undertake, if our Bid is accepted, to commence the Works as soon as is reasonably possible after the receipt of the Engineer's notice to commence, and to complete the whole of the Works comprised in the Contract within the time stated in the Appendix to Bid.*

4. *We agree to abide by this Bid until the date specified in ITB Clause 16 [insert date], and it shall remain binding upon us and may be accepted at any time before that date.*

5. *Unless and until a formal Agreement is prepared and executed this Bid, together with your written acceptance thereof, shall constitute a binding Contract between us.*

6. *We understand that you are not bound to accept the lowest or any bid you may receive.*

7. *We certify/confirm that we comply with the eligibility requirements as per ITB Clause 3 of the bidding documents.*

Dated this _____ day of _____ 20 _____

Signature _____ in the capacity of _____

duly authorized to sign bids for and on behalf of _____

[in block capitals or typed]

Address: _____ Witness: _____ Address: _____ Occupation _____

Form of Invitation for Bids
[letterhead paper of the Employer]

To: [name of Contractor] _____ [date]

[address]

Reference: [Insert IBRD Loan No. or IDA Credit No.]

[Contract Name, and Identification No. _____ / _____]

Dear Sirs:

We hereby inform you that you are prequalified for bidding for the above cited contract. A list of prequalified and conditionally prequalified Applicants is attached to this invitation.

On the basis of information submitted in your application, you would [not] (insert if appropriate) appear eligible for application of the domestic bidder price preference in bid evaluation. Eligibility is subject to confirmation at bid evaluation.

We now invite you and other prequalified Applicants to submit sealed bids for the execution and completion of the cited contract.

You may obtain further information from, and inspect and acquire the bidding documents at, our offices at [mailing address, street address, and cable/telex/facsimile numbers].

A complete set of bidding documents may be purchased by you at the above office, on or after [time and date] and upon payment of a nonrefundable fee of [insert amount and currency].

All bids must be accompanied by a security in the form and amount specified in the bidding documents, and must be delivered to [address and exact location] at or before [time and date]. Bids will be opened immediately thereafter in the presence of bidders' representatives who choose to attend.

Please confirm receipt of this letter immediately in writing by cable, fax, or telex. If you do not intend to bid, we would appreciate being so notified also in writing at your earliest opportunity.

> *Yours truly,*
> *Authorized signature*
> *Name and title*
> *Employer*

1.1.1.5   Specification

Specification is to describe the Employer's tendering projects in technical language, and propose technical standards and procedures during execution. Contractor's engineers of cost need to study the Specification when calculate the tendering price, so do Contractor's procurement personnel before procurement of materials as well as project managers and technicians in charge of construction.

Employer's management staff shall know more about specifications so as to ensure their ends to be met.

※ **Discussion**: How to apply this sub-clause into Chinese projects?

When applying FIDIC into domestic projects, domestic compulsory "legal regulation" shall be differentiated from the specification. [6]

For example, if the Works include work on an existing facility, the Contractor might be required to phase the work in a particular way in order to minimize the disruption to the continuing operation of the facility.

The specification may include the matters referred to some or all of the following sub-clause (GPPC's page 3).

1.8 Requirements for Contractor's Documents

1.13 Permissions being obtained by the Employer

2.1 Phased possession of foundations, structures, plant or means of access

4.1 Contractor's designs

4.6 Other contractors (and others) on the Site

4.7 Setting-out points, lines and levels of reference

4.14 Third parties

4.18 Environmental constraints

4.19 Electricity, water, gas and other services available on the Site

4.20 Employer's Equipment and free-issue material

5.1 Nominated Subcontractors

6.6 Facilities for Personnel

7.2 Samples

7.4 Testing during manufacture and/or construction

9.1 Tests on Completion

13.5 Provisional Sums

1.1.1.6 Drawings

Specification and Drawings are the documents where the Employer specifies all matters not covered by the Conditions of Contract, including the location of the Site, the scope of the works, the details listed on GPPC's page 3, details of how each part of the Works is required to be constructed, and (possibly) a program of work.

Drawings mentioned hereafter are those specified in contract, and amendment or supplement provided by Employer in execution of works.

FIDIC clearly states that for Employer, whether to provide basic design drawings or working drawings depends on the requirements in other specifications of Contract.

※ **Discussion**: According to CONS, does Employer provide all drawings needed in construction? If no, then where does Employer specify the scopes and types of drawings?

Refer to 4.1 Contractor's General Obligations. FIDIC defines that the drawings shall be provided by the Employer, it's defined so in order to prevent the collaboration between the Contractor and the design institute, the act of which may hugely increase the investment input and deprive the Employer of chances to make profits. [7]

1.1.1.7 Schedule

Schedules include documents often presented by means of tables and sheets, which are issued with tender documents, to be completed by tenderer, including Bill of Quantities, Data Schedule, Unit Price Analysis Schedule and Daywork Schedule. Bear this in mind that all "documents" titled with schedule namely belong to contract documents.

BILL OF QUANTITIES

The objectives of the Bill of Quantities are:

（1）to provide sufficient information on the quantities of Works to be performed to enable bids to be prepared efficiently and accurately;

（2）when a contract has been entered into, to provide a priced Bill of Quantities for use in the periodic valuation of Works executed.

In order to attain these objectives, Works should be itemized in the Bill of Quantities in sufficient detail to distinguish between the different classes of Works, or between Works of the same nature carried out in different locations or in other circumstances which may give rise to different considerations of cost. Consistent with these requirements, the layout and content of the Bill of Quantities should be as simple and brief as possible.

BILL OF QUANTITIES

The Bill of Quantities should be divided generally into the following sections:

（1）Preamble;

（2）Work Items（grouped into parts）;

（3）Daywork Schedul

（4）Summary.

BILL OF QUANTITIES

Sample

Bill No. 1: General Items

Item no.	Description	Unit	Quantity	Rate	Amount
101	Performance Guarantee	sum	item		
102	Insurance of the Works	sum	item		
103	Allow for maintenance of Works for 12 months after completion	month	12		
203	—etc.—				
Total for Bill No. 1					
（Carried forward to Grand Summary, p.　　）					

Bill No. 2: Earthworks

Item no.	Description	Unit	Quantity	Rate	Amount
201	Excavate topsoil to maximum depth 25cm and stockpile for reuse, maximum haul distance 1 km	m^3	95,000		
202	Excavate topsoil to maximum depth 25 ~ 50cm, and dispose	m^3	15,000		
203	—etc.—				
Total for Bill No. 2					
（Carried forward to Grand Summary, p.　　）					

Grand Summary

General Summary	Page	Amount
Bill No. 1 General Items		
Bill No. 2 Earthworks		
—etc. —		
Total for Daywork (Provisional Sum)		
Subtotal of Bills	(A)	
Special Provisional Sum included in subtotal of bills	(B)	5,400,000
Total of Bills Less Specified Provisional Sums (A-B)	(C)	
Add Provisional Sum for Contingency Allowance	(D)	[sum]
Bid Price (A + D) (Carried forward to Form of Bid)	(E)	

1.1.1.8　Tender

A complete set of "Tender" documents may also contain auxiliary documents such as the early schedules, subcontract plan, equipment list, construction guide, key staff list, Contractor's on-site organization diagram, construction site arrangement, labor source, etc.

Being the core of "Tender", "Letter of Tender" is usually prepared and annexed to "Tender" by Employer, completed and used as formal offer by Contractor.

1.1.1.9　Appendix to Tender

"Appendix to Tender" lists out the main items of the contract conditions as well as the reference number.

Although the Employer may complete all items, he might prefer to require tenderers to complete various items. Normally, experienced Contractor can read what underlies the data the financial condition of Employer and possibility of cooperation. "Appendix to Tender" is an important document demands Contractor's consideration and study.

"Appendix to Tender" requires signature on each page. The requirements on these details reflect on the FIDIC spirit of rigorousness. [8]

They're comprised in the "schedule", and some specific works allow the possibilities without Daywork Schedule, which circumstances are specified with "if any".

1.1.1.10　Bill of Quantities

They're comprised in the "schedule", and some specific works allow the possibilities without Daywork Schedule, which circumstances are specified with "if any".

1.1.2　Parties and Persons

1.1.2.1　Party

The Parties to the Contract are defined to be the Employer and the Contractor only. All other persons or units whoever might get involved in the Works are regarded as either the Employer's personnel or the Contractor's personnel. The Engineer is also sort of special personnel of the Employer.

1.1.2.2   Employer

Is it right to call a manager or a boss of real estate company "Employer"? No, he is one of the Employer Personnel. [9]

1.1.2.3   Contractor[10]

1.1.2.4   Engineer

The Engineer acts in a special way, "person" herein as it's so named but refers to a consulting company in majority of the cases. "Person" can be either natural person or legal person, and includes corporations. In western countries, the Engineer can be either a corporation or a person. Under the current circumstances in China, the "Engineer" refers to the superintendence company and the authorized representative from the company is called chief engineer. The Engineer is the real administrator of the Works and the most important role of all.

1.1.2.5   Contractor's Representative

The Contractor's Representative is often included in the key staff list, which is annexed to the Letter of Tender and submitted to the Employer.

In China, this address is often replaced by "project manager", who is assigned by the Contractor.

1.1.2.6   Employer's Personnel

The Employer's personnel would include those involved in inspection and testing, but would typically not include all the Employer's other contractors on the Site The Engineer is clearly defined to be the Employer's personnel, hereby alter the qualities of "independence" and "impartiality" which are embodied in the definition and description of the previous editions.

1.1.2.7   Contractor's Personnel

The Contractor's Personnel include all subcontractors' employees on the Site, and others assisting the Contractor's execution of the Works.

1.1.2.8   Subcontractor

Part from these types, there's another subcontractor—Nominated Subcontractor. (Refer to 4.5)

1.1.2.9   DAB

(1) The Panel persons are jointly appointed by the Parties,

(2) A panel of one or three persons, to whom a dispute between the Parties is initially referred for Adjudication, which concluded with the Board's decision in accordance with the Contract. Generally, the decision will be binding, unless and until it is revised in an amicable settlement,

arbitration or litigation.

1.1.2.10 FIDIC[11]

1.1.3 Dates, Tests, Periods and Completion

1.1.3.1 Base Date

Base Date is a new term and mainly used for price adjustment.

1.1.3.2 Commencement Date

The Commencement Date is the reference date for the Time of Completion and the Contractor's completion obligation under Clause 8.

Administration of the Contract may be facilitated by redefining the Base Date and Commencement Date as particular calendar dates, in the Contract Agreement.

1.1.3.3 Time for Completion

(1)Time means a period of time rather than a fixed point of time.

(2)It's calculated from the Commencement of Date.

(3)It's the time specified until the completion of the Works.

(4)It's specified in the Appendix to Tender.

(5)It's related to either the whole Works or a Section.

(6)If the Contractor acquires any extension, the Time for Completion will be extended for a similar period of time.

1.1.3.4 Tests on Completion

(1)It's conducted before the whole Works or a Section is taken over by the Employer. Time needed for tests on completion shall be included in the time for completion.

(2)Its content and procedures are illustrated in the specifications.

(3)Additional tests agreed by both parties or required by the Employer shall be instructed as a Variation.

(4)Tests shall be carries out under Clause 9.

1.1.3.5 Taking-over Certificate

Usually, Contractors wish to receive the certificate as soon as possible, after which the responsibility of custody of the Works will be passed to the Employer, and Retention Money can also be refund. Hereafter, the Works comes to the stage of defect notification period. [12]

The general sequence of events (接收顺序) is as follows:

—the Contractor completes the Section or Works;

—the Contractor carries out tests defined as the Tests on Completion;

—the Employer takes over the Section or Works, and;

—the Tests after Completion are carried out, if any.

1.1.3.6 Tests after Completion

(1)It has to be clearly specified in Contract otherwise it can be ignored.

（2）If any, they shall be carried out according to the specifications in the Particular Conditions.

（3）It shall be carries out as soon as the Work or a Section is completed.

Tests after Completion are rarely spoken of under CONS.

1.1.3.7 Defects Notification Period

（1）The expression recognizes the most significant aspect of this period, the notifying if defects by the Engineer to the Contractor. [13]

（2）"The works" here means the Work or a Section which has been taken over by the employer and taking-over certificate has been issued to the Contractor. [14]

（3）Length of the "Period" is specified in the Appendix to Tender. [15]

（4）It can be extended under 11.3 extension of Defects Notification Period.

（5）The period commences on the completion of the Works or a Section, and the completion date is subject to the date in the taking-over Certificate. [16]

1.1.3.8 Performance Certificate

① It's to certify that the Contractor has fulfilled all his contract obligations. The receipt of this certificate to Contractor means the Works is completed. [17]

② To help the Contractor get the Performance Security back. [18]

1.1.4 Money and Payments

1.1.4.1 Accepted Contract Amount

The Accepted Contract Amount is indeed the tender price offered by the Contractor. Another possibility is if there's something wrong with the tender price calculation which is discovered during the period of tender valuation, the Employer can modify the price. And the tender price will become effective with the confirmation from the Contractor.

1.1.4.2 Contract Price

We can learn from the definition that rather than a "static" procedure, the final price is the settlement price calculated upon the completion of the Works which has taken into account the accumulated adjustments of price during the execution of the Works.

※ **Discussion**: The difference between "Accepted Contract Amount" and "Contract Price"?

More than often, the amount stated in the Letter of Acceptance and hereby accepted by the Employer is the modified price. This amount is rather than the effective contract price which can only be determined after the Works is completed but just the contract price by name. [19]

Rather than a "static" procedure, the final price is the settlement price calculated upon the completion of the Works which has taken into account the accumulated adjustments of price during the execution of the Works. [20]

1.1.4.4 Final Payment Certificate

The Final Payment Certificate is one of the payment certificates, which is issued under the Clause 14.13. The issue of this certificate means the due payment to the Contractor will be paid soon.

1.1.4.5　Final Statement

In fact, the final statement draft is an application submitted to the Engineer by the Contractor, inquiring the Engineer to issue the Final Payment Certificate. After the approval from the Engineer, the draft effectively turns to a Final Statement. Under such premise that the Engineer has issued to the Employer the Final Payment Certificate based on the Final Statement will the Contractor receive the final payment.

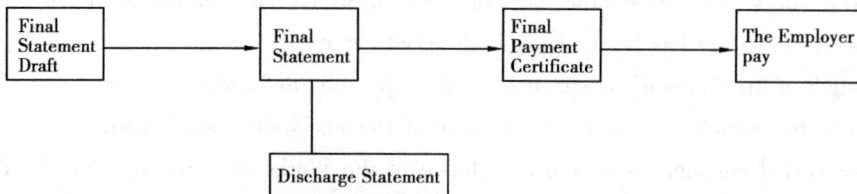

1.1.4.6　Foreign Currency

In order to differentiate it from local currency, so is it named foreign currency.

1.1.4.7　Interim Payment Certificate

There're basically two sorts of payment certificates, one is the Interim Payment Certificate, the other is the Final Payment Certificate.

1.1.4.8　Local Currency

The currency of the country where the project locates.

1.1.4.9　Payment Certificate

Including the interim payment certificate and the final payment certificate.

1.1.4.10　Provisional Sum

The sum is often shown in fixed number or sometimes in the form of the percentage of the tendering price, and it's usually embodied in the Bill of Quantities.

※ **Discussion**：Does the provisional price constitute part of the Contract Price?

After the study of the definition of "Contract Price", we can be sure that the provisional sum does account for part of the Contract Price.

The provisional sum is prepared for：

（1）Contingency costs may occur in the execution of the Works. i. e. costs related to the Daywork. [21]

（2）In tendering, for certain part of the Works, research hasn't gone to such an extent that detailed information can be provided by the Employer for tenderers to offer the fixed unit price. [22]

（3）In tendering, the Employer hasn't decided yet whether certain work shall be included in the work schedule of the Contract. [23]

1.1.4.11　Retention Money

Actually it's a sort of cash deposit(现金保证金), which shares the same virtues with the

Performance Security, aiming to provide the guarantee that Contractors will fulfill his obligations in execution of the Works, otherwise the Employer will be entitled to draw the money and complete the work, which was supposed to be done by the Contractor. [24] to remedy the defects during the Defects Notifying Period. Meanwhile, if the account is overdrawn for interim payment, the Employer can compensate it with that from the Retention Money. [25]

The Retention Money together with the Performance Security will be legally binding to the Contractor. [26]

Up to 50% of retention money shall be returned to the Contractor when the Works is taken over. [27]

1.1.4.12   Statement

Statement includes the monthly statement, statement upon the completion of the Works and the final statement.

1.1.5   Works and Goods

This clause mainly concerns about the "tangible" input (可见的投入) such as materials, plant, machinery, etc. and output of "products and semi-products" (成品和半成品) such as the completed Works or a Section.

1.1.5.1   Contractor's Equipment[28]

※ **Discussion**: Does the Contractor's equipment include the equipment used or owned by the subcontractor?

Yes, it does.

1.1.5.2   Goods

Goods almost covers all things needed in construction.

1.1.5.3   Materials

The materials here exclude those used in the "Temporary Works".

"Supply-only-materials" mean the Contractor provides only supply according to the Contract, excluding any "processing" after procurement which will change the materials into part of the Permanent Works.

1.1.5.4   Permanent Works

Permanent Works will be handed over to the Employer after the works has been completed and thus is listed under the glossary of the Employer's belongs. [29]

1.1.5.5   Plant

"Vehicles" usually belongs to the "Contractor's Equipment" and "vehicles" here means those which form part of the permanent works.

For example, in a petrol pipe project, the measurement station of which needs water-supply during the operation, a scheme is devised to transport water from places far away by lorry with water tank. This lorry with water tanks provided by the Contractor is regarded as sort of Plant and forms part of the

Permanent Works.

1.1.5.6 Section

※ **Discussion**：What's the meaning of section in these conditions?

section of the Works or unit works? Refer to note 4.

1.1.5.7 Temporary Works

The temporary works include：houses and offices on construction site, construction pavement, temporary bridge, cofferdam in hydro-projects, labour sandstone system, concrete mixture, processing workshops, experiment rooms, facilities for security and lightening, etc. [30]

Generally, after the completion of the Works, all temporary works need to be dismantled, though some may be preserved for usage during the operation of the Works.

1.1.5.8 Works

Including the temporary works and the permanent works.

1.1.6 Other Definitions

1.1.6.1 Contractor's Documents

※ **Discussion**：Under CONS, the Contractor undertakes the construction referring to the design provided by the Employer, what kind of documents do they have to prepare by himself?

Referring to 4.1, The Contractor's obligations（承包商的义务）. [31]

※ **Discussion**：The contractor has many design documents, and is the Contract demanded to submit all of them to the Employer?

Referring to 1.10.

No, some documents are not defined as "the Contractor's documents".

1.1.6.2 Country

Some "linear" shape projects（线型工程）like pipe or road projects may cross over some countries borderlines.

※ **Discussion**：Will the country in which the Site is located always be the country of the Employer?

Generally speaking, yes, except for BOT or BOO projects with foreign investment. [32]

1.1.6.3 Employer's Equipment

In the Specification, details of the Equipment like type, brands, specification, origin of fuel shall be specified. In the contrary, if such things haven't been mentioned at all, the implication of this is that the Employer won't provide to the Contractor any Equipment. [33]

1.1.6.4 Force Majeure

Referring to Clause 19.

1.1.6.5 Laws

1.1.6.6 Performance Security

Possibilities remain thatthere may be several performances securities or no performance securities at all. It's defined so, giving consideration to some Employer have no requirements on performance securities. [34]

1.1.6.7 Site(现场)

Sites include:

①sites used for the Permanent Works and the Temporary Works;

②sites where the Plant and the Materials are stored and warehouses;

③sites for office and living;

④others so named as "sites" stipulated by the contact. [35]

1.1.6.8 Unforeseeable

If a Contractor wants to demonstrate something is unforeseeable, he/she will have to demonstrate these things beforehand:

①It's possible to foresee it before submission of the tender documents, which means unforeseeable during the preparation of tender. [36]

②He must be an experienced Contractor, which means whatever he does, be it before the award of contract or after that, shall be regarded as behaviors of Contractor with rich experience (i. e. by putting forward questions, undertaking site survey, reading through tender documents, etc). Put it in another word, "failure of foreseeing" is caused by objective reasons but not lacking of experience. [37]

It's reasonably unforeseeable. It's always difficult to get a full appreciation of what "reasonable" means. When encounter such a reasonably unforeseeable matter, the Employer will often attribute this to the Contractor's lacking of experience. And the phrase of "reasonably unforeseeable" often relates to affairs such as natural conditions, extrinsic impediment, contamination, etc. [38]

1.1.6.9 Variation

Referring to Clause 13 "Variations".

中文参考

[1] 中标函是"特定某个投标函"的中标函。

[2] 中标函是否等同于雇主对承包商"你可以进场了"的通知?

[3] 在没有此中标函的情况下,"中标函"一词就指合同协议书,颁发或接收中标函的日期就指双方签订合同协议书的日期。

[4] 投标函是投标人的要约,邀请招标人进入一个有法律效力的合同。

[5] "投标函"不长,但是当它被对应的中标函接收后就形成了一个有法律效力的合同。

[6] 国内使用 FIDIC 合同需要区别我国强制性"法定规范"和合同规范。

[7] 按 FIDIC 的定义,图纸由雇主提供,这是为了斩断承包商与设计院之间的关联关系。国内两者串通以变更增加投资来变相牟取私利的情况很严重。

[8] "投标书附录"要求页页签字。FIDIC 合同在这些细节上的要求体现了其严密性。

[9] 某房地产公司老板被称为雇主,对否? 否。他是雇主人员。

[10] 承包商又称为"施工单位""总包"。

［11］国际咨询工程师联合会。

［12］接收证明是指业主在接收工程之后颁发给承包商的一个证书,以证明工程按照合同已经实质性竣工。从此,工程进入缺陷通知期。性质:物权移交。

［13］缺陷通知期是指工程师通知承包商修复工程缺陷的期限。

［14］上述的工程是业主已经接收并颁发给承包商接收证书的工程或区段。

［15］缺陷通知期期限从工程竣工日期开始计算,而竣工日期则以接收证书中证明的竣工日期为准。

［16］缺陷通知期期限的长短在投标函附录中写明。

［17］履约证书证明合同已经被正式履行完毕。竣工验收和接收证书等都不能算作工程师对工程的完全认可。只有拿到履约证书,才证明承包商完全履行了合同。

［18］承包商可以凭履约证书拿回进场前提交的履约担保。

［19］合同价格是一个实际价格,而中标合同金额只是一个预测的名义上的价格。

［20］合同价格的计算是一个相对动态的过程,考虑到了工程执行当中所有的累计的调整。

［21］工程实施过程中可能发生业主方负责的应急费、不可预见费等,如计日工涉及的费用。

［22］在招标时,对工程的某些部分,业主方还不可能确定到使投标者能够报出固定单价的深度。

［23］对某些工作,业主方希望以指定分包商的方式来实施。

［24］保留金的目的是保证承包商在工程执行过程中恰当履约,否则业主可以动用保留金去做承包商本应修复的工程缺陷,因此在我国又称为保修金。

［25］同时,如果在期中支付过程透支了工程款,业主还可以从保留金中予以扣除。

［26］保留金与履约保函一起共同构成对承包商的约束。

［27］工程接收完成的时候,承包商可拿回50%的保证金。

［28］在我国被称为"承包商的施工机具"。

［29］永久工程要在工程结束之后移交给雇主,所以它呈列在雇主所有物的目录当中。

［30］临时工程包括:施工营地的住房、办公室、施工便道、人工砂石料系统、混凝土拌和系统、加工车间、实验室以及安全和照明设施等。

［31］承包商对其文件、临时工程,以及永久设备和材料的设计负责,但不对永久工程的设计或规范负责,除非有明确规定。

［32］一般是除了BOT和BOO项目以外。

［33］在规范中对业主提供的设备应有具体规定。如果在规范中没有提及,则意味着业主方不向承包商提供任何施工机具。

［34］本条款的措辞表明有的时候有几个履约保函,有时完全没有。这种定义的原因是因为有些雇主不要求履约保函。

［35］①永久工程和临时工程用地;②永久设备和材料的存放地、仓库等;③办公和生活营地;④合同明文规定的其他作为现场的用地。

［36］不可预见,是指一个有经验的承包商在提交投标书之前不能合理预见:其不可能在提交投标书之前预见该事件,即在承包商编制投标书的过程中无法预见。

〔37〕承包商必须是一个有经验的承包商,其行为是有经验的,比如:答疑会上问问题,做现场勘查,仔细研究投标文件。

〔38〕承包商没有预见到该事件是合理的,如自然条件、外部障碍、污染等。

Note

1.我们国家的验收规范:比如,住宅工程实际是最终用户物业公司与业主来接收。现在有一种趋势,雇主会直接安排这种实质接收人参与到接收组里,这意味着承包商要直接面对最终用户。由于与最终用户验收之间有着标准适用上的冲突,就极易出现工程通过工程师验收,雇主却以质量缺陷为理由迟迟不接收的情况。解决办法?

2."缺陷通知期"和"责任期"的区别?

(1)缺陷通知期要比责任期的内容广。比如,雇主使用不当造成的工程缺陷,按缺陷通知期说法,承包商应该来维修,至于费用可以再谈。责任期就不同,至少字面上只有承包商原因造成的缺陷,承包商才有责任来修。

(2)缺陷通知期的提法对雇主很有利。

(3)公平合理。

(4)缺陷通知期比责任期的时效定义要严密一些。

3."缺陷通知期"和"质量保修期"的区别?

国内合同描述缺陷通知期为"质量保修期",这个定义就相对窄多了。

按"质量保修期"定性,国内合同在工程竣工移交雇主的那一刻起,就意味着除质量保修之外的所有合同内容"履约完毕"。

此外,质量责任的定性很不明确,比如,我们国家的质量验收规范有允许偏差项目,规范意义上,这是明文规定允许"缺陷",而不能归结为质量问题。

4.单位工程的英文原词是"section",有人翻译为"单位工程",笔者认为其字面意义是指可分割的一个整体的某个部分,这个"部分"到底是"整体"的哪一块并不确定,所以它不是单位工程,而是"部分工程"。在FIDIC条件下,雇主有权就部分工程进行先验收、先接收、先使用,这与"单位工程"的概念差别很大。例如,一个商住楼项目,雇主要求在主体结构施工到三层时,承包商先行移交底层工程先做商业开业。而此时底层结构有大量的管线设备及建筑通道等未完工程,要将底层以某种"单位工程"的形式交出去似乎不可能。只能把不影响后面施工的能使用的部分先移交给雇主,让雇主以商业开业的要求去配机电及装修等工程。就是这样先移交的工程部分,也可能遗留大量的与将来完工工程的接口问题,也有当前使用的供电供水等问题。这个先移交给雇主的"部分工程"整体情况与"单位工程"应该有所区分。所以"section"翻译成"单位工程"是译者的一个失误。

FIDIC条件下,有"section",也有"part"。两者的区别在于"section"是招标时就明确要求先移交的部分工程,而"part"通常指合同签订后雇主变更要求先移交的部分工程。在合同意义上,两者区分很严格。

Vocabulary

laudable　可嘉的;值得赞美的;值得称许的
Something that is laudable deserves to be praised or admired.

execute　执行;实施;贯彻

If you execute a plan, you carry it out.

procurement　（为军队或其他组织的）采购,购买

Procurement is the act of obtaining something such as supplies for an army or other organization.

legally binding　有法律约束力

This document is legally binding.

nominate　（为工作或职位）提名,推荐

If someone is nominated for a job or position, their name is formally suggested as a candidate for it.

memoranda　（备忘的）记录;非正式商业书信,便函;节略;便笺

unforeseeable　不能预见的;不可干预;不可预见

force majeure　不可抗力

defect　缺点;缺陷;毛病;瑕疵

A defect is a fault or imperfection in a person or thing.

notify　通知;告知

If you notify someone of something, you officially inform them about it.

specification　规格;具体要求

A specification is a requirement which is clearly stated, for example about the necessary features in the design of something.

permanent　永久的;永恒的

Something that is permanent lasts for ever.

appendix　（书末的）附录

An appendix to a book is extra information that is placed after the end of the main text.

personnel　（组织中的）人员,职员

The personnel of an organization are the people who work for it.

1.2　Interpretation

(1) Gender, when these languages are used as contract languages, disputes concerning about "gender" may occur, thus does it specifically indicate one gender include all genders. [1]

(2) it also indicates that different meaning may be expressed when in different form of either singular or plural. i. e. damage, damages. The former means loss, injury, but the latter means money asked from or paid by a person causing loss or injury. [2]

(3) Thus important documents are seldom "electronically made" in prevention of disputes. [3]

1.3　Communications

Six types of formal communications—approvals, certificates, consents, determinations, notices and requests are required to be in writing and allows the party issuing a communication to decide upon the method of transmission, namely by hand, mail, courier or electronic.

The successful delivery of message is critical to the effectiveness of communications.

For instance, Electronic transmission is preferred nowadays among these communications types. But how could the delivery to its recipient be confirmed and reflected to its sender in time?

It's usually done by notifying the sender with fax, on which the signature of the recipient and the fax number and time work well as legal proofs. These issues always relate to time, and many litigation pleas are objected by the courts simply because they're out of the time of legal effectiveness. Resolution of the problem of "time" :

In prevention of time delay, documents needed to be countersigned and include such sentences like "Please make sure to reply within _____days", or to insert a column with items of

    ☐ *reply needed;*

    ☐ *instant reply needed;*

    ☐ *replay within a week needed;*

    ☐ *no need of reply, etc.*

to be ticked and sent back.

※ **Discussion**: an implied claim provision.

Approval, certificate, consents and determinations shall not be unreasonably withheld or delayed". [4]

Assume you were a Contractor, the approval or consent you applied for had been postponed deliberately by the Engineer, so were certificates and determinations withheld, while at the completion of the Works, arbitrator made verdict that the Contractor should be entitled with right of extension. How would you respond in such circumstances?[5]

Suggestion is made to quote this claim provision and claim for losses. Disputes may occur when decide on whether it's "unreasonably withheld or delayed". In such case, the Contractor may turn to the applicable contract law for help. For instance, it's stated in the Contract Law in China that for any delay of the execution of the Works caused by the Employer (or the Engineer), the contractor shall be compensated for the loss he has suffered.

1. 4　Law and language

The law governing the Contract must be stated. The law typically will affect the interpretation of these Conditions, such that some provisions may have different consequences in different jurisdictions.

The ruling language only relates to a part of the Contract for which different versions have been written in different languages.

The language for communications should be stated in the Appendix to Tender, if there's no such statement, then the language used to write the contract will be taken as the communication language.

It's common for a contract to be in two language versions, i. e. the middle-east countries regard Arabic as the official language but also use English in their daily lives. And in a Contract, Arabic is usually defined as the ruling language and English is for communication.

1.5 Priority of Documents

Contract Documents-as referred to 1.1.1.1—are a package of documentsincluding the Contract Agreement, the Letter of Acceptance, the Letter of Tender, these Conditions, the Specification, the Drawings, the Schedules, and the further documents (if any) which are listed in the Contract Agreement or in the Letter of Acceptance.

An underground tunnel of a project was invisible from the design drawings. The Engineer didn't discern such a mistake until the coming to the end of the work. The Contractor was obliged to reject the work and redo it by procuring more materials. This also caused two weeks of suspension of work for the construction personnel in charge of underground work. The Contractor claimed for what he had suffered.

Sub-clause 1.5 If an ambiguity or discrepancy is found in the documents, the Engineer shall ① issue any necessary interpretation or clarify the document ambiguity ② issue instruction to the Contractor to follow ③ give certification, if the Engineer accept such facts that the instruction will cause additional payment to the Contractor and the discrepancy is what an experienced Contractor can't reasonable foresee, and instruct the Employer to compensate the Contractor.

The Contractor can only claim for additional payment entitled under this sub-clause and some extension of time but not extra profits that in some other cases may also be entitled to.

The Engineer replied after consideration and took it as acceptable. Since the Contract afforded additional costs by following the Engineer's instruction and the discrepancy was what the Contractor couldn't t reasonably foresee before the events, which resulted in two weeks of suspension of the Works and idleness of the Contractor's equipment and personnel. Thus the Contractor is entitled by sub-clause 1. 5 for additional payment and extension of time.

※ **Discussion**: the necessity of setting the priority of documents.

The interrelationship of the above documents shall be complementary to each other rather than being contradictory to each other. While actually, the compilation of contract documents takes long time and wide participation of a large number of editors, which will unavoidably result in inconsistency or contradiction. In order to resolve these problems, in cases where the same subject matter is covered several times in different parts of the Contract, this Sub-clause provides an order of precedence of the documents.

The priority of the documents are as follows:

1.	Contract Agreement	constituted by both offer and acceptance
2.	Letter of Acceptance	replace the contract agreement when the it's absent
3.	Letter of Tender	need to be confirmed by the Letter of Tender
4.	Particular Conditions	these prevail over the general conditions
5.	General Conditions	

For the documents above, both of the Contractor and the Employer share the same, while for the documents below, they follow the principle that Employer's documents should have priority over the Contractor's documents[6]

6.	Specifications	basic technical data which are the reference used for the compilation of the drawings and the schedules
7.	Drawings	
8.	Schedules	the work starts when all the above documents have been well prepared and noticed to be ready for use

If there's an ambiguity or discrepancy within a particular contract document, Sub-clause 1. 5 and 3. 3 empower the Engineer to issue as clarification or instruction.

For instance, in an oversea construction project, white cement is preferred in the work of mosaic joint pointing in wash rooms as specified in the B. Q. , while it's replaced by Portland cement in the Specifications and the Drawings.

Disputes occurred as to which kind of cement should be used. The Employer voted for white cement, but the Contractor intended to use Portland cement in order to economize the project costs. Also different sets of documents applied for each option. In the last resort, the Engineer proceeded to make decisions, and the principle of the Priority of Documents was quoted and supports went to the Contractor, because the Specifications and the Drawings prevailed over the B. Q. If the Employer insisted on using white cement, the Engineer would instruct variations based on the Clause 13 "Variation and Adjustment" requiring the contractor to make a new offer, taking into account the extra costs. Finally, the Employer compromised the aesthetic standard for the saving of cost, and the use of Portland cement was determined. This enabled a save of at least $100,000 to the Contractor.

1.6 Contract Agreement

The Contract agreement consists of 3 parts: ①all the terminologies to be used in the Contract documents that have been defined in a particular way. ② all the schedules to be used in the Contract documents. ③ clarification of the offers and acceptances from the Parties. i. e. the Contractor promises to carry on the Works in accordance with the Contract, the Employer guarantee that the payment will be paid to the Contractor as stated in the Contract.

Structure analyzed

The Parties shall enter into a Contract Agreement within 28 days after the Contractor receives the Letter of Acceptance, unless they agree otherwise. The Contract Agreement shall be based upon the form annexed to the Particular Conditions. The costs of stamp duties and similar charges (if any) imposed by law in connection with entry into the Contract agreement shall be borne by the Employer.	第一句话:签订合同协议书的时间 第二句话:合同协议书的格式 第三句话:确定印花税和类似费用的承担者

1.7 Assignment

※ **Discussion**: reasons for the 2nd type of assignment?

As we well know, a large-scale project demands huge amount of expenditures at the early stage, often enough, the advance payment of the Employer is insufficient for this amount of expenditure and the Contractor may need to finance the difference by applying for loan from the banks. Generally, banks or financial institutes will require the Contractor to secure their loans with the due payment or those which will become due, and sometimes even to open a new account for the remittance of the due moneys.

1.8 Care and Supply of Documents

If a Party becomes aware of an error or defect of a technical nature in a document which was prepared for use in executing the Works, the Party shall promptly givenotice to the other Party of such error or defect.

※ **Discussion**: If some problems occur to the technical documents of one party, which results in the failure of the execution of part of the Works, is it possible for the party to shirk the responsibility and shift the blames to the other party, with the excuse that they're not notified by the errors or defects?

We can rather regard the notification as one of the operation procedure specified for the purpose of "effective management", advocating the relationship of cooperation and team spirit.

1.9 Delayed Drawings or Instructions

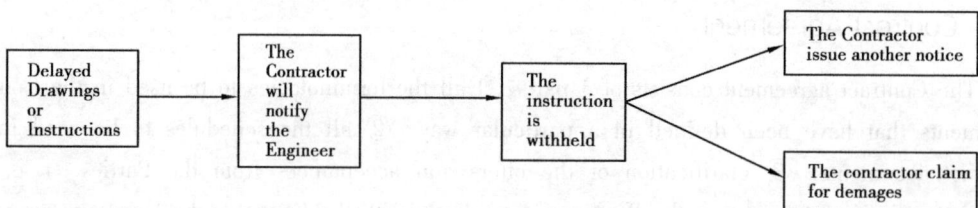

The Contractor should be reminded: ① to take the initiatives (主动) to give notice to the Engineer rather than wait positively (被动). The notice should include details of the drawings or instructions and the reasons why they're needed, with the supporting details of the construction plans and arrangements approved by the Engineer, and the requirements of the Engineer on Site. ②their work should be in compliance with (符合) the contract requirements (合同要求) and make sure not to grant the Engineer chances (不给工程师机会) to find any excuses (理由) and show disapproval (反对) of the claims.

In a road engineering project, the Engineer proposed to regroup passages and culverts for the purpose of road upgrading and relevant drawings are due to the responsibility of the Engineer. Such proposals had delayed the submission of revised drawings comparing with the stipulated time in contract, and the Contractor claimed for compensation. While on the whole, the design variation benefited the Employer by economizing engineering costs.

Sub-clause 1.9, the Contractor shall give a further notice to the Engineer and shall be entitled subject to Sub-Clause 20.1 [Contractor's Claims] to: (a) an extension of time for any such delay, if completion is or will be delayed, under Sub-Clause 8.4 [Extension of Time for Completion], and (b) payment of any such Cost plus reasonable profit, which shall be included in the Contract Price, if the Contractor suffers delay and/or incurs Cost as a result of a failure of the Engineer to issue the notified drawing or instruction within a time which is reasonable and is specified in the notice with supporting details. ②The Contractor has given notice to the Engineer whenever the Works are likely to be delayed or disrupted if any necessary drawing or instruction is not issued to the Contractor within a particular time, which shall be reasonable.

The contract and specifications specify that all the sewers and their correct location, altitude, angles are to be measured and confirmed by the Engineer. There're altogether more than 200 sewers in this engineering projects. As what the Contractor notified, the Engineer should issue all relevant construction drawings with particular details within half month after the commencement of the works, otherwise, the Contractor should be entitled to claim for the incurred costs and the delays he suffered. The Engineer determined that sub-clause 1.9 state it's unreasonable for the Engineer to submit all the drawings about more than 200 sewers within such a short time. Based on the approved progress program, only 20 drawings are required to be issued in half a month and they had already reached to the Contractor. The Contractor's claim was revoked.

1.10 Employer's Use of Contractor's Documents

Contractor's Documents include a variety of design documents including computer software, models, operations and maintenance manuals and other manuals and information of a similar nature (referring to 1.1.6.1).

After sign on the contract, permission will be granted to the Employer for use of the Contractor's documents. The Employer will be entitled to use the Contractor's documents during the working life of the Works and even communicate with the third parties about these documents.

※ **Discussion**：Copyrights

The Contractor shall be deemed（by signing the Contract）to give to the Employer a non-terminable（不可终止的）transferable（可转让的）non-exclusive（非排他性的）royalty-free（免版税）license（许可证）to copy, use and communicate the Contractor's Documents, including making and using modifications of them（可做修改）.

※ **Highlight**：The Employer is entitled（被赋予权力）to use the Contractor's Documents for the Works（为工程）, but he is not entitled to use them for other purpose.

1.11 Contractor's Use of Employer's Documents

The Employer's consent must be given in writing, and is not to be unreasonably withheld or delayed, in accordance with sub-clause 1.3. It may be reasonably for the Employer to withhold consent if the Contractor declined to accept reasonable conditions in respect of secrecy or of restriction on use.

1.12 Confidential Details

In order to protect the Contractor's rights（保护承包商的权利）, and prevent the Engineer from demanding too much（要求太多）, this provision is specified by asking the Engineer to act in accordance with following requirements：

①The request from the Engineer must be reasonable（要求合理）.

②The information can only be used to verify（核实）the Contractor's compliance with（遵守）the Contract.

※ **Discussion**：What kind of information shall be kept as confidential?

As far as civil engineering industry（工程行业）in concerned, they can be unique processes（独特的工艺）which are gained by the construction companies through years of experiences and used to improve the work efficiency and add to competence（提高竞争力）in the industrial circles. Such processes are called "know-how"（技术诀窍）, which is different from patent（专利）and not under the protection of laws. Once published, these processes will no longer be of any value to their companies.

1.14 Joint and Several Liability

There may be pros（赞成的意见）and cons（反对的意见）considering constituting a joint venture（合资企业）, consortium（联合体）or other incorporated grouping（联合团体）.

The united forces may turn out to be a great advantage when their role is complementary to each other, hence making it easier for them to win the contract.

While therein lie also disadvantages that there may be conflicts between the members and difficulties in project management.

中文参考

［1］没有性别的区分，一种性别包含其他所有性别。

〔2〕单数形式的词亦包括复数含义,复数形式的词亦包括单数含义。

〔3〕正式合同文件很少用电子版的,是为了防止纷争发生。

〔4〕六种沟通方式:颁发批准书、证明、同意函、确定、通知和请求。

〔5〕工程师要求承包商赶工,而且承包商也按其要求进行了赶工,为此承包商同时提出了工期索赔,但是当时工程师没有批准延期,最终仲裁员裁定承包商有权延期。如何看待这个问题?承包商如何处理?

〔6〕以上的文件,雇主和承包商共享用一套;以下的文件,雇主和承包商各自有一套。雇主的文件优先于承包商的文件。

Note

此处的承包商文件在中国类似"工程档案",承包商文件版权归承包商。比如雇主出租办公楼,铺面承租者就可能要求业主提供相关工程档案资料来了解铺面的工程情况,以便安排装修等事宜。

Vocabulary

gender　性别

A person's gender is the fact that they are male or female.

singular　单数的;单数形式的

The singular form of a word is the form that is used when referring to one person or thing.

plural　复数的;复数形式的

The plural form of a word is the form that is used when referring to more than one person or thing.

consortium　(若干人或公司组成的)财团,联合企业

A consortium is a group of people or firms who have agreed to co-operate with each other.

complementary　相互补充的;相辅相成的

Complementary things are different from each other but make a good combination.

patent　专利权

A patent is an official right to be the only person or company allowed to make or sell a new product for a certain period of time.

entitled　给予…权利;给予…资格

If you are entitled to something, you have the right to have it or do it.

withhold　拒绝给予;扣留

If you withhold something that someone wants, you do not let them have it.

delay　使延期;使延迟;推迟

If you delay doing something, you do not do it immediately or at the planned or expected time, but you leave it until later.

If there is a delay, something does not happen until later than planned or expected.

terminable　有期限的,可终止的

transferable　可转让的;可转移的

If something is transferable, it can be passed or moved from one person or organization to another and used by them.

non-exclusive　非独家的

shirk the responsibility　逃避,规避(责任、义务);偷懒

If someone does not shirk their responsibility or duty, they do what they have a responsibility to do.

shift the blames to the other party　推卸,推诿,转嫁(责任)

If someone shifts the responsibility or blame for something onto you, they unfairly make you responsible or make people blame you for it, instead of them.

notify　通知;告知

If you notify someone of something, you officially inform them about it.

2　The Employer

In general, the obligations of the Employer specified in Contract include:

(1) To appoint an Engineer to oversee (监督) the daily operation of the Works, who acts impartially(公正) and complies with the criteria of professional ethics.

Under 3.4 if the Employer intends to replace the Engineer, notice is required to be given to the Contractor. And the Employer shall not replace the Engineer without the consent from the Contractor. The degree of the Engineer's independence is one of the risk factors that the Contractor has to take into consideration in tendering. And normally the replacement of the Engineer is not encourage.

(2) To provide all the information needed in the design and the construction to the Contractor, and ensure the authenticity(真实性) of the information.

(3) To hand-over the site to the Contractor

Site is defined in the Specifications or the Drawings. Without the hand over of the site, the contractor won't be able to proceed to work.

(4) Not to interfere in(不要干扰) the construction of the Works

For instance, the Employer entrusts the Engineer to give instructions which are not specified in the Contract and lead to the change (increase or decrease) of the amount of work. This shall be regarded as sort of interference and enable the Contractor to claim for extension or compensation.

(5) To nominate (提名)a Subcontractor

If the subcontractor who is nominated by the Employer has interfered with the construction of the Works, it's the Employer who shall take the responsibility and compensate for the loss.

(6) To make sure that due payment will be paid in time. What tops the list of all the obligations for the Employer is to pay the Contractor, which is also the basic requirement to the Employer in FIDIC. And what accounts is to "be in time".

2.1   Right of Access to the Site

For the Employer, he is deemed to provide the Site and the facilities in time, otherwise the Contractor shall be compensated for the loss he has suffered.

For the Contractor, if he wants to claim for compensation, he must: to give notice in time and make sure that the Employer's failure was not caused by an error or delay by the Contractor.

The Employer is required to make the Site available to the Contractor within a prescribed time. In additional to that, the Employer is also required to give processions of any foundation, structure, plant or means of access, also in the time and manner stated in the Specification.

But the second sentence of the sub-clause states that other parties may also have right of access to, and procession of, the Site.

※ **Highlight**: The Employer is only required to grant the Contractor the "right" of access to the Site, it being that there is a route along which access either is already physically practicable or can be constructed by the Contractor. In other words, the practicable difficulties is getting to and from the Site are to be solved by the Contractor.

2.2   Permits, licenses or Approvals

Sub-clause 2.2 follows the general provision contained in sub-clause 1.13(b)—the Contractor shall give all notices, pay all taxes, duties and fees, and obtain all permits, licenses and approvals, as required by the laws in relation to the execution and completion of the Works and the remedying if any defects. [1]

It's the Contractor who owes the liability to the Employer (承包商对雇主承担责任) for obtaining all permits (许可证), licenses (执照) or approvals (批准). And the Employer is required to provide reasonable assistance, the extent of which depend upon the relationship between the Employer and the Contractor and how the Works goes on. This "reasonable assistance" may, for example, comprise the authentication (公正) of the Contractor's application documentation, but it would not be reasonable for the Contractor to expect the Employer to do anything which the Contractor can do himself.

The Employer has no obligation under sub-clause 2.2 to provide any "reasonable assistance" unless and until (除非并直到) he receives the Contractor's request (要求), which must be in writing in accordance with sub-clause 1.3.

2.3   Employer's Personnel

Requirement of two Cs: "Cooperation" and "Compliance with regulations".

Cooperation: The Employer's personnel (雇主的人员) and contractors (承包商) are required to cooperate with the Contractor's coordination efforts (协调努力), and take actions in respect of safety procedures (安全流程) and environmental protection (环境保护).

Compliance with regulations: i.e. Anyone on site must put on safety helmet, or 50 yuan will be fined, irrespective of being the personnel of the Employer, the Contractor or the third party. Under clause 4, there're also similar requirements imposed on the Contractor. The Corresponding subclauses are 4. 5 Cooperation, Safety and Environment Protection. The restrictive stipulations conform to the standpoint of impartiality of FIDIC. [2]

2. 4　Employer's Financial Arrangements

The Employment is required to provide reasonable evidence of financial arrangements when requested. The "reasonable evidence" means bank certificates and the like. Nowadays, it's frequent for the Employer to withhold the project payments against the Contractor, which often results in the default on the obligation of the Contractor This provision is specified in order to diminish the happening of such cases and perfect the management of obligation fulfillment.

The evidence is required to demonstrate the Employer's ability to pay the Contract Price, which typically would be the estimated final Contract Price at the time of the request but excluding the effect of adjustment which have not yet become available. For example, it would usually be unreasonable to add a contingency to allow for the possibility of a future event resulting in an adjustment.

Tenderers would be entitled to be concerned at such deletion of this Sub-clause, especially if the Employer has been unable to replace it by some other form of assurance (GPPC'S Annex G, for example). The Contractor will be entitled to (after 21 days' notice) to suspend work, or reduce the rate of work, if the Employer fails to submit the evidence requested under Sub-clause 2. 4. Termination provides the ultimate remedy.

2. 5　Employer's Claim

This Sub-clause prescribes the procedure to be followed by the Employer if he considers himself to be entitled to any payment under or in connection with the Contract, or he considers himself to be entitled to an extension of the Defects Notification Period.

In the case of a payment have been claimed, the Engineer may include it as a deduction in Payment Certificates. If the Employer considers himself to be entitled to any payment under or in connection with the Contract, he is thus required to follow the procedures prescribed in this sub-clause, and is not entitled to withhold whilst awaiting the outcome of these procedures.

Sub-clause 2. 5 requires the Employer to adhere to a claims procedure, which is specified with less precision than the procedure imposed on the Contractor (who may be more familiar with preparing claims than many Employers).

Particulars may be given at any time, but excessive delay in their submission may be construed as an indication that the Employer will not be proceeding with the notified claim.

The following sub-clauses provide the supportive evidences for the Employer's claim against the Contractor: refer to Appendix "Counterclaim of the Employer".

中文参考

[1] 见 1. 13(b)遵守法律。

对于法律中要求的与实施、完成工程和修补缺陷有关的各项事宜,应由承包商发出通知、支付税款、关税和费用,并获得所有的许可、许可证和批准;承包商应保障雇主免遭其未做到上述要求的后果的损失。

[2] 比如,进场人员都必须带安全帽,谁没带就罚 50 元,不分雇主或是承包商或是第三方。对应的是要求承包商的 4.6"合作"和 4.8"安全"4.18"环境保护"。这个体现 FIDIC 在对双方要求的公平立场。

Note

雇主开具的支付保函范例格式

合同简要介绍＿＿＿＿＿＿＿＿＿＿＿＿

受益人名称和地址＿＿＿＿＿＿＿＿＿(合同定义为承包商的法人)＿＿＿＿＿＿

我们已经得知＿＿＿＿＿＿(填入合同定义为"雇主"的法人,以下称为"委托人")被要求开具银行保函。

应委托人的要求,我们(填入银行名称)＿＿＿＿＿＿在此不可撤回地承担在我方收到你方书面要求及说明下列情况的书面声明后,向你方＿＿＿＿＿＿受益人/承包商支付总数不超过(填入"保函金额",用文字表示)＿＿＿＿＿＿的一笔或多笔款额。

(a)对于按照合同应该支付的款额,委托人未能在合同规定的应支付此款额的期限期满后 14 天内完全支付,则未付清的款项将由指定的担保人支付。

(b)委托人未支付的数额。

任何支付要求必须附以一份关于委托人未完全支付的款额的【证明收款权利的文件列表】。要求支付的文件必须有你方签名,签名必须经你方银行或知名的公共机构证实。我方必须在此处,于(填入预计的工程缺陷责任期满后 6 个月的日期)或之前,收到你方经证实的要求和声明,在上述日期之后,本保函期满并应返还给我们。

除上文规定外,本保函受＿＿＿＿＿＿的法律的约束,并受国际商会出版的编号为 458 的"即付保函的统一规则"的约束。

日期＿＿＿＿＿＿＿＿＿＿   签名＿＿＿＿＿＿＿＿＿＿

Vocabulary

default   不履行;未支付

If a person, company, or country defaults on something that they have legally agreed to do, such as paying some money or doing a piece of work before a particular time, they fail to do it.

counterclaim   反诉状,索赔

impartial   不偏不倚的;公正的;无偏见的

Someone who is impartial is not directly involved in a particular situation, and is therefore able to give a fair opinion or decision about it.

due to   由于;因为

If an event is due to something, it happens or exists as a direct result of that thing.

ultimate   最后的;最终的

You use ultimate to describe the final result or aim of a long series of events.

access   进入(权);通道;路径

If you have access to a building or other place, you are able or allowed to go into it.

3　The Engineer

The role of the Engineer is described as follows:

①he's employed by the Employer to undertake the administration of the Work;

②he's one of the Employer's personnel, rather than an impartial intermediary;

③he exercises the authorityattributable to the Engineer as specified in or necessarily to be implied from the Contract;

④he exercise a special authority as approved by the Employer.

And, In general, the obligations of the Employer specified in Contract include:

①To appoint an Engineer to oversee the daily operation of the Works, who acts impartially and complies with the criteria of professional ethics.

②To provide all the information needed in the design and the construction to the Contractor, and ensure the authenticity of the information.

③To hand-over the site to the Contractor.

Site is defined in the Specifications or the Drawings. Without the handover of the site, the contractor won't be able to proceed to work.

④Not to interfere in the construction of the Works.

⑤To nominate a Subcontractor.

⑥To make sure that due payment will be paid in time.

For instance, the Employer entrusts the Engineer to give instructions which are not specified in the Contract and lead to the change (increase or decrease) of the amount of work. This shall be regarded as sort of interference and enable the Contractor to claim for extension or compensation.

3.1　Engineer's Duty and Authority

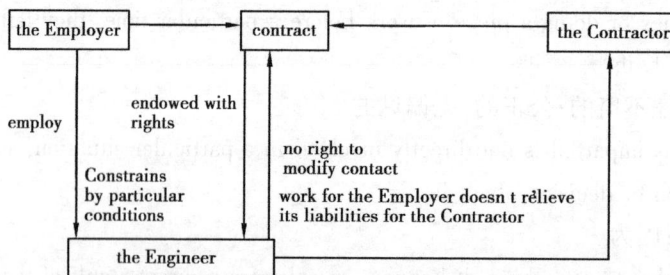

The Engineer should carry out his duties and exercise his authority in professional manner, utilizing the "suitable quality engineers and other professionals".

When examine the tender documents and considering the role of the Engineer, tenderers may take account of such matters as:

——the Engineer's technical competence and reputation particularly in relation to reviewing Contractor's Documents,

——the degree of independence indicated by the status of the appointed Engineer, namely whether he is an independent consulting engineer, and

——the practical consequences of any constraints on the Engineer's authority.

And in the B. Q. , there's an item named "the Engineer's preliminaries", specifying that the Contractor has to provide the Engineer with things like vehicles, fuel, fax machine, telephone, etc. and bear all the relevant costs. All these (excluding those which have been consumed) will be reverted to the Contractor after the accomplishment of the Works.

※ **Discussion**: What's the role of an Engineer?

Make a figurative illustration: if a project is, say, a particular "product", then the Engineer is identified with the supervisor of the manufacture of this "product", and his approval can be taken as a permission to enter into the next working procedure and an acknowledgment of what have already been done. It is to ensure that the manufacture procedure of the "product" will be in compliance with the Contract specifications and industrial conventions. The Contractor has to guarantee the hand-over of a qualified final product to the Employer, the Employer is the purchaser of the product, and the Engineer is employed to ensure the qualification of the product.

The Engineer is in no way under the obligation to the Contactor, but they two may be in frequent contact with each other in work, and probably, the Contractor may think of it the most difficult to cope with the Engineer.

Consultancy work is of high technical value added and consultancy engineer is the talent with expertise of technical management. For example, as quoted from a piece of article published many years ago, the figure shows that the annual salary of an English Engineer is $80,000 which seems incompatible with their duties. From the observation of the writer, all that the Engineer has done throughout the whole project is as simple as signing his name on the working drawings and issuing a confirmation letter to the Contractor, which won't relieve the Contractor from any responsibility he has under the Contract according to sub-paragraph(c).

Ever since the contract has been signed, both of the Employer and the Contractor will be obliged to follow the instruction of the Engineer as far as the instructions are workable. Until and unless they can no longer put up with the contract obligations, the case will be submitted for international arbitration. The Engineer has to explain on his instructions in the arbitration, and all the previous decision may be questioned, examined or modified, which forces the Engineer to make sensible decisions.

In international projects, the consultancy fees account for about 10% of the total project investment, which is inversely proportional to the Contract Price, much higher than that in domestic projects, which is around 1% ~4%.

For example, as described by a piece of article, in a World Bank project, all that the Engineer has

done is as simple as to sign his name on the working drawings and issuing a confirmation letter to the Contractor which won't relieve the Contractor from any responsibility except as otherwise stated in these Condition:

（c）any approval, check, certificate, consent, examination, inspection, instruction,notice, proposal, request, test, or similar act by the Engineer（including absenceof disapproval）shall not relieve the Contractor from any responsibility he hasunder the Contract, including responsibility for errors, omissions, discrepanciesand non-compliances. [1]

3.2 Delegation by the Engineer

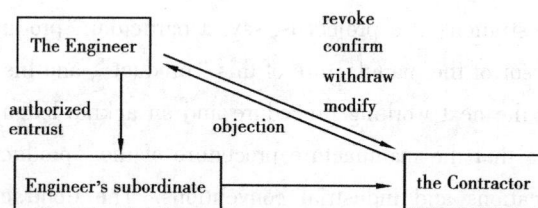

Under CONS, the Engineer is empowered by the Employer to administer the whole Works. In some complex projects, the Engineer may need to delegate the authority to his assistants and let the contract know about to what extent the assistant had been allowed to issue instructions.

The Employer should ensure that there are sufficient assistants and that they comply with the criteria in the second-paragraph of this sub-clause. They're included within the definition of "Employer Personnel". If the assistants have issued instructions beyond the authority they have been delegated to, the Contractor is entitled to reject such kind of instructions, failing which the Contract has to undertake the consequences themselves.

※ **Discussion:** An assistant has finished this examination of the work of the Contractor, and the Contractor has proceeded on to the next working procedure, while later on, the Engineer rejects the work when he arrives at the construction site.

Is the Engineer entitled to act like this?

Yes, because he has right to reject the work which the assistant fails to disapprove. Refer to the sub-paragraph（a）.

（a）any failure to disapprove any work, Plant or Materials shall not constitute approval, and shall therefore not prejudice the right of the Engineer to reject the work, Plant or Materials. [2]

3.3 Instructions of the Engineer

Under CONS, the Contractor executes the Works in accordance with the Engineer's instructions, and with designs which has been carried out by（or on behalf of）the Employer. The Engineer is empowered to issue instructions, and the Contract is generally obliged to comply.

The Contractor is especially concerned whether the instructions issued but by the Engineer are beyond what's specified in the Contract, Theoretically, if the instructions do go beyond the limits, they constitute Variations, and Clause 13 applies. While in practice, the Engineer often instructs the Contractor to do certain work without indicating whether the instruction should be treated as Variation or not.

Under such circumstances, the Contractor should be able to distinguish the Variations from the instructions and raise a protest against the unfair judgment of the Engineer.

It may even be necessary for immediate oral instructions to be given, although they should be avoided wherever possible, in case the Contractor will be exposed to various kinds of risks. So detailed procedures are specified for an instruction which is nor immediately confirmed in writing. The procedure requires prompt confirmation or denial and alleged oral instruction, in order that its validity or invalidity can be established as soon as possible.

3.4 Replacement of the Engineer

Under CONS, the Engineer has a major role in the administration of the Contract, particularly with respect to issuing Variations and Payment Certificate, and reviewing any Contractor's Documents.

※ **Discussion**: If the Employer considers the Engineer is incompetent, does he has the right to replace the Engineer?

Employers understandably consider that there should be no restriction imposed on replacing the Engineer. While tenderers may not want the Employer to be replaced because the replacement of the Engineer often will interrupt the continuity of the operation of the Works, thus cause the Contractor to suffer delay or incur cost.

Sub-clause 3.4 provides a fair and reasonable compromise between the conflicting desires of the Parties.

3.5 Determinations

Under CONS, unless otherwise agreed by both parties, the Engineer shall not delegate the authority to determine any matter in accordance with Sub-clause 3.5.

The function of the Engineer has been changing all along the evolution of the FIDIC edition. In the 3rd edition in 1977, the Engineer is still clearly defined to be "an independent party". When came to 1987, the word of "independent" could be found nowhere and the verse changed to "act impartially". And in the new edition of 99, the provision where the verse "act impartially" is comprised has been cancelled. Instead, in sub-clause 3.5, "to make a fair determination" appears to be the main task of the Engineer. Moreover, another function of the "Engineer" as "an arbitrator" has also been replaced by "DAB", which is a recently defined term in the new edition that comes out in 1999.

(1) the determination comply with the Contract provisions.

(2) the Engineer has taken due regard of all relevant circumstances.

(3) the Engineer has consulted both parties, rather than just follow the ideas of the Employer.

When make determinations, in practice, the Engineer may fist make an interim determination, indicating his intention to review it when further particulars are presented to him, and meanwhile including the appropriate adjustment in Interim Payment Certificate.

中文参考

［1］工程师的任何批准、审查、证书、同意、审核、检查、指示、通知、建议、请求、检验或类似行为（包括没有否定），不能解除承包商依照合同应具有的任何责任，包括对其错误、漏项、误差以及未能遵守合同的责任。

［2］未对任何工作、永久设备及材料提出否定意见并不构成批准，也不影响工程师拒绝该工作、永久设备及材料的权利。

Note

1.工程师作用的不足：FIDIC 条件中规定的工程师作用的不足，唯一明显值得讨论的来自两个虚拟困难。有人说这两个困难有碍于业主和承包商之间合理公平地行使其权力。这两个困难是：

（1）工程师由业主雇佣且支付酬劳，因此就必须对业主承担契约责任，以及忠诚于他必须依赖求得过去和将来雇佣机会的业主；

（2）作为工程设计者，当承包商就设计变更或延误交图及延误发出指示而提出索赔时，工程师有时会因为他自己违约而作出不承认违约的决定。

2.除了 FIDIC 合同条件，世界上很多地区使用的合同条件都规定了工程师的权力和责任，唯有我国例外。

Course work: According to the new edition of the FIDIC Contract Conditions for Construction, give a detailed description about the role of the "Engineer"? 200 words or above.

Vocabulary

delegate   代表；（尤指）会议代表；授（权）；把（职责、责任等）委托（给）

A delegate is a person who is chosen to vote or make decisions on behalf of a group of other people, especially at a conference or a meeting.

If you delegate duties, responsibilities, or power to someone, you give them those duties, those responsibilities, or that power so that they can act on your behalf.

preliminary   预备的；初步的

Preliminary activities or discussions take place at the beginning of an event, often as a form of preparation.

protest   抗议；提出异议；反对

If you protest against something or about something, you say or show publicly that you object to it. In American English, you usually say that you protest it.

amend   修改；修订

If you amend something that has been written such as a law, or something that is said, you change it in order to improve it or make it more accurate.

revocation   废止，撤回

reverse　逆转,彻底改变(决定、政策、趋势等)

When someone or something reverses a decision, policy, or trend, they change it to the opposite decision, policy, or trend.

dispute　争吵;吵闹

A dispute is an argument or disagreement between people or groups.

proceed　接下来做;接着做

If you proceed to do something, you do it, often after doing something else first.

4　The Contractor

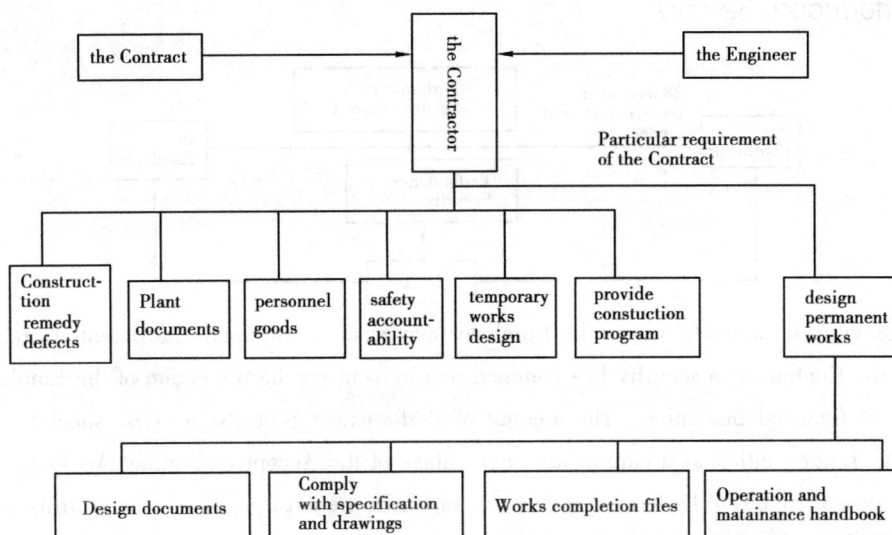

4.1　The Contractor's General Obligations

According to the contract of FIDIC, the obligations of the Contractor are listed in order as follows:

(1) to complete the Works;

(2) to take certain measures to complete the Works (采取措施完成工程);

(3) to take responsibilities for the measures taken to complete the Work (including the obligation of design stipulated in the Contract) (包含合同中注明的设计义务).

Hereby costs incurred corresponding to the obligations listed above(以上义务产生相对费用), and they're also stated in the B. Q. (工程量清单中):

(1) the relevant costs to the Works;

(2) the costs for the measurement (因采取的措施而产生的费用) taken to complete the Works include organization fees (组织费用) of employees and goods(雇员和货物), the expenditure for purchase of scaffold (购买脚架) used in the temporary Works;

（3）Incurred costs when take the corresponding responsibilities include maintenance fees occurred for remedying defects（修补缺陷）, insurance premium and charges for letter of guarantee, etc.

This Sub-clause specifies the Contractor's general obligations and requires the Contractor to design to the extent which is cleanly described in the Specifications.

Fitness for purpose if the basic criteria with which Contractor designed Works must reply. It is therefore not essential for example, for a contract documents to specify that roofs must be resistant to local weather conditions（sun, rain, snow, etc.）because such obvious requirements are imposed on the Works by this sub-clause, and are probably also implied by applicable laws.

4.2　Performance Security

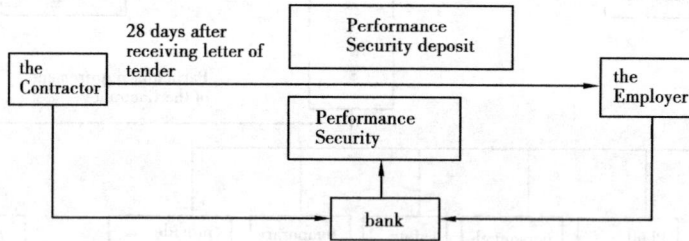

In international contracts, where the Employer may wish to anticipate the potential problems of default by the Contractor, a security is a common requirement for the protection of the Employer and of the project financial institution. The amount of Performance Security must be special in CON's Appendix to Tender, either as a sum or as a percentage of the Accepted Contract Amount.

There're many types of Performance Security, of which the most popular is the security issued by banks, hence have the name of the Performance Bank Guarantee. This security is usually 10% ~ 15% of the Accepted Contract Amount. This type of security can be subdivided into two:

（1）A "Conditional" security（有条件的保函）requires certain conditions to be satisfies before it may be called（cashed）（兑换）, the conditions typically being an arbitral award（仲裁裁决）or evidences（证据）like: the Contractor has been notified（承包商被通知）, reasons have been stated（原因被呈明）, agreement of the Contractor has been obtained（获得了承包商的同意）, etc. This type of performance security provides less scope for unfair calls, and is typically preferred by the Contractors.

（2）An "unconditional" or "on-demand" security（无条件的保函）without pre-conditions, which can be directly called（直接兑换）on banks if only the Employer considers it to be appropriate.

FIDIC used to adhere to the principle of using "conditional" security, while the example form annexed to the Contract Conditions in the new edition is proved to be of the "unconditional" type, reflecting its conceptrevolution. [1]

In practice, the Contractor needs to be attentive to the specific stipulations in the Performance

Security concerning amount, validity period and conditions, under which the Employer is entitled to claim.

Speaking of the Performance Security, usually, the Employer will make some improvements on the standard form which is annexed to the GPPC, in different aspects as follows:

(1) Deleting the passage from the example form that requires the Employer to make explanation on their default, so as to make it applicable for the security to be called on demand.

(2) Banks are not supposed to provide answers to any queries from the Contractor.

(3) No acts under the Contract or any illegal provisions will relieve the Contractor from their responsibilities under the Performance Security.

* The Employer shall not make a claim under the Performance Security, except foramounts to which the Employer is entitled under the Contract in the event of:

(1) failure by the Contractor to extend the validity of the Performance Security asdescribed in the preceding paragraph, in which event the Employer may claim the full amount of the Performance Security, [2]

(2) failure by the Contractor to pay the Employer an amount due, within 42 days after thisagreement or determination, [3]

(3) failure by the Contractor to remedy a default within 42 days after receiving the Employer's notice requiring the default to be remedied, [4]

(4) circumstances which entitle the Employer to termination irrespective of whether notice of termination has been given. [5]

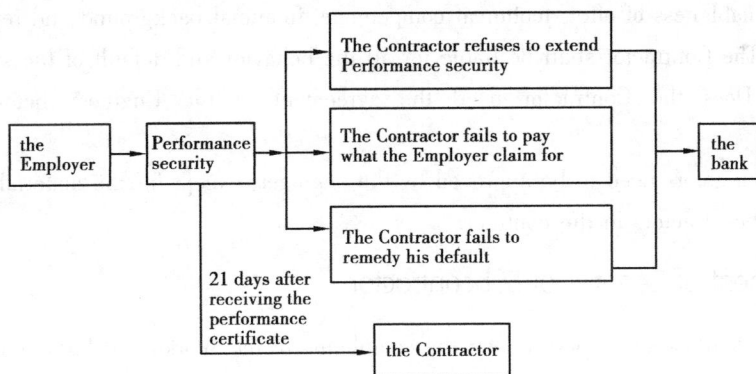

4.3   Contractor's Representative

The role of the Contractor's representative is of great importance and essential to the final success of the project. It's called "project manager" of the Contractor in China. The Contractor's Representative is the individual responsible for the performance of the Contractor's obligation under the Contract, including directing the Contractor's personnel and Subcontractors.

There're some basic criteria to judge whether the provisions are effective or not, one of which depends upon whether it's favorable to the smooth operation of the project and the improvement of work efficiency.

The last sentence specifies that the representative and all these persons shall be fluent in the communication language. Undoubtedly, if only people from different parties could be able to communicate with one language, we can reasonably expect great improvement in the work efficiency.

Unless the Contractor's Representative is named in the Contract, the Contractor shall, prior to the Commencement Date, submit to the Engineer for consent the name and particulars of the person the Contractor proposes to appoint as Contractor's Representative.

The Works commenced in parallel to contract operation, and the Employer was actively involved in site meetings, problem discussion and communications. Later on when substantial contractual diversification occurred, both parties looked back through the whole case and found out the contract defect concerning the Contractor's Representative. The consent of his appointment was withheld. The Employer defaulted on his contract obligation for variation and the Contactor shifted the blame to the Employer and refused to implement his duties. All of the correspondences and agreements signed by the Contractor's Representative were deemed as ineffective.

Sub-clause 3. 4 provides no ground for both to stand against each other, since the time limit of giving the consent is not specified, thus caused a dilemma for two parties.

4. 4 Subcontractor

Different from that of the Contractor, the performance of the Sub-contractor directly affect the whole Works. Four factors have to be taken into consideration when evaluating the candidates of sub-contractor: reasonableness of offer, technical competence, financial background and reputation.

※ **Highlights**: The Contractor shall be liable for all the behavior and default of the subcontractor.

※ **Discussion**: Does the Contractor need the agreement of the Engineer before appointing subcontractor?

Other subcontractors need to be approved by the engineer, except for the material supplier and the appointed subcontractors in the contract.

4. 5 Assignment of Benefits of Subcontractor

The Defects Notification Period follows the completion of the Works and lasts about one year.

※ **Discussion**: the sub-contractor to supply mechanical and electrical equipment (supplier) promises to the Contractor more than one year's Defects Notification Period referring to the subcontract and the applicable law. After the relevant Defects Notification Period specified for the Contractor expires whilst that of the subcontractor has not run out, problems may occur and the equipment can no longer work, then to whom shall the Employer turn and claim for compensation?

CONS 4. 5 is only likely to be applied if the Employer becomes aware of the Subcontractor having a continuing and assignable obligation. And the General Conditions do not require the Contractor to advise the Employer that a Subcontractor's obligations extend beyond the relevant Defects Notification Period.

Obviously not the Contractor, since the expiry of the contract has relieved him from responsibility of maintenance. And neither the sub-contractor for there's no contracts between him and the Employer.

If only prior to the date, the Engineer instructs the Contractor to assign the benefits of such obligation to Employer will the Contractor be obliged to obey.

And the Contractor shall have no liability to the Employer for the work carried out by the Subcontractor after the assignment.

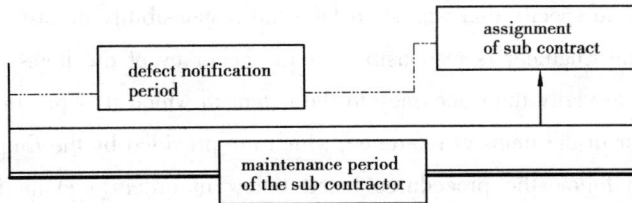

```
                                                    ┌──────────────────┐
                                                    │   assignment     │
                                                    │ of sub contract  │
                                                    └──────────────────┘
              ┌─────────────────────┐                        ▲
              │ defect notification │                        │
              │ period              │                        │
              └─────────────────────┘                        │
      ┌──────────────────────────────────────────────────────┐
      │        maintenance period                            │
      │        of the sub contractor                         │
      └──────────────────────────────────────────────────────┘
```

CONS 4. 5 is only likely to be applied if the Employer becomes aware of the Subcontractor having a continuing and assignable obligation. And the General Conditions do not require the Contractor to advise the Employer that a Subcontractor's obligations extend beyond the relevant Defects Notification Period.

4. 6 Cooperation

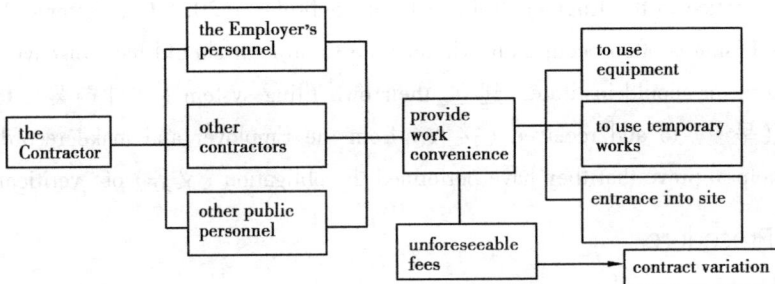

```
                    ┌──────────────────┐
                    │ the Employer's   │
                    │ personnel        │                      ┌──────────────┐
                    └──────────────────┘                      │ to use       │
┌──────────────┐    ┌──────────────────┐   ┌───────────┐      │ equipment    │
│ the          │    │ other            │   │ provide   │      └──────────────┘
│ Contractor   │────│ contractors      │───│ work      │      ┌──────────────┐
└──────────────┘    └──────────────────┘   │ convenience│     │ to use temporary│
                    ┌──────────────────┐   └───────────┘      │ works        │
                    │ other public     │                      └──────────────┘
                    │ personnel        │   ┌───────────┐      ┌──────────────┐
                    └──────────────────┘   │unforeseeable│    │ entrance into site│
                                           │ fees        │    └──────────────┘
                                           └───────────┘      ┌──────────────┐
                                                              │ contract variation│
                                                              └──────────────┘
```

For some large-scale or expansion projects, the Contractor may not have the exclusive right of access to, and possession of, the Site. In addition to the Employer's Personnel, the Contractor must also allow the Employer's other contractors to carry out their work.

Several subcontractors and contractor carry out their work simultaneously on the same Site, and sometimes the Employer's personnel also join, which unavoidably lead to chaos. In such cases, cooperation is needed in order to maintain high efficient work on the Site. "Cooperation" is also specified to be one of the Contractor's obligations in Contract considering promoting the cooperation between the Parties.

If instructions are given under the first sentence of this sub-clause, the Contractor is expected to have allowed in his Tender for Cost which an experienced contractor would reasonably have foreseen. To the extent that the cost was not reasonably foreseeable by an experienced contractor, taking account of the information available to tenders, the instruction constitutes a Variation and Clause 13 applies.

4.7　Setting Out

The first step the Contractor will take at the commencement of the Works is to send their surveyors to the Site to make survey and confirm the location of the Works. The original points, lines and levels of reference are specified in the Contract or notified by the Engineer. And the Contractor is responsible for setting out the Works, based upon items of reference.

This sub-clause if to specify that who shall take the responsibility in case of mistakes.

Under CONCS, the Engineer is responsible for the accuracy of the items of reference, but the Contractor is required to verify their accuracy to the extent to which it is practicable to do so.

When errors occur in the items of reference, which are provided by the Employer the Contractor has to take steps and follow the procedures listed below in order to claim for compensation or extension:

(1) to demonstrate that the Contractor suffers delay or incurs Cost form execution of work which was necessitated by an error in the original reference provided by the Employer. [6]

(2) After that, to further demonstrate that an experienced contractor could not reasonably have discovered such errors and avoid this delay or cost, even after they have made reasonable efforts to do so.

(3) To give notice to the Engineer subject to the Sub-clause 20.1 Contractor's claims.

※ **Discussion**: Disputes often occur as to whether the Contractor should have discovered the errors.

So the Contractor should institute（建立）their own filing system（文件档案）, to examine the files submitted（呈递）to and received（接收）from the Employer and make records（做记录）, which at least help to prove that they have performed the obligation（义务）of "verification"（证实）.

4.8　Safety Procedure

This sub-clause is to propose the safety procedure in construction to the Contractor from the view point of humanism and protection of the benefits of the public.

(1) *In fact, to the Contractor, the work of safety procedure relatively no only to his social image but also to cause him a great many problems concerning management on the Site. For example, for the work conducted in mid-air, after the happening of an accident, the work efficiency rate and attendance rate may drop dramatically.*

(2) *What's more, some prequalification documents about project tendering contain the item of accident rate, requiring the Contract to complete the report about the finished work. This works as one of the criteria examine the Contractor's pre-qualification.*

4.9　Quality Assurance

According to the conventions in the modern construction management, the Contractor is required to institute a quality assurance system in accordance with the details stated in the Contact, requiring the Contractor's personnel to comply with.

Talking about the quality assurance, you may think of the ISO 900 series. They're the ser ies of international standards made by the Technology Committee of IOS/TC 176, of which IOS 9001 applies to the Civil Engineering industry.

ISO 9001 standard is widely adopted in the construction companies with high level of management. So a contractor with an awareness of the modern management method and a desire for participation in international competition should introduce in the ISO 900 standard in the management of the company and the projects, and strive for the acknowledgement of authentication of the ISO 900 quality system. This will help them not only with the exploration of the international market but also the improvement of the work and management efficiency(提高工作和管理效率).

If this sub-clause is to apply, details of the quality assurance system should be included in the Contract, and could have been proposed by tenderers.

4.10   Site Data

Site data generally included hydrological （水文）, geological （地质） and environmental （环境） conditions. Due to the reason that it's almost completely impossible （几乎完全不可能） for the Contractor, nor does the Employer to obtain all the data relevant （相关数据） to the Site conditions before the commencement （开始） of the Works, the "uncertainties"（不确定因素） of the Site condition become an underlying risk factor （潜在危险因素） in the execution of the works. Thus how to fairly divide the risks between the Employer and the Contractor becomes the hot issue that all Contractors concern about.

For the Employer, he hall make available to the Contractor data which came or come into his possession either before or after the Base Date. Failure in this respect may have significant consequences. In some countries, negligent or intentional withhold of data may entitle the Contractor to termination, and consequential personal injury may result in private or criminal liability.

The Contractor is responsible for interpretation of the Site data, and for obtaining other information, so far as was practicable. The practicability of obtaining information will already depend upon the time allowed for the preparation of the tender.

Cautious attitude is necessary to deal with this kind of site conditions issues, please refer to the suggestions as follows：

（1）To study carefully the site data provided by the Employer, especially those that can be interpreted in different ways （不同的方式）.

（2）To conduct a site survey（现场勘查）.

（3）To ask the Employer to clarify the Discussions in case ambiguity （含糊不清） occurs, by taking chance of the meeting （标前会议）before tendering.

（4）To study under what conditions （在什么条件下）will the Contractor be entitled to claim （可以被授权索赔）.

（5）To study how to create advantageous（有利） but reasonable （合理） conditions for claim before tendering or in the executing of the works. reasonable conditions for claim before tendering or in the executing of the works.

※ **Discussion**: What's the result after the interpretation and valuation of the Contractor on the site data?

To such an extent the site conditions will affect the project expenditures that if the site risks are overvalued, the Contractor's offer will inevitably become less competitive; in the contrary, if the Contractor gives a much lower appraisal to the risks, the happening of which will cause a great loss to the Contractor.

4.11 Sufficiency of the Accepted Contract Amount

In order to prevent that the Contractor asserts the tendering price has not covered all contract contents due to the omission of certain items, and further raise the claim against the Employer, the contracts of the international projects specify that offer is apt to cover the contractor's entire obligation under the Contract. [7]

4.12 Unforeseeable Physical Conditions

※ **Discussion**: Construction takes long time, large span of space, complicated processes and requires work to be done in the open air. These features determine that the construction work is easily affected by external physical conditions, which may further prolong the working period and increase the costs. Then who shall take the responsibility, the Employer or the Contractor?

This sub-clause not only protects the Contractor if the physical conditions were not foreseeable, but also protects the Employer by providing a method of dealing with the possibility of inaccuracies in the data referred in sub-clause 4.10.

Note the limitation to the Site, for this sub-clause does not entitle the Contractor to compensate in respect of conditions encountered at "any additional areas" which may be obtained by the Contractor? Having encountered physical conditions which he considers may be both adverse and unforeseeable, the Contractor should promptly issue a note as soon as practicable, so that the Engineer:

—has the maximum opportunity to carry out an inspection and assess for himself whether the described conditions were unforeseeable, taking account of the Contractor's reasons set out in the notice, and

—may consider initiate a Variation in order to lessen the losses which might otherwise be sufficient by the Employer.

Having given such prompt notice, the Contractor is entitled to an extension of time and reimbursement of the Cost. In other words, the payment due should normally be the sum of:

(1) the original contract value;

(2) the additional Cost attributable to the extent to which the physical conditions actually encountered are Unforeseeable.

4.13   Rights of Way and Facilities

During the execution of the Works, both of the equipment and personnel of the Contractor's need to be transported to and from the Site. And the public roads will be at the disposal of the Contractor and his personnel of they're along the Site. In the contrary, the contractor may need to obtain some special or temporary ways if the Site locates at the remote place.

※ **Discussion**: Who shall be responsible for obtaining the rights of way?

This sub-clause specifies that the responsibility of obtaining the special or temporary rights of way will be of the Contractor's. [8]

This means the Contractor need to carry on a detailed research when conducting the site survey about the roads or routsthat need to be used in the execution of the Works, as well as whether some private roads are passable, or some temporary and specific roads need to be constructed, etc. All these factors need to be presented to the Contractor before he makes an offer.

4.14   Avoidance of Interference

Construction work may bring an adverse effect to the surrounding environment such as noise, pollution and traffic jams, etc. This sub-clause is specified to constrain the Contractor to interfere with the public as little as practicable. In international projects, such restrictions are not only stated in the Contract but also in the applicable laws of different states.

(1)*For instance, when excavating the ground at the center of cities with high population density, it will be advisable to also sprinkle on the dusty roads.*

(2)*In another example, in China, it's proclaimed in many cities that all the construction work which will produce noise must pause during the period when the university entrance examinations take place.*

4.15   Access Route

A great deal of equipment will need to be transported to and from the Site during the execution of the Works, especially some heavy-duty equipment. Thus it's important to ensure that there will be access to the Site.

The word "route" indicate something which can be represented as a line on a map, typically overland without implying that a road to the site exists. It is only assumed that there is a route by which access would be physically practicable. The Contractor is entitled to make use of the route without negotiation with its owners, but his entitlement does not indicate that the route is suitable for transport. The wording of the Sub-clause does not preclude the possibility that he might to construct a road along the route.

If the Site is totally surrounded by land owned by the third party, the Contractor should clarify:

(1)the alignment of the route through the third parties' lands, along with the Employer will be granting the right of access;

(2) how the Contractor can gain access, for example, whether access will be hindered by third parties' control measures.

Two decisions of the courts demonstrate the principles involved in apportioning responsibility for providing access to site.

In the case of Penvidic Contracting Co Ltd v International Nickel Co. of Canada Ltd. , the contract involved the laying of track and top ballasting on a railroad. Penvidic was the contractor and work to properly grade and sub-ballast was constantly delayed by the failure of other contractors the right of way in front of its machinery. In addition the International Nickel Co failed to obtain the necessary way leaves and permissions to cross various hydro lines and highways. It was held that the extent of possession or access provided by an Employer would vary with the nature of the work and the circumstances. In the case of a new project the main contractor would normally be entitled to exclusive possession of the entire site in the absence of express terms to the contrary. A term would normally be implied that the site would be handed over within a reasonable time and, in most cases, with a sufficient uninterrupted possession to allow the contractor to carry out his obligations by the method of his choice. It was held that International Nickel Co had failed to do so and that this was a breach of contract entitling Penvidic to damages.

In LRE Engineering Services Ltd v Otto Simon Carves Ltd. Simon Carves was the contractor for building works at steelworks at Port Talbot. LRE were subcontractors and had completed a very substantial proportion of the works when a steel strike broke out. The activities of pickets at the site prevented LRE from completing the work until some considerable time later, causing them to incur considerable additional costs. LRE maintained that Simon Carves was in breach of contract in that it had an absolute obligation to see that there was available entry to the site at all times. This was not accepted. It was held instead that the term "access" had more than one meaning in the relevant Clause. In one part of the clause it meant "physical means of access" since that part also referred to the condition of the access. Another part placed an obligation on Simon Carves to "afford access" to LRE. On this interpretation it was held that there was no breach of contract. Simon Carves had provided LRE with the opportunity of entering the site by the required means of access. The fact that they were prevented from doing so was not a breach of contract.

4.16   Transport of Goods

This sub-clause specifies that the Contractor has to take full responsibility for the transportation of any Plant or a major item of other Goods, he is required to give notice of the intended arrival of the objects and to indemnify the Employer in respect of claims arising from their transport.

And Goods must be insured when they are within the country.

4.17   Contractor's Equipment

Contractor's equipment, which included Subcontractor's equipment, is deemed to be intended for the execution of the Works, and not for use elsewhere.

※ **Discussion**：Any use of the Contractor's equipment other than to project execution?

Some of the Equipment are quite expensive, when such equipment are retained（滞留）in the Site of the Works，they are considered to act as a special role of "guarantee"（担保）. Literally（字面上）, there's no strict definition（严格定义）on this sort of "guarantee", while in practice（现实中）, when disputes arise between the Contractor and the Employer, especially when the project faces with the possibility if suspension（暂停）which is caused by the Contractor, the Employer will distrain upon（扣押）these equipment as a method of protection of their benefits.

Consent is required before major items leave the Site, especially for transport vehicles, which come forth and back through the Site daily.

4.18   Protection of Environment

The protection of environment has been the focus among global issues and attracted more attention from different countries. Because the construction tends to cause pollutions to environment, there have been more strict requirements imposed on construction procedure which are stated in the international construction contracts in recent years.

In some countries, the protection of environment arouses great interest of people especially in countries relying on the tourism as the main source of national income. Such countries also have very stern environment protection laws.

A Contractor who has been well equipped with the techniques of modern management should be equally taught how to handle the problem of protection of environment in construction. For this issue not only relatively to their obligation under the Contract or law, but also to the build-up of social image of the company.

The contractor is required by this sub-clause to take all reasonable steps to protect the environment and is required to limit emission to specified value. If he fails to do so, the Contractor would be liable.

（1）*compulsory cease of work during the national entrance examination to university*（国内工程高考期间强制停工）.

（2）*government compulsory limit on night work in urban area*（市区内晚间施工的政府强制性限制与管制）.

（3）*compulsory expert demonstration on excavation engineering scheme*（基坑围护方案强制性专家论证）.

（4）*compulsory protection on surrounding architecture*（强制性对周边建筑的保护）.

4.19   Electricity, Water and Gas

On the construction Site, electricity, water and gas are necessities for the staff to live on, usually solved by the Contractor himself, which doesn't exclude the possibilities that these can be provided to the Contractor under charge, if only at the convenience of the Employer. The first sentence of the sub-clause excluded the Employer's responsibility, except to the extent (if any) to which he has undertaken to male specified services available.

If the Employer is to make any of these services available, details and prices must be given in CON'S Specification. If the Contractor will need to rely upon the continued availability of a service, the Contractor should indicate who bears the cost of a failure in the supply. It may be reasonable for the Employer to be responsible for services which he controls, and for other specifies services to be at the risk of the Contractor.

4.20 Employer's Equipment and Free-Issue Material

The provisions entitle the Contractor to use whichever of these things are described as being available, in CONS' Specifications.

This sub-clause refer to (关于) the possibility of two categories of items (两类物品) being made available to (提供给) the Contractor:

(1) Employer's equipment, which is under charge.

(2) "free-issue materials", free of charge.

The Employer will provide to the Contractor the equipment under the conditions that rates will be charged, which has an equal effect of renting. The details are included in the CONS' Specification such as: rates charged by the Employer, equipment specification and status, calculation of operation time, which party is responsible for equipment maintenance and providing operators, fuel and equipment. Typically, the Employer rents out the equipment with more favorable conditions comparing.

For free-issue materials, you can also find details of the materials availability, arrangements and particular requirements in the CONS' Specifications. Sensitive issues include the place for delivering the materials and time arrangement.

During the execution of the project, when water pressure test was carried on, tube burst. Grounded on such evidence, the Contractor proclaimed that the Employer should be responsible for the materials he provided, and replenish new materials. Moreover, the Contractor also claimed for compensations of both cost and time for his retest.

The Employer reasoned that "after this visual inspection, the free-issue materials shall come under the care, custody and control of the Contractor" and he was no longer liable for any shortage, defector default. It's most probably that tubes were damaged on the way of transportation from the hand-over site to the construction site. And the Contractor should do the retest at his afford.

In general conditions, for any problems occur to the "free-issue materials", the Contractor's obligations of inspection, care, custody and control shall not relieve the Employer of liability for any shortage, defect or default not apparent from a visual inspection.

They came into an agreement that the Employer is liable for resupplying materials and compensate the Contractor for costs excluding time. The following stipulations shall be comprised into the contract as to "free-issue materials":

(1) *Both of quantity and quality standard;*

(2) *Time;*

(3) *Place;*

(4) *Division of the obligation in case of problems.*

4.21　Progress Reports

The Employer and the Engineer learn the progress of the construction work and manage the Contractor through Progress Reports, which are important management documents.

In practice, before the submission (呈递) of the first report, the Contractor will negotiate with (同…讨论) the Engineer and determine the format (格式) of monthly report, on which the monthly reports will be based.

With the growing popularity of the use of computer, especially after the applied software have been used for the purpose of construction management, it has become much easier and more convenient to work on a report and submit it subsequently.

In addition to the items listed from (a) to (h), there are more that are required to be included into the reports like the number of the monthly accidents about quality and according remedying measures, for example, the notice issued by the Employer or the Engineer when quality defects of the Contractor have been discovered, which is called Non-performance Report.

If the reports have not been submitted in time, the Engineer is entitled to reject the application of the Interim Payment Certificate by the Contractor.

Progress report includes:

(1) *progress chart and illustrations* (进度图表及详细说明);

(2) *site photos* (现场照片);

(3) *examination certificate of equipment and materials* (设备材料检验情况);

(4) *provide specific personnel numbers and equipment items* (详细的人员数量及设备细目);

(5) *relevant documents on material quality guarantee* (材料质量保证相关文件,这个国内多是专项申报);

(6) *filing of claim documents* (索赔文件备案);

(7) *safety items* (安全事项);

(8) *progress comparison* (进度对比). [9]

4.22　Security of the Site

This sub-clause states that the Contractor is responsible for the security work. In practice, the contracts may specify that the Contractor has to recruit security guards from specialist security companies to ensure the safety of the Site and protects the Site against theft and sabotage.

For some particular Plant, for example, the warehouse for storage of dynamite, which is used for explosive work, may requires the local troops to be on guard. During the execution of the Works, the events with adverse effect may happen one after another, for instance, staff member is shot or kidnapped, etc. and these will hamper the normal progress of the Works. Facing with such projects with high risks, the Contractor has to not only give risk evaluation in tendering but also take certain precautions in the construction period.

4.23 Contractor's Operation on Site

The Contactor should carry out their work on the Site in compliance with certain rules, for example: do not cause inconvenience to the occupier of the adjacent land, properly arrange the activities on the Site, etc.

The Contractor is required to confine his operations to:

—the Site,

—any additional areas, which do not become parts of the Site.

These agreed areas are obtained by the Contractor, the Engineer is not responsible for them, Plant and Materials are not required to be delivered thereto, and Permanent Works are not executed thereon.

The equipment or materials shall be put at the place to which they are appointed rather than being willfully disposed of, which may cause accidents.

For instance, once in a project, a driver placed a bulldozer on the ground to be backfilled before he was off the duty. That night, the heavy rain caused the collapse of the ground and the bulldozer slid into a deep ditch. As the result, the Contractor suffered a great loss.

This lesson proves that a clear site will contributes to high efficient work.

4.24 Fossils

Many countries, especially those highly civilized ancient countries, owns laws of relic protections. And there're also chapters with similar title in construction contract. In this sub-clause, fossils and other antiquities are the property and also the liability of the Employer.

The Contractor is required to give notice upon discovering of the finding, and await instructions for dealing with it.

※ **Discussion**: Any practical problems arising from this?

This clause doesn't set restrictions on the Contractor concerning the right of claims but encourages the Contractor to make efforts to protect the findings and specifies that it's one of his obligations.

Coursework: Please analyze the structure of sub-clause 4.3 and translate it sub-clause 4.3 into Chinese, since it provides a good contract module to imitate.

中文参考

［1］承包商一般愿意使用有条件的保函。FIDIC 以前坚持使用"有条件的"保函,但是在 1999 年新的版本中,变成了"无条件"的保函,这是 FIDIC 合同条款的一个变革。

［2］承包商未按上述规定延长履约保证的有效期,此时业主可以将该履约保证全部没收。

［3］在双方商定或工程师决定后的 42 天内,承包商没有支付已商定工程师决定的业主的索赔款。

［4］在收到业主方发出的补救违约的通知之后 42 天内,承包商仍没有补救。

［5］业主有权终止合同的情况。

［6］证明业主方提供的原始数据出错。

［7］除非合同中另有规定,接受的合同款额应包括承包商在合同中应承担的全部义务(包括根据暂定金额应承担的义务,如有时)以及为恰当地实施和完成工程并修补任何缺陷必需的全部有关事宜。

［8］承包商应自费去获得他需要的特别或者临时道路的通行权,包括进入现场的此类通道。

［9］进度对比,国内多在会议上说明,很少承包商能够自行以文件的形式明确进度的精细状况。

Note

1. 履约担保(4.2)的知识点:

(1)在投标书附录中规定履约担保的保证的金额和币种。

(2)承包商自费取得履约担保,并在收到中标函 28 天内向业主提交履约担保,并向工程师送一份副本。

(3)履约担保应由业主批准的国家或地区的银行或担保机构提供,并采用专用条款所附格式,或业主批准的其他格式。

(4)履约担保的作用主要是确保承包商按照合同完成工程,因此应确保履约担保直到承包商完成工程的施工、竣工及修补完任何缺陷前持续有效和可执行。就算在合同的履约担保的条款中规定了履约担保的有效期限,但承包商在期满前 28 天仍未能取得履约证书,承包商应将履约担保的有效期延长至工程竣工和修补完成任何缺陷时为止。

(5)业主在收到履约担保后,应在投标书附录中规定的时间或者按照第 8.3 款的规定给予承包商进入现场、占用现场的权利。

(6)业主在收到履约证书的副本后 21 天内发放履约担保。

(7)业主对履约担保提出的索赔。在履约担保中规定了其期满日期,但承包商在期满前 28 天仍未能取得履约证书,承包商又未应业主要求将履约担保的有效期延长至工程竣工和修补完成任何缺陷时为止。业主可以索赔履约担保的全部金额。(4.2)

2. 承包商应对其所需的所有电力、水及其他服务的供应负责,并完全承担相关风险。

但是,如果雇主方便的话,也可以代办,并可在"规范"中注明收费价格和相关细节。但是雇主先行申报施工用临电临水,再交由承包商来做会存在问题。一个是雇主在申报施工用临电临水时会有意无意地将容量申报的小一些,容易造成承包商进场后电水用量紧张的问题,甚至会发生容量严重不足而不得不临时追加容量申报的事情;另一个,雇主提供电水燃气的接入,就得雇主负责。

3.(1)"甲供材料"简单来说就是由业主方(甲方)提供的材料。这是在甲方与承包方签订合同时事先约定的。甲供材料一般为大宗材料,比如钢筋、钢板、管材以及水泥等,当然施工合同里对于甲供材料有详细的清单。

(2)我们指的甲供材就是主要指以前的3大材,现在的4大材,以前是水泥、钢筋、木材,现在增加燃料油。

(3)甲供材料的优点是可以减少投资,避免因不熟悉地方行情高价买货。对于施工方而言,优点就是可以减少材料的资金投入和资金垫付压力,避免材料价格上涨带来的风险。对于甲方而言,甲供材料可以更好地控制主要材料的进货来源,保证工程质量。

施工方不能赚到材料和合同之间的价差,而甲方前期投入的资金数量较大。

4.外部障碍条件是指承包商现场遇到的外部天然条件、人为条件、污染物等,包括水文条件和地表以下的条件,不包括气候条件。

Vocabulary

vocabulary　(某人所掌握的)词汇,词汇量

Your vocabulary is the total number of words you know in a particular language.

adequacy　适当;恰当

Adequacy is the quality of being good enough or great enough in amount to be acceptable.

consumable　消耗性的

Consumable goods are items which are intended to be bought, used, and then replaced.

as-built　竣工;完工

coordination　协调

Co-ordination means organizing the activities of two or more groups so that they work together efficiently and know what the others are doing.

dismantle　拆卸;拆开;拆除

If you dismantle a machine or structure, you carefully separate it into its different parts.

reassemble　重组;重新整合;重新装配

If you reassemble something, you put it back together after it has been taken apart.

enforceable　可执行的;可强制执行的

If something such as a law or agreement is enforceable, it can be enforced.

revoke　取消,废除,撤销(许可、法律、协议等)

When people in authority revoke something such as a licence, a law, or an agreement, they cancel it.

possession　占有;拥有

If you are in possession of something, you have it, because you have obtained it or because it belongs to you.

rectify　纠正;修正;矫正

If you rectify something that is wrong, you change it so that it becomes correct or satisfactory.

alignment　结盟;联合

An alignment is support for a particular group, especially in politics, or for a side in a quarrel or struggle.

dimension   方面;部分

A particular dimension of something is a particular aspect of it.

be subject to   受支配;从属于;可以…的;常遭受…

institute   建立(体系等);制定(规章等);开始;开创

If you institute a system, rule, or course of action, you start it.

contingency   可能发生的事;不测之事;突发事件

A contingency is something that might happen in the future.

hydrological   水文学的

indemnify   保证赔偿

To indemnify someone against something bad happening means to promise to protect them, especially financially, if it happens.

exclusively   排他地;独占地;专有地;完全地

Exclusively is used to refer to situations or activities that involve only the thing or things mentioned, and nothing else.

nuisance   讨厌的人;麻烦的事情

If you say that someone or something is a nuisance, you mean that they annoy you or cause you a lot of problems.

hazardous   (尤指对健康或安全)有危险的,有危害的

Something that is hazardous is dangerous, especially to people's health or safety.

surplus   过剩;剩余;过剩量;剩余额

If there is a surplus of something, there is more than is needed.

fossil   化石

A fossil is the hard remains of a prehistoric animal or plant that are found inside a rock.

archaeological   考古学

Archaeology is the study of the societies and peoples of the past by examining the remains of their buildings, tools, and other objects.

authentication   鉴别;鉴定

If you authenticate something, you state officially that it is genuine after examining it.

strive for   奋斗,争取;谋求;讲求

5   *Nominated Subcontractor*

5.1   Definition of Nominated Subcontractor

In accordance with the second sentence of sub-clause 4.4, "the Contractor shall be responsible for the acts or default of any Subcontractor (including Nominated Subcontractor)". The Employer and the Engineer should not deal directly with a nominated Subcontractor (or with any

Subcontractor) but should only deal with the Contractor (unless he agrees otherwise).

Subcontractor is preferred by the Contractor in some large-scale projects, with the agreement obtained from the Engineer. While the Employer may wish to subcontract some work about he key parts or Plant to specialist companies with rich experience, which they're also keen on and trusted, to ensure the work quality and that their particular needs will be met.

In the Contract, "nominated Subcontractor" means a Subcontractor:

(1) who is stated in the Contract as being a nominated Subcontractor, or

(2) whom the Engineer, under Clause 13 [Variations and Adjustments], instructs the Contractor to employ as a nominated Subcontractor.

After reading this provision, we get to know that Nominated Subcontractor shall be determined before the Contract is signed, otherwise the instruction issued by the Engineer to employ a Subcontractor constitutes Variation under Clause 13.

But there're apparent advantages of instructing the employment of a nominated Subcontractor because the Employer or the Engineer can:

(1) choose the Specialist company;

(2) participate the choice of plant;

(3) avoid participation in co-ordination of the interface between the Nominated Subcontractor and the Contractor's Works.

Here're also some advices on those who wish to become subcontractors:

Unless they can be certain of the profitability of the subcontracted projects, they're advised not enter into a subcontract in a haste, because normally the Contractor is harsh to the subcontractor.

The first choice they may consider is to join the Contractor to constitute a join-venture, consortium or other unincorporated grouping of two or more person, under which they will take the joint and several responsibility to the Employer and gain more chances in negotiation.

5.2　Objection to Nomination

※ **Discussion**: Is the Contractor obliged to accept the Nominated Subcontractor who is chosen by the Employer?

If the Contractor wishes to object to the nomination, he must do so promptly.

If the Contractor wishes to object to the nomination, he must do so promptly, describing all the grounds on which his objection are based. This sub-clause has listed the most likely grounds for objection under CONS Contract, though the grounds need not to be restricted to those described in the subparagraphs. Because the Contractor has to take the whole responsibility for the quality and working period of the Works, thus it may diverge from FIDIC's intention by enforcing the Contractor to employ any subcontractor when he's unwilling to do so.

Objection reasons:

(1) Sufficient proofs to show that this subcontractor is incapable, insufficient in resources or

incompetent in financial background[1]（该分包商能力不足,资源不足或者财力不足）;

（2）No clear statement that if the subcontractor defaults on his duties, the Contractor will not be not exempted from losses[2];

（3）No guarantee that if any problems occur to the subcontractor's work, the subcontractor himself will take full responsibilities and subsequent result[3]（如果分包的工作出了问题,分包商将为之承担一切责任,以及此类责任的后果）.

※ **Discussion**: How can the Employer react to such an objection?

The sub-clause provides the Employer with a possible resolution of the objection, namely indemnification. That is to say, if only the Contractor raise reasonable objection, the Employer can't insist on employing any subcontractor unless he can indemnify and hold the Contractor against and from the consequences of all the matters.[4]

5.3   Payment to Nominated Subcontractor

Structure analysis of this sub-clause:

（1）The Contractor shall be paid the amounts which he pays to the nominated Subcontractor, and the Engineer is required to certify such actual amounts.

（2）"Other charges" here means the Overheads and Profits the Contractor he has collected from the Employer for the Work he has carried out to manage the subcontractors. It is usually a percentage of the Sub Contract Price and is specified in the Appendix to Tender or the Schedules.

（3）Provisional sum shall be used when Plant, Materials or services are to be purchased by the Contractor from a nominated Sub-contractor, as stated in 13.59 provisional sum.[5]

5.4   Evidence of Payment

The Engineer is entitled to request the Contractor to supply reasonable evidenced of previous payment, though normally he would not do so unless he has reason to believe that the Contractor is in default under the Sub-clause.

The snag in construing this provision is that we can hardly understand why shall the Engineer pay directly to the subcontractor and subsequently claim it back from the Contractor?

※ **Discussion**: Shall the Contractor be liable to the Employer for the default of the sub-contractor?

Normally, the Contractor shall be liable to the Employer, especially when problems occur to the working processes or provided materials, except the Employer insists on employing the subcontractor irrespective of the reasonable objection from the Contractor and indemnify the Contractor against all possible losses.

In such a case, if the delay of the work of the subcontractor affects the Contractor, the Contractor will be entitled to claim for extension of time. And the failure of completing the work in time will incur costs to the Employer. Because the Contractor has been exempted from the liability to the Employer, the Employer can't claim for compensation from the Contractor, neither will the Contractor pass on the liability to the subcontractor. The subcontractor can almost succeed in defaulting on his obligations.

In order to solve this sort of problem, in practice, the Employer is apt to sign an agreement with the nominated subcontractor, stipulating the Nominated Subcontractor has to perform his obligations under the agreement. Correspondingly, the Employer will undertake to the subcontractor that if the Contractor fails to pay the due amount, the Employer will pay directly to the Nominated Subcontractor.

An construction project of office building（办公楼）for rent. The construction period（建设期）is 18 months. Management fees（管理费）are 12.5% of the total contract price. While the handover（接收）of the construction period is postponed（延迟）, and the Contractor claimed for damages. One of the reason is that the Nominated Contractor（制订分包商）breached the contract（违反合同）. And the failure of completing the work in time will incur costs to the Employer. In order to solve this sort of problem, in practice, the Employer is apt to sign an agreement with the nominated subcontractor, stipulating the Nominated Subcontractor has to perform his obligations under the agreement.

Summary chart of this clause：

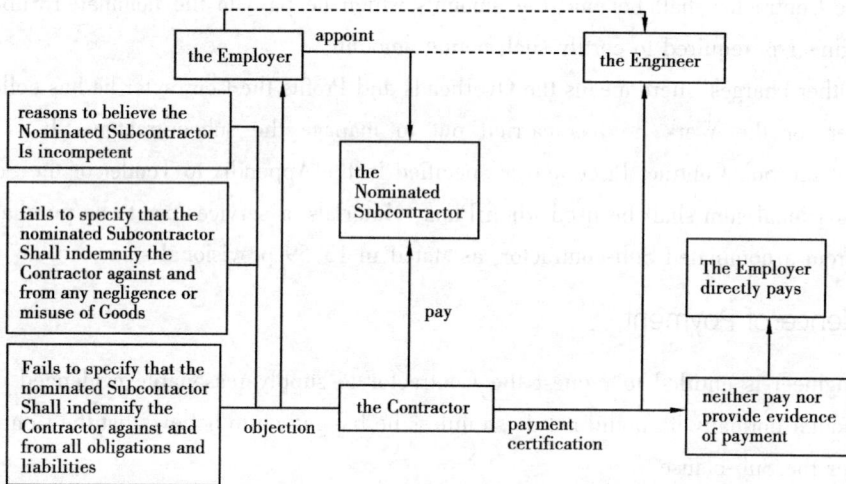

Coursework：What's the difference between "Subcontractor"（4.4）and "Nominated Subcontractor"?

Hints for this question：5 aspects include Selection Rights, Contents, Source of payment, Protection from Employer, Contractor's undertakings.

中文参考

［1］该分包商能力不足、资源不足或者财力不足。

［2］如果该分包商一方渎职或者误用材料,承包商不会因此而遭受损失。

［3］如果分包的工作出了问题,分包商将为之承担一切责任,以及此类责任的后果。

［4］本条款为雇主提供了一条可能的解决承包商反对的方法,即保障。也就是说,如果承包商提出合理的反对意见,雇主不能坚持使用任何分包商,除非他能保障承包商免于承担所有事情的后果。

［5］通常指定分包商承担的工作从主合同中的暂定金额中支付。

Note

1. 定义:指定分包商是由业主(或工程师)指定、选定,完成某项特定工作内容并与承包商签订分包合同的特殊分包商。合同条款规定,业主有权将部分工程项目的施工任务或涉及提供材料、设备、服务等工作内容分包给指定分包商实施。

(1)考虑到某部分施工的工作内容有较强的专业技术要求,一般承包单位不具备相应的能力。

(2)在合同关系和管理关系方面与一般分包商处于同等地位。

(3)对其施工过程中的监督、协调工作纳入承包商的管理之中。

Vocabulary

exempt   被免除的;被豁免的

If someone or something is exempt from a particular rule, duty, or obligation, they do not have to follow it or do it.

discharge   清偿(债务)

If someone discharges a debt, they pay it.

breach   违反,破坏(条约、法律或承诺)

If you breach an agreement, a law, or a promise, you break it.

postpone   推迟;使延期;延缓

If you postpone an event, you delay it or arrange for it to take place at a later time than was originally planned.

6   *Staff and Labor*

6.1   Engagement of Staff and Labor

This sub-clause removes any implication of obligation on the part of the Employer to provide personnel, except to the extent (if any) that the Employer has undertaken to do so.

The arrangement of the staff and labour depends on specific circumstances. For those the Contractor has brought with him along from their home country, the Contractor has to provide them with housing by building up new houses near the Site or inside, or rent the local houses for them. For the local staff, if the construction site is not far from the local community, the contractor will provide means of transportations. He is in no way under the obligations of providing housing nor feeding, but he has to ensure the drinking water on the Site is available. [1]

Whatever the Contractor like to do, he must verify the labor contract and make sure it will be in compliance with the local labour law.

6.2 Rates of Wages and Conditions of Labour

By integrating this sub-clause into sub-clause 6.4 will they two constitute an integral clause concerning labor. It's specifically stated in consideration to the following two factor:

(1) Only if the rates of wages and conditions of labour (工资标准及遵守的劳动条件) are higher than the general level (普通水平), can they recruit (招收) qualified staff and labour (合格的人员), so as to ensure the quality and progress (质量和进度) of the work.

(2) To protect the benefits of the workers (工人的利益) in case the labour laws (劳动法) of the country where the project locates (项目所在国) haven't been well established (建立不完善), and the Employer can also avoid (避免) getting involved in (卷入) unnecessary disputes (不必要的纷争) about wages and work conditions (工资和劳动条件).

This sub-clause reminds us that when conducting marketing census in the Employer's country, the investigation into the local general level of wages will help to improve the accuracy of tendering price.

6.3 Persons in Service of Employer

This sub-clause tends to protect the benefits of the Employer. It is also reasonable to allow the Contractor to undermine the Employer's activities, either on project or elsewhere, by encouraging the Employer's Personnel to transfer their employment to the Contractor. Without such prohibition, the confidential particulars of the Contractor may get released. Without such prohibition, the confidential particulars of the Contractor may get released. [2]

6.4 Labour Law

Labour law in different countries may be different to each other but all cover the same issues:
(1) recruitment procedure (招聘程序) and discharge procedure (解聘程序);
(2) Lowest rates of wages (最低工资水平);
(3) Welfare conditions (福利条件), such as the labour safety utensils;
(4) Social insurance (社会保险) or Employer liability insurance (辅助责任险);
(5) Sickness leave and vacation with pay (病假和带薪假期);
(6) Working time and over-time pay (工作时间和加班费), etc.

6.5 Working Hours

The Employer may wish to specify the working hours, besides, the Employer's Personnel may also wish to know the Contractor's working hours in advance, in order to plan and manage their activities.

Under CONS, if the Engineer wishes to specify working hours, they should be stated in the Appendix to Tender (投标函附录). If the Employer's Personnel (雇主人员) wish to know the Contractor's intentions (承包商的意愿), the item in the Appendix to Tender (投标函附录) may be left blank (空白) in the tender documents (投标文件), to be completed by each tenderer (投

标人自行填写).

※ **Discussion**：Is the Contractor allowed to work over-time in holidays?

The viewpoint of the Employer may diverge from that of the Contractor due to this reason. If the Contractor wants to work on the locally recognized days of rest (公共休息日), then the Employer or Engineer may need to correspondingly arrange overtime work (加班) too in order to ensure the Contractor's work will be in accordance with the Specifications, and such a decision will require the Employer to give extra overwork pay (加班费) to their personnel. But on the whole, the Employer and the Contractor agree on the same target to complete the Works as soon as possible, thus normally the application for overwork form the Contractor will be approved.

6.6 Facilities to Staff and Labour

The sub-clause removes any implication of obligation on the part of the Employer to arrange facilities for the Contractor's personnel.

The requirement of providing necessary facilities by the Contractor is also included in the "service range" of the Contractor or the "requirements of the Employer" of which the facilities included：the on-site offices (现场办公室) of the Employer, office facilities (办公设备) such as computers, telephones, fax-machine, and transportation vehicles (交通工具), etc. The content and amount of the providings (供应的内容和数量) must be clarified (澄清) before tendering, for example, whether the Contractor is also required to afford the relevant costs (相关成本) such as fuel charges (燃油费) and telephone fees (电话费)?

But it may be difficult to establish what accommodation and facilities are "necessary" until the effects of their inadequacy have become apparent.

6.7 Health and Safety

There're many factors threatening health and safety of the personnel during the execution of the Works and accidents often happen unexpectedly：

As an experienced administrator, the Contractor should be discreet in dealing with these matters：He's supposed to maintain the balance between he construction progress and safety, appoint qualified engineer to deal with safety issues, provide adequate training about safety to project staff, make complete and feasible safety rules and specific measures to implement these rules. Stipulations of this sub-clause coincide with the No. 167 Convention of the International Labour Organization.

6.8 Contractor's Superintendence

In order to guarantee the smooth operation and safety of the Works, it's required that the Contractors has to provide all necessary services and undertakes that he will perform the obligations under the Contract.

It may be difficult to establish what is "necessary" and how many are "sufficient" under this sub-clause, and these relate the quantity and quality requirements of the superintendence. Specifically, superintendence includes the following aspects：

①scope management；②time management；③cost management；④human resource management；⑤risk management；⑥quality management；⑦communication management.

Highlights：normal management staff should be a specialist in at least one aspect and an excellent superintendent should be both a specialist in one aspect and a generalist in all the above aspects.

6.9　Contractor's Personnel

High level of management（高水平的管理）and achievement（成就）depends upon use of high quality management staff（高质量管理人员）and technicians（技术人员）.

This sub-clause shows the demands（要求）on the Contractor's Personnel quality（承包商人员的质量）, which comprise technical（技术）and professional ethics（专业道德）.

The Engineer is entitled to remove any person employed on the Site or Works, including the Contractor's Representative, so that the overall quality of the personnel can be ensured. Typically, the Contractor may readily be persuaded to remove the person, and such removal by agreement is preferable to enforcement under this sub-clause.

Meanwhile, in order to prevent the Engineer misusing such entitlement, restrictive conditions of (1)，(2) and (3) are specified.

(1)persists in any misconduct or lack of care；

(2)carries out duties incompetently or negligently；

(3)fails to conform with any provisions of the Contract；

(4) persists in any conduct which is prejudicial to safety, health, or the protection of the environment.

And if the Contractor demonstrates that the opinion of the Engineer was unreasonable and unfounded, the Contractor may be entitled to compensation under applicable law.

6.10　Records of Contractor's Personnel and Equipment

In order to facilitate the evaluation of claims and Variations, it is necessary to establish basic record-keeping from the commencement of t a contract. The providing of the data and details will be greatly helpful for the Employer to know about the project progress.

In practice, the records also provide a good source for both parties to trace up and support their claims if disputes arise. For instance, the Employer may accuse（指责）the Contractor of their fault（错误）which is proved by such records showing the Contractor's insufficient input（不足的投入）of personnel and equipment. The Contractor's claims（承包商索赔）for extension of working period may be rejected on grounds of this.

The data required to be submitted must be included in each of the Contractor's reports, in accordance with Sub-clause 4.21 (4).

6.11　Disorderly Conduct

The happening of riots during the execution of the Works may add to the complication of project management.

In international projects, it happens frequently for workers to go on strike and the interests of the local staff conflict with that of the foreign staff.

This sub-clause specifies that the Contractor has to take responsibility for these events in order to reduce the happening of such riot and preserve the peace near or on the site afterwards.

中文参考

［1］承包商没有责任安排住房或膳食,但是他需要确保现场的生活饮用水的提供。

［2］承包商不应从雇主的人员中招收或试图招收职员或劳工。

Vocabulary

engagement　约会;约定

An engagement is an arrangement that you have made to do something at a particular time.

feeding　养;喂;饲养

If you feed a person or animal, you give them food to eat and sometimes actually put it in their mouths.

unavoidable　不可避免的;无法阻止的

If something is unavoidable, it cannot be avoided or prevented.

precaution　预防措施;防备

A precaution is an action that is intended to prevent something dangerous or unpleasant from happening.

epidemics　(疾病的)流行,传播

If there is an epidemic of a particular disease somewhere, it affects a very large number of people there and spreads quickly to other areas.

superintendence　指挥,主管,监督

prejudicial　有害的;不利的

If an action or situation is prejudicial to someone or something, it is harmful to them.

replacement　替代;替换;取代

If you refer to the replacement of one thing by another, you mean that the second thing takes the place of the first.

outstanding　(款项)未支付的,未结清的

Money that is outstanding has not yet been paid and is still owed to someone.

riotous　(行为或事件)狂欢的,喧闹的,放纵的

You can describe someone's behaviour or an event as riotous when it is noisy and lively in a rather wild way.

7 *Plant , Materials and Workmanship*

7.1 Manner of Execution

This sub-clause specifies general requirements in respect of the manner in which the Works are to be executed. More detailed requirements will be derived from other provisions in the Contract.

Three rules are specified to be followed when executing the Works（执行工程）for the Contract:

（1）the first rule requires the Contractor just to follow what's specified in the Contract; [1]

（2）the second is additional to the first one, the recognized good practice will become the standard when no exact construction methods are specified; [2]

（3）the third raises the requirements on the construction manner from the views of safety of the facilities and materials. [3]

The sub-paragraph prohibits the use of hazardous materials. In this context, there're different hazardous situations（危险材料的使用）:

Many manufacturing processes（生产流程）are hazardous（危险的）but do not result in hazardous "Materials"（危险材料）① Materials must not require the use of hazardous Site procedures; ② Materials must nor be hazardous thereafter, during their working life or during any subsequent procedures for their demolition and disposal.

Under CONS, the Engineer is not empowered to relax this provision of the Contract. If he consents to the use of Materials which are subsequently found to be hazardous, the Contractor will have to replace the Materials.

7.2 Samples

This sub-clause specifies that the Contractor has to submit to the Engineer samples of Materials prior to using the materials in the Works.

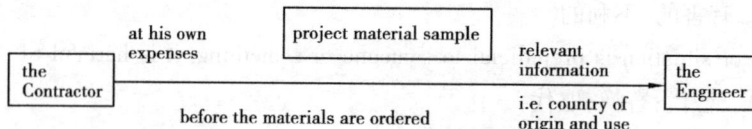

In practice（实际中）, when large bulk of cement（大批量水泥）is required, the Contractor will claim on relevant data（相关数据）of the cement directly from the manufacturer（制造商）according to the Specification and design requirements.

After acquiring（得到）the technical data（技术数据）, the Contractor will submit（交给）them to the Engineer asking for their consent（同意）before he gives the order to the manufacturer（订购前）, so as to avoid the dilemma（窘境）that the Engineer refuses to use the purchased Materials（购买

材料).

Some contracts specify（要求）that certain Plant requires the permits（同意）of the Employer before orders are given and can only be purchased（购买）from the supplier（供应商）who are on the list（名单上）approved by the Employer.

7.3   Inspection

Inspection is one of the ways of quality control.

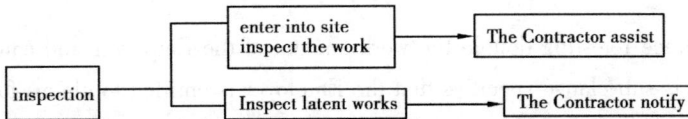

And the contract specifies the Contractor is obliged to give the Employer's Personnel full opportunity to inspect and test.

This sub-clause comprises two parts: the first part specifies that the Employer's Personnel are to be given all reasonable access to inspect and test materials and workmanship and the Contractor is obliged to assist the Employer's Personnel to carry out these inspection and test.

The second part lists the procedure to examine the Works, including the procedure of packaging, storage and check-up before transportation.

This sub-clause states that "the Engineer shall then either carry out the examination, inspection, measurement or testing without unreasonable delay", but no specific time limits are specifies. it should be considered to give a specific time limit to redefine an "unreasonable delay" in the Particular Conditions.

7.4   Testing

Testing can be classified into 3 types: ①testing carries during the execution of the Works（工程执行中进行的检验）;②tests on Completion（完成时的测试）;③ tests after Completion.

Under CONS, there're only the first two sorts of Tests(完成后的测试).

Under CONS, there're only the first two sorts of Tests(前两种测试).

Additional tests would be instructed as Variations under Clause 13.

7.5   Rejection

※ **Discussion**: How if the testing result doesn't comply with the Contract provisions and the Materials or Workmanship are found to be defective?

The first paragraph applies if, following any of the activities described in sub-clause 7.3 or 7.4, something is found to be defective. The contractor is then required to remedy the defects and make the thing comply with the contract.

There're typically two reasons if the Engineer rejects the Work of the Contractor. The first due to the defects of the work itself（工程本身的缺陷）, for example, cracks（裂缝）are found on the concrete（混凝土）which is made by casting（浇筑）. The other is the failure of keeping in compliance with（遵守）the Contract though no flaws（瑕疵）can be found in the product itself, for instance（比如）the Contract specifies that the origin（产地）of the UPS applying to the works shall be France, while the Contractor purchase the UPS from Singapore manufacturer.

In practice, it's possible that the two parties do not agree with each other as to the testing result because of lack of explicit statement of testing standard. In order to prevent the Engineer from misusing his right, this sub-clause requires him to give the reasons when he rejects the work of the Contractor.

※ **Claim clause**：Since retesting double the work amount of the Employer and cause him to double pay his personnel, this sub-clause specifies that the Employer is entitled to claims for incurred costs. This is a fair decision because retesting is caused by the fault of the Contractor.

7.6 Remedial Work

※ **Discussion**：After the Material, the Plant and the workmanship have been tested and approved. Shall the Engineer withdraw from（撤走）further issuing any instruction（发布指令）?

This sub-clause consists of two parts：first, the Engineer is empowered to issue instructions, second, which party shall pay the costs.

Regardless of the previous approval to the completed work of the Contractor, if the Engineer finds the approval work fails to comply with the contract subsequently, he is allowed to issue instructions, requiring the Contractor to replace any Plant or Materials or re-execute the Works. It's a typical provision that the approval of the Engineer won't relieve the Contractor from any obligations under the Contract, which ultimately are to provide to the Employer Works in compliance with the Contract.

It's a typical provision that the approval of the Engineer won't relieve the Contractor from any obligations under the Contract, which ultimately are to provide to the Employer Works in compliance with the Contract.

The second part shows that apparently, this is a provision about "Employer's claims" but indeed an implied provision of "Contractor's Claim".

Contractor's Claim：if the Contractor follows the Engineer's instruction and execute some work which has exceeded the scope of the Contract, he's also entitle to claim against the Employer. [4]

7.7 Ownership of Plant and Materials

Typically, it's specified that before the Plant and Materials are installed or consumed（被安装或消耗）in the Works, their ownership belongs to the Employer. The change in ownership occurs as soon as the Contractor is entitled to payment and not when he subsequently receives payment.

Under sub-paragraph（b）, the change in ownership occurs as soon as the Contractor is entitled to payment and not when he subsequently receives payment. While when the change of ownership occurs, the Contractor most probably hasn't been entitled with payment in full and the promised payment might not have been realized. This may be against the applicable law in some countries, thus it's specified that the precondition is "to the extent consistent with the laws of the Country".

7.8   Royalties

The Contractor is typically entitled to use the earth, rock and other natural materials for any earthwork which may be required on the Site, without paying the Employer for these Materials. But if the Contractor needs to obtain Materials outside the Site, he has to negotiate with the owner of the origin place and pay for what he wants.

Sewage treatment station is often built-up inside the Site, and thoughtful treatment methods have been specified in the Contract provisions as to the disposal of materials from demolitions and excavations and of other surplus material, for example, some rubbish must be burnt and some other must be buried. If it's unallowable to dispose the rubbish on the Site, then the Contractor has to dump the rubbish outside, all at his own cost.

中文参考

[1] 按照合同所述执行。

[2] 如果没有具体的建筑方法,公认的良好惯例就是标准。

[3] 要求安全的设备材料。

[4] 如果承包商未能遵守该指示,则雇主有权雇用其他人来实施工作,并予以支付。

注:上述[1][2][3]条称为合同执行过程当中的 3 个原则。

Note

1. 检查中不论以前是否进行了检验或颁发了证书,工程师仍可以指示承包商:

(1)将工程师认为不符合合同规定的永久设备或材料从现场移走并进行替换;

(2)把不符合合同规定的任何其他工程返工并重建;

(3)实施任何因保护工程安全而急需的工作,无论因为事故、不可预见事件或是其他事件。

2. 除非规范中另有规定,承包商应为下列各项支付所有矿区使用费、租金或其他费用:

(1)从现场外获得的原材料;

(2)对拆除及开挖的材料和其他剩余材料(无论是天然的或合成的),但不包括合同中规定的现场内的弃土区。

3. 在 7.4 节理想状态下,双方希望顺利合作,不想延迟检验,毕竟都想让工程按时完成。然而,显示会有很多突发事件打断工程的进行,因此最好在特殊条款中特别定义一下什么是"unreasonable delay"。

Vocabulary

recognized   公认的,经过验证的;认可的;普遍接受的

apparatus　器械;器具;仪器;设备

Apparatus is the equipment, such as tools and machines, which is used to do a particular job or activity.

additional　额外的;附加的;添加的

Additional things are extra things apart from the ones already present.

promptly　立即;马上;及时

If you do something promptly, you do it immediately workmanship.

skill　工艺;手艺

Workmanship is the skill with which something is made and which affects the appearance and quality of the finished object.

rejection　拒绝;摒弃;剔除物

encumbrance　拖累;障碍;累赘

An encumbrance is something or someone that encumbers you.

disposal　（废物等的）丢掉,清理,销毁,处理

Disposal is the act of getting rid of something that is no longer wanted or needed.

8　Commencement, Delay and Suspension

Progress management is a main part of the project management. Time, costs and quality are the criteria to judge whether a project a successful or not. In view of the project progress, factors that are in connection with time management included commencement of work, progress, completion of work, defect notification period and extension of working period. Clause 8,9,10,11 are all about time management.

8.1　Commencement of Works

The Engineer shall give the Contractor not less than 7 days' notice of the Commencement Date. Commencement of work is an important milestone in the execution of the Works. The Contractor concerns the most about when to commence the work after receiving the Letter of Acceptance.

The notice should be given soon after the Contract becomes legally effective （法律上有效） and need only state:

"We hereby give notice （通知）, in the term of Sub-clause 8.1 of the Conditions of Contract （合同条款）, that the commencement Date （开工日期）shall be…"

The Contractor will commence the preparation of the Works after he receives the Letter of Acceptance, but will be prevented from making appropriate arrangement if the notification is purposely withheld by the Employer. The idle equipment and personnel will incur costs to the Contractor, thus limitation is set to be "within 42 days after the Contractor receives the Letter of Acceptance".

8.2　Time for Completion

Time for completion means a period of time, which is more often called "working period" in China. The Contractor has to complete all the work within this period of time, and enable the Works to be able to stand up to the valuation stipulated in the sub-clause 10.1 "conditions for taking-over", and make the Works to be ready for being taken-over by the Employer, unless the Contractor has successfully claimed for extension. If different parts of the Works are required to be completed within different Times for Completion, these parts should be defined as Sections; in the Appendix to Tender under CONS. Precise geographical definitions are advisable, in order to minimize ambiguity regarding each party's responsibility when the Employer take over a Section.

8.3　Programme

Time limits in connection with program are specified:

(1)the Contractor shall submit time programme (进度计划) to the Engineer within 28 days after receiving the notice;

(2) The Engineer shall, within 21 days after receiving a programme, gives notice to the Contractor stating the extent to which it does not comply with the Contract(它与合同不一样的地方).

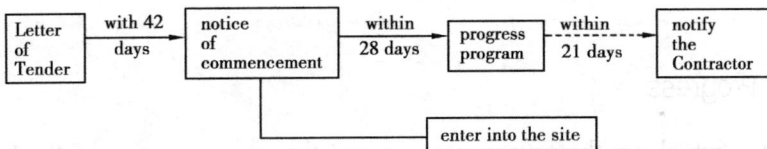

Contractor should revise the program whenever the previous program is inconsistent with: ①actual progress; ②the Contractor's obligation; ③his intention.

※ **Discussion**: Program verse Contract documents?

Program is drafted and submitted by the Contractor to the Engineer after the Contract is signed. And program is more of reference document, the provision of which will be invoked by the Contractor in execution of Works; It doesn't alter the role of either party, nor relieve either party from their responsibility under the Contract.

If the specific date of hand-over of Site is neglected in the Appendix to Tender, then the program provides a reference time schedule for the Employer to make arrangement until the hand-over of the Site to the Contractor.

Besides, it may also work as criteria for the work of the Engineer, whether to issue instructions or drawings.

※ **Discussion**: How if the Contractor fails to submit the program in time?

This sub-clause doesn't provide a solution if the Contractor fails to submit it in time. On the whole, the delay of submission of program won't cause a big problem to the Employer. While in order to simulate the Contractor to act properly in submitting program, it's advisable to add one more condition for payment, which is: the Employer, needn't pay the Contractor before the Contractor submit the program.

8.4 Extension of Time for Completion

Sub-clause does not include a description list of all events which can give rise to an extension but gives examples (a) to (e).

These events comprise two types: ①the delay of time for completion caused by the failure of the Employer; ②delays caused by external impediment.

8.5 Delays caused by Authorities

※ **Discussion**: If the authorities' act delay or disrupt the Contractor's Work, which party shall be blamed for?

The disruption of the authority enable the Contractor to claim for extension of time only if the Contractor's claim can be substantiated by his proofs that these requirements listed in this sub-clause as (a), (b), (c) are perfectly met. [1]

The execution of the Works is often affected by the public policies and regulations such as the construction noise control in special times imposed by the Department of Environmental Protection and the pipeline projects control in the free trade districts, etc.

8.6 Rate of Progress

Based on this Sub-clause the Engineer can control the rate of progress of the Contractor. It's mainly about that under two circumstances the Engineer can require the Contractor to increase the work hours and the number of Contractor's Personnel and Goods at the risk and cost of the Contractor's. and pay the Employer his incurred additional costs for the increase of work amount.

Two problems may arise in practice.

(1) How if the Contractor refuses to obey the Engineer's instruction?

It seems that only sub-clause 15.2 (Termination of the Employer) will apply to this situation, which may be inapplicable in practice unless the Contractor's progress has fallen far behind the programme and the Employer is unconfident that Contractor can complete the Works in time.

(2) Assume that the Contractor did as the Engineer required, and also raised the claims for extension of working time but failed to get the approval from the Engineer. If the Contractor finally accomplishes his tasks in time, and succeeds in getting extension of time from the arbitrator, will the Contractor be entitled to claim for reimbursement for the increase of his work amount?

Two solutions: first, the notice from the Engineer can be regarded as a constructive change order, which has altered the original working period, thus claims for compensation can be entitled under the clause 13, Variations. Second, the final result of time grants proves the Engineer has unreasonably withheld the determinations to grant the Contractor extension of time, which is against the stipulations in sub-clause 1. 3 and hereby constitutes a breach of contract. The Employer is deemed to be liable for this. [3]

8. 7 Delay Damage

The concept of "Delay damages" is widely accepted in international projects and regarded as reasonable and effective binding mechanism.

They may require the sum to have been calculated as:

—a reasonable estimate of the Employer's losses or foregone benefits, which may be equivalent to financing charges for the Contract Price per day, plus

—the daily cost of the Employer's Personnel involved in supervising the execution of the Works during the period of prolongation. [2]

For the limit of the delay damage, if it is to be stated, the usual percentage in international contracts generally varies between 5% and 15%.

Damages vary from penalty as stipulated in laws, the amount of the former is equal to the loss the Employer suffers for the default of the Contractor, and the later is means of punishment whose amount is usually mush higher than the real loss. The standard of "delay damages" is determined by the Employer before the contract is signed as reasonable estimation to the damages, thus may be inconsistent with the actual loss.

If the Employer considers himself to be entitled t be paid delay damages, he is required to give particulars in accordance with Sub-clause 2. 5. Sub-clause 2. 5 concludes by stating that the Employer is not entitled to withhold the amount from payments due to the Contractor, unless and until the procedures described in Sub-clause 2. 5 has been followed.

8. 8 Suspension of Work

Even if it is obvious that certain works must be suspended, for example, because of a flood season, there's no duty under the Contract to instruct a suspension. It is obvious that certain works must be suspended, for example, because of a flood season,In these obvious cases, it is the Contractor who is at risk if he persists in executing work which should obviously be suspended.

If and to the extent that the cause is notified and is the responsibility of the Contractor, the following sub-clause 8. 9, 8. 10 and 8. 11 shall not apply, otherwise, you can find the entitlement of the Contractor to be compensated in these three sub-clauses.

8. 9 Consequences of Suspension

(1)This sub-clause sets out the procedure to deal with a suspension.

First, he gives notice under CONS. Although no time limit prescribed for him to give the notice, he should do so as soon as possible after he receives the instruction to suspend. The Contractor's entitlement for claims have been clarified and what remains is to determine the costs incurred during the suspension period, due to the idle equipment and personnel and on site overheads.

(2)How to calculate the incurred costs during the suspension period?

The Employer normally won't agree to pay full working rates because both of the equipment and personnel are just stand-by, for example, in a negotiation, both parties finally agreed on a rate which is 70% of the Unit Contract Price.

＊The Contractor shall not be entitled to an extension of time for, or to payment of theCost incurred in, making good the consequences of the Contractor's faulty design, workmanship or materials, or of the Contractor's failure to protect, store or secure inaccordance with Sub-Clause 8.8 [Suspension of Work].

8.10　Payment for Plant and Materials in Event of Suspension

If the Works is under normal progress, the only entitlement of payment of Plant and Materials would be under the Clause 14 and the payment would follow the normal procedures stated therein. But the suspension of work may affect the procurement of Plant and Materials. For a suspension which is not due to the Contractor's shortcomings, he becomes entitled to payment for the suspended Plant and Materials, after 28 days, if he takes the necessary actions for them to become the Employer's property.

8.11　Prolonged Suspension

※ **Discussion**: While in case the Contractor is unwilling（不愿意）to wait, will he be entitled to take further actions（进一步措施）?

This sub-clause tends to protect the benefits of the Contractor because though entitlement of claims is granted, excessive delay may foil the plan of the company and cause him some problems. So the Contractor can make choice from the options provided in this sub-clause by either omitting the affected part of the work or terminating the whole works.

8.12　Resumption of Work

If the Contractor didn't choose to omit part of the work nor terminate the whole work, then the resumption of work has to follow the procedures specified in this sub-clause.

This sub-clause requires a joint examination on the Works before the resumption of works starts and the Contractor has to make good any deterioration or defect in or loss of the Works.

※ **Discussion**: Which party is to pay the incurred cost?

Refer to 8.9.

If the Contractor suffers delay and/or incurs Cost from complying with the Engineer'sInstructions, the Engineer and shall be entitled subject toSub-Clause 20.1 [Contractor's Claims] to:

(1)an extension of time for any such delay, if completion is or will be delayed,under Sub-Clause 8.4 [Extension of Time for Completion],

(2)payment of any such Cost, which shall be included in the Contract Price.

The Contractor shall not be entitled to an extension of time for, or to payment of the Cost incurred in, making good the consequences of the Contractor's faulty design, workmanship or materials, or of the Contractor's failure to protect, store or secure in accordance with Sub-Clause 8. 8 [Suspension of Work].

中文参考

[1] 虽然合法当局的打扰可以作为承包商索赔工期的一个原因,但同时提出了3个条件,也就是说:只有承包商提出证据,证明自己的做法符合这3个条件,才能获得索赔工期的权利。

[2] 雇主损失或预知利润的合理估计,相当于合同价格的每天融资费用和在拖延期间参与监督工程实施的雇主人员的每天费用。

[3] 两种解决方法:第一种,可以将工程师的赶工通知看作一项可推定的变更命令,即工程师变更了新的合同工期,进而按变更的原则提出经济索赔;第二种,如果最后裁定承包商有权获得延期,这证明了工程师"没有正当理由"而扣发了给予承包商的延期决定,违反了1.3款的规定是一种违约,业主方应承担相应责任。

Note

(1)竣工时间指的是一个时间段,不是指的一个时间点;开始计算竣工时间的日期为开工日期;竣工时间是完成工程的时间;竣工时间可以指整个工程的竣工时间,也可以指某一区段的竣工时间;如果承包商获得某一段工期的延长,则合同竣工时间为原竣工时间加上延长的那段时间。

(2)误期损害赔偿(Liquidated Damages Delay)是 FIDIC 合同中的一个重要概念。无论是雇主、工程师或承包商都希望通过对这一概念的不同解释来维护自身的利益。误期损害赔偿在业内常被称为"延期罚款"或"固定违约金"。中华人民共和国《合同法》第一百一十三条规定:"当事人一方不履行合同义务或者履行合同义务不符合约定,给对方造成损失的,损失赔偿额应当相当于违约所造成的损失,包括合同履行后可以获得的利益……"

误期损害赔偿属于一般损害赔偿的范畴,专指承包商由于自身原因造成的误期导致工程不能按期完工而向雇主作出的赔偿。而固定违约金的概念则较为宽泛,它不仅可以指合同双方约定的误期损害赔偿,也可指双方在合同中约定的其他固定金额的违约赔偿。因此误期损害赔偿可以是"固定违约金"中的一种,而固定违约金未必仅是"误期损害赔偿"。

"新红皮书"取消"清偿性"这一提法,似乎意味着它不再强调误期损害赔偿必须是雇主损失的真实估算,从而使它多少带有固定违约金的色彩。

Vocabulary

commencement　开始

The commencement of something is its beginning.

take-over　接管,接收

inconsistent　不能始终如一的;时好时坏的

Someone or something that is inconsistent does not stay the same, being sometimes good and sometimes bad.

anticipate　预期;预料;预计

If you anticipate an event, you realize in advance that it may happen and you are prepared for it.

proposal　提议;建议;提案

A proposal is a plan or an idea, often a formal or written one, which is suggested for people to think about and decide upon.

disruption　中断;扰乱;混乱

When there is disruption of an event, system, or process, it is prevented from continuing or operating in a normal way.

fall behind　落后;下降;退后;逾期(付款等)

faulty　(设备等)有问题的,有毛病的,出故障的

A faulty piece of equipment has something wrong with it and is not working properly.

suspension　暂停;延缓

The suspension of something is the act of delaying or stopping it for a while or until a decision is made about it.

jointly　共同地,联合地,连带地

deterioration　恶化; 变坏; 退化; 堕落

9　Tests on Completion

Clause 9 is intended to be applicable to any type of tests which the Contractor is required to carry out at completion, before the taking-over procedures described in Clause 10.

9.1　Contractor's Obligations

This sub-clause specifies the Contractor's obligations when carrying out tests on completion, the preconditions of tests, the particular circumstances he needs to make allowance for, etc.

The tests on Completion are the tests which are required by the Employer in order to determine whether the Works (or a section, if any) have reached the stage at which the Employer should take over the Works or Section. Tests on Completion must be specified in detail in CONS' Specification.

It's specified at the beginning of this sub-clause that the Contractor needs to provide the documents in accordance with sub-paragraph (d) of sub-clause 4.1 (Contractor's General Obligations).

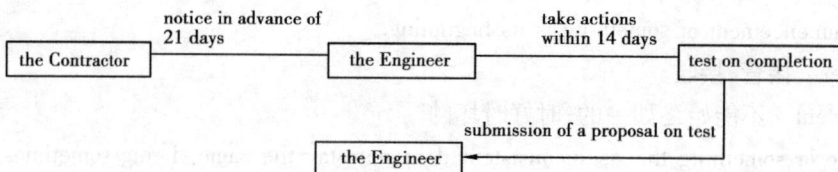

※ **Discussion**: What kind of the documents are these?

They're the Contractor's Documents. Please refer to the definition of 1. 1. 6. 1 "Contractor's Documents" means the calculations, computer programs and other software, drawings, manuals, models and other documents of a technical nature (if any) supplied by the Contractor under the Contract.

9. 2 Delayed Tests

This provision deals with two situations separately; first, it's the default of the Employer, the other, default of the Contractor.

—If the Tests on Completion are delayed by the Employer, the immediate effect is the applicability of Sub-clause 7. 4 (the fifth paragraph, the Contractor can claim according to 20. 1).

—If the delay is excessive, Sub-clause 10. 3 becomes applicable, which entitles the Contractor to compensations for carrying out Tests on Completion during the Defects Notification Period. [1]

—If the Tests on Completion is delayed by the Contractor, The Employer's Personnel can make their own arrangements to carry out the tests at the risk and cost of the Contractor. The Contractor should first be given the opportunity to rectify his default. If Tests are thereafter carried out by the Employer's Personnel, the Contractor is required to accept the results of the Tests, although he is not entitled to receive a report. [2]

9. 3 Retesting

If the Engineer requires this Plant, Materials or workmanship to be retested, the tests shall be repeated under the same terms and conditions. If the rejection and retesting cause the Employer to incur additional costs, the Contractor shall subject to Sub-clause 2. 5 Employer's Claims pay these costs to the Employer.

If tests are repeated after the cause of previous failures has been remedies, and it seems likely that other related work may have been affected by the remedied work, that other work may therefore need to be retested.

9. 4 Failure to Pass Tests on Completion

This sub-clause provides three solutions if the Works or a Section fails to pass the Tests on Completion repeated under Sub-clause 9. 3, the Engineer shall be entitled to:

(1) order further repetition of Tests on Completion under Sub-Clause 9. 3;

(2) if the failure deprives the Employer of substantially the whole benefit of theWorks or Section, reject the Works or Section (as the case may be), in whichevent the Employer shall have the same remedies as are provided in sub-paragraph (c) of Sub-Clause 11. 4 [Failure to Remedy Defects];

(3) issue a Taking-Over Certificate, if the Employer so requests. [2]

There's no limit on the number of repetition which may be ordered. And if the Contractor cannot carry out the remedial works, the Employer may apply Clause 15 or seek agreement to a reduction in the Contract Price. Typically, he might first indicate the reduction he would require, and seek the

Contractor's agreement prior to the issue of a Taking-over Certificate. If agreement cannot be reached prior to the issue of the Taking-Over Certificate under sub-paragraph (3) then sub-paragraph (1) or (2) could be applied.[3]

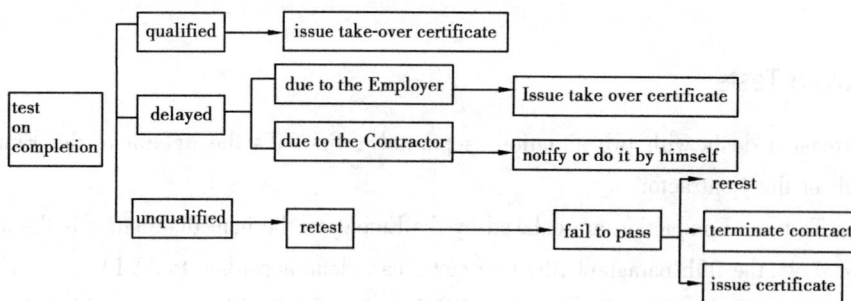

中文参考

[1] 本款对业主和承包商延误竣工检验的情况分别进行了规定:如果竣工试验被业主延误的话,直接适用第7.4款的第五大段;如果延误时间过长,则适用第10.3款,该款使承包商有权在缺陷通知期限内进行竣工试验得到补偿。

[2] 如果试验是由于承包商的缘故被延误的话,雇主人员可以自行进行这些试验,实验的风险和费用应由承包商承担,但首先应给承包商机会修正其违约。如果此后试验由雇主人员进行,承包商要接受试验结果,但无权得到试验报告。

[3] 对指令的重复次数没有限制。如果承包商不能进行修补工作,雇主可以运用第15条,或争取就减少合同价格达成协议。一般地,雇主可能首先表明他要求的减少额,并在颁发接受证书前争取承包商的同意,如果根据(3)项在颁发证书前不能达成协议,这时可以适用(1)项或(2)项。

Note

未能通过竣工实验时,工程师有权:

(1)下令根据第9.3款(重新试验)再次重复竣工试验;

(2)如果此项试验未通过,使雇主实质上丧失了工程或分项工程的整个利益时,拒收工程或分项工程(视情况而定),在此情况下,雇主应采取第11.4款(未能修补缺陷)(c)项规定相同的补救措施;

(3)如雇主要求,颁发接收证书。

Vocabulary

allowance　（定期发给的）津贴,补助

An allowance is money that is given to someone, usually on a regular basis, in order to help them pay for the things that they need.

repetition　（常指令人不快的事件的）反复发生,重复出现,重演

If there is a repetition of an event, usually an undesirable event, it happens again.

10   Employer's Taking Over

10.1   Taking-over of the Works and Sections

Except as stated in Sub-Clause 9.4 [Failure to Pass Tests on Completion], the Work sshall be taken over by the Employer when (i) the Works have been completed in accordance with the Contract, including the matters described in Sub-Clause 8.2 [Time for Completion] and except as allowed in sub-paragraph (a) below, and (ii) a Taking-Over Certificate for the Works has been issued, or is deemed to have been issued in accordance with this Sub-Clause.

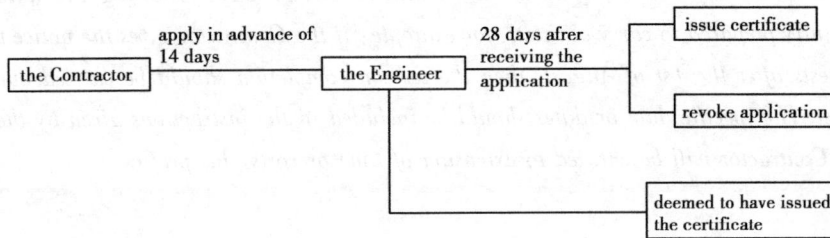

the Contractor	apply in advance of 14 days	the Engineer	28 days afrer receiving the application	issue certificate
				revoke application
				deemed to have issued the certificate

Sample form of Taking-over Certificate for the Works

Having received your notice under Sub-clause 10.1 of the Conditions of Contract, we hereby certify that the Works were completed in accordance with the Contract on _____ (date), except for minor outstanding work and defects (which include those listed in the attached Snagging List and) which should not substantially affect the use of the Works for their intended purpose.

The Contractor should learn from the sub-clause that he needn't wait until all the outstanding works has been finished to apply for a Taking-Over Certificate, but act as soon as the Works or Section have been completed in accordance with the Contract being aware that the minor outstanding work and defects won't affect the use of the Works or Section. [1]

Drawing a conclusion by referring to both of the Clause 9 and Clause 10, the whole test procedure can be divided into 8 stages: [2]

①Preparation for Tests on Completion; ②Applying for Tests on Completion; ③Submitting documents; ④Tests on Completion; ⑤Tests on Completion completed; ⑥Applying for Taking-over Certificate; ⑦Issuing of Taking-over Certificate; ⑧ Taking-over by the Employer.

10.2   Taking Over of Parts of the Works

This Sub-clause grants the Employer right of taking over any part once it has been completed. Because most of these decisions of taking-over are made without notifying the Contractor at advance, the Contractor's arrangements of work may be affected. Under this circumstance, the Contractor is entitled to payment of any such Cost plus reasonable profit.

It's possible that the Employer may use any part of the Works before the Taking-Over Certificate is issued. It's specified that the part which is used shall be deemed to have been taken over by the Employer, and the Engineer shall grant the Contractor opportunity to carry out the tests on completion on this part, and the tests shall be done within the Defects Notification Period. [3]

10.3 Interference with Tests on Completion

Typically, the Tests on Completion are the events which immediately precede completion and taking over. It is therefore reasonable that if such tests are prevented by the Employer, he becomes responsible for the relevant Works or Section: not just the part.

When the first sentence mentions 14 days, it doesn't indicate which day is the beginning of the 14 days period. But as shown in the context, it should be the 14 days following the date when the Contractor is fully prepared to carry out tests, for example: if the Contractor gives the notice that he will be ready for tests after the 1st of August, then the test on completion should be carried out before the 15th of August. The specific date or dates should be included in the instructions given by the Engineer, otherwise the Contractor will be entitled to extension of time or costs plus profit.

10.4 Surface Requiring Reinstatement

This sub-clause specifies that a certificate shall not be deemed to certify completing of any ground or other surfaces requiring reinstatement, but depend upon whether it has been stated in the Taking-Over Certificate. If not, this work shall be regarded as part of the outstanding work to be completed by the Contractor during the Defects Notification Period.

While this sub-clause covers only a Section or part of the Works, which may lead to misunderstanding that if the certificate is about the Whole Works, then it shall be deemed to certify the completion of the grounds or surfaces requiring reinstatement even if they're not stated in the Taking-Over Certificate. Which is obviously not the truth. Thus it's advisable to modify the relevant sentence and change it into "a certificate for a Section or part of the Works or the whole Works".

中文参考

[1] 承包商阅读本款应知道,他不必等到工程已经全部完成才提出接收证书的申请。只要是工程已经基本完成,剩下的扫尾工作或小缺陷并不影响工程的使用功能时,就可以提出申请。

[2] 整个工程验收程序大致可以分为 8 个阶段:

①准备好竣工检验;②申请竣工检验;③提交竣工资料;④开始竣工检验;⑤通过了竣工检验;⑥申请接收证书;⑦签发接受证书;⑧业主接受工程。

[3] 本款还提出了业主在接收之前使用工程的情况,规定出现这种情况,即认为业主接收了该部分工程,同时要求工程师给予承包商机会进行该部分的竣工试验,承包商应该在该部分的缺陷通知期内完成该检验。

Note

除非接收证书中另有规定,区段或部分工程的证书并不认为可以证明任何需要恢复原状的场地或其他地表面的工作已经完成。

Vocabulary

deem   认为;视为;相信

If something is deemed to have a particular quality or to do a particular thing, it is considered to have that quality or do that thing.

substantially   非常地;巨大地

If something changes substantially or is substantially different, it changes a lot or is very different.

cease   停止;终止

If you cease something, you stop it happening or working.

remainder   剩余部分;剩余物;余下的人(或物)

The remainder of a group are the things or people that still remain after the other things or people have gone or have been dealt with.

interference   干涉;干预;介入

Interference by a person or group is their unwanted or unnecessary involvement in something.

reinstatement   (法律、做法等的)恢复;(设施等的)修复

The reinstatement of a law, facility, or practice is the act of causing it to exist again.

11   *Defects Liability*

11.1   Completion of Outstanding Work and Remedying Defects

※ **Discussion**: Which day is the beginning of the defects notification period?

Please refer to the definition 1.1.3.7 of the Defects Notification Period and see which day is the commencement date of this period. "It's the period specified in the Contract for notifying defects, calculated from the date which the Works (or, possibly, a Section) are completed and taken over."

※ **Discussion**: Does the work to be implemented during the defects notification period refer only to defects remedying?[1]

Under Sub-clause 10.1, the Contractor is entitled to a Taking-Over Certificate notwithstanding that some work, namely outstanding work, may still be incomplete. This sub-clause stipulates that except for the responsibility to remedy defects or damage before the expiry date of the Defects Notification Period, the Contractor also has to complete the work which is outstanding within such reasonable time.

As to the scope of the "outstanding work" and to what extent shall the defects be remedied, they shall be subjected to the conditions required by the Contractor It is desirable for there to be a joint inspection of the Works or Section, which should be conducted a few days before the expiry of the Defect Notification Period and should be attended by representatives of the Parties, and the Engineer.

The Employer is also obliged to notify the Contractor if a defect appears or damage occurs but not remedy by himself, unless he has demonstrable grounds for believing that the Contractor would fail to carry out the work with the necessary skill and care.

11. 2 Cost of Remedying Defects

The defects of the Works can either be caused by the Contractor or some other reasons. If its attributable to the Contractor, he will have to pay the costs and take corresponding risks, otherwise, it's the Employer who shall take the responsibilities.

※ **Discussion**: Have you found any problems with this statement?

As stated in the text, it's the Employer who shall notify the Contractor if it's found to be of other reasons, and the Employer may justifiably refuse to give the notice if such an action will incur costs to himself. [2]

Suggestion: What is more practicable is to organize a joint inspection by both parties. And we can put much reliance on the inspection result showing who shall be accountable for the defects.

11. 3 Extension of Defects Notification Period

The circumstances stated in the first paragraph may have occurred before or after taking-over, and may have been due to the Contractor's shortcomings. If the Contractor is not responsible for the defect or demands, the remedial work would constitute a Variation and entitle the Contractor to additional payment（追加付款）, including compensation for the extension of the Defects Notification Period. If it's not due to the Contractor's shortcomings, the Employer will be entitled to extend the Defects Notification Period but no more than 2 years.

And if a defect prevents the Works, Section or a major item of Plant being operated for a certain number of days, the Employer is entitled to require the Defect Notification Period to be extended by that number of days.

11. 4 Failure to Remedy Defects

Before the Employer take use any of the three suggested measures, he must make sure:

(1) to give an advance notice to the Contractor about the date on or by which the defect or damage is to be remedied and the date should be prescribed to be within a reasonable period of time.

(2) that the defects are due to the Contractor's shortcoming.

What constitutes "reasonable" must depend on such factors such as the proximity of the Site to the Contractor's equipment and personnel, the delivery period for replacement Plant, and the operational status of the Works.

11. 5   Removal of Defective Work

Some defects may not be suitable to be remedied on site, or will incur high costs, for example, the defects in some large equipment. Under such circumstance, it's recommended for the equipment to be demolished and sent to the manufacturer to be fixed, the remedial work is necessary to be carried out off the Site.

The Employer can't withhold the consent unreasonably but may impose reasonable conditions, for instance, requiring the Contractor either to increase the amount of the Performance Security or to provide another form of security. The requirements may do the Employer good, but will unavoidably incur costs to the Contractor. Therefore Contractor can benefit from his reputation, a reflection of "credit value" in commercial society. [3]

11. 6   Further Tests

If repetition of tests is instructed by the Engineer, the Contractor must carry out such work. If the Contractor refuses to carry out the tests, the Employer can refer to 9. 2 "Delayed Tests" to protect his own benefits.

And if the Contractor considers none of the sub-paragraph of sub-clause 11. 2 applies and that he is therefore entitled to be paid for repeating a test, he should promptly respond to the instruction by giving notice and detailed particulars of his claims in accordance with the procedure specified in sub-clause 20. 1. And the Employer can extend the Defects Notification Period by referring to the 11. 3 (Extension of Defects Notification Period) in such case in order to protect himself.

11. 7   Right of Access

The Contractor needs to obtain the right access in order to remedy defects or carry out necessary examination work during the Defects Notification Period.

This sub-clause is a comprehensive provision, taking into consideration both of the needs for the Contractor to carry out the remedial work and the needs of security of the Employer since some projects are of high confidentiality.

11. 8   Contractor to Search

Because the Contractor is the executant of the Works, if anything wrong occurs to the Works, the Employer may wish the Contractor to conduct the research for the cause.

Since the result of search relates to the liability of both parties, thus it's required that the Contractor has to conduct the research under the guidance of the Engineer, so as to ensure the objectiveness of the research.

Unless the defect is to be remedied at the cost of the Contractor under Sub-Clause 11. 2 [Cost of Remedying Defects], the Cost of the search plus reasonable profit shall be agreed or determined by the Engineer in accordance with Sub-Clause 3. 5 [Determinations] and shall be included in the Contract Price. [4]

The remedying work are divided into two types under Sub-Clause 11. 2 [Cost of Remedying Defects],if and to the extent that the work is attributable to:

(1) any design for which the Contractor is responsible,

(2) Plant, Materials or workmanship not being in accordance with theContract,

(3) failure by the Contractor to comply with any other obligation.

They shall be executed at the risk and cost of the Contractor, otherwise, they shall be borne by the Employer. [5]

11. 9 Performance Certificate

The Performance Certificate provides written confirmation that the Engineer:

(1) considers that the Contractor has completed his performance of obligations under the Contract;

(2) accepts the Works.

The Performance Certificate should be issued within 28 days after the latest of the expiry of the Defect Notification Periods, unless the Contractor is then known to have outstanding obligations. For example, these obligations include further Contractor's Documents to be supplied, tests to be passed, searched to be completed, and defects to be remedied. In this case, the Performance Certificate should be issued as soon thereafter as the Contractor has supplied all the Contractor's Documents and completed and tested all the Works. It may be difficult to establish how soon is "as soon as", but normally it won't exceed the limit of 28 days after the Contractor has completed all the outstanding work.

For example, these obligations include further Contractor's Documents to be supplied, tests to be passed, searched to be completed, and defects to be remedied.

※ **Discussion**: How if the Performance Certificate is delayed or withheld by the Engineer after the Contractor has completed all of his obligations?

Because issue of Performance Certificate is associated with the refund of retention money and return of Performance Security, if it's delayed or withheld, the Contractor's interests may be damaged. In such a case, the Contractor is advised to invoke sub-clause 1. 3 (communications) "certificates, consents and determinations shall not be unreasonably withheld or delayed".

11. 10 Unfulfilled Obligations

It's most probably that when the Performance Certificate is issued, both parties still have unfulfilled obligations such as:

(1The Employer still have not made all the payments due under the Contract(雇主可能没有根据合同支付所有应付款项);

(2) The Employer still have not released all the Performance Security(没有返还履约担保);

(3) The Works do not comply with the Contract (because of latent defects for example)(工程

随后发现没有完全遵守合同, 比如是因为隐蔽工程缺陷);

(4) The Contractor applies for the Final Payment Certificate(承包商未申请最终支付证书);

(5) The Engineer issues the Final Payment Certificate(工程师未签发最终支付证书);

(6) Disputes get to be solved(索赔争端解决);

(7) The site needs to be cleared(现场没清理).

11.11   Clearance of Site

The Contractor may retain on the Site reasonable amount of Plant and Materials in order to complete the outstanding obligation and remedy defects during the Defect Notification Period. But upon receiving the Performance Certificate, the Contractor has to remove any remaining Contractor's Equipment, surplus materials, wreckage, rubbish and Temporary Works from the Site.

※ **Claim Clause**：

This Sub-clause specifies that the Contractor has to clear the Site within 28 days after receiving the Performance Certificate in prevent of the Contractor's long term take-up of the Site, otherwise the Employer is entitled to dispose of any remaining items.

中文参考

[1] 缺陷通知期内的工作仅包含修补缺陷吗?

[2] 但这在实际操作中不太可行,因为条款规定,应由雇主来通知承包商,如果发现是由其他原因引起的话,但雇主一般不会这么做,因为这样他自己要承担相应的费用。

[3] 承包商的信誉会给承包商带来一定的"信誉",这也是商业社会"信用价值"的体现。

[4] 除非此类缺陷已依据第11.2 款【修补缺陷的费用】,由承包商支付费用进行了修补,否则调查费用及其合理的利润应由工程师依据第3.5 款【决定】作出商定或决定,并加入合同价格。

[5] 本款对修复缺陷的工作分为两类:一类是由于承包商的原因造成的,承包商自己承担修复缺陷所产生的维修费用及在维修过程中所遭遇的风险;另一类是其他原因造成的,则由业主方负担一切的费用和风险。

Note

针对承包商不履行在缺陷责任期的修复义务,业主可采取 3 种规定的处理方式,雇主可(自行):

(1) 以合理的方式由自己或他人进行此项工作,并由承包商承担费用,2.5 款【雇主的索赔】;

(2) 要求工程师依据第3.5 款【决定】对合同价格的合理减少额作出商定或决定;

(3) 对整个工程或不能按期投入使用的那部分主要工程终止合同。

Vocabulary

removal   消除;去除

The removal of something is the act of removing it.

attributable　可归因于…的,可归结于…的

If something is attributable to an event, situation, or person, it is likely that it was caused by that event, situation or person.

suspension　暂停;延缓

The suspension of something is the act of delaying or stopping it for a while or until a decision is made about it.

expire　到期;期满;失效

When something such as a contract, deadline, or visa expires, it comes to an end or is no longer valid.

dispose　处理,处置; 安排

restore　使恢复;使康复;使复原

To restore someone or something to a previous condition means to cause them to be in that condition once again.

12　*Measurement and Evaluation*

Clause 12 is based upon the principle that the Works are to be valued by measuring the quantity of each item of work under Sub-clause 12. 2 and applying the appropriate rate per unit or the appropriate lump-sum price under Sub-clause 12.3. Alternatively, GPPC 114 refers to the possibility of replacing Clause 12 by appropriate Particular Conditions, for a lump-sum contract or a cost-plus contract. [1]

12.1　Works to be Measured

This sub-clause provides two sorts of measurements; the first is to conduct on-site measurements which are supposed to be done by a join activity by the representative of the Contractor and the Engineer. The second is to measure the items from records. It's the Engineer who should prepare the records.

FIDIC Contract is unit price contract, which emphasizes on the separation of quantity and price, so to speak, the quantity can vary but the unit price remains unchanged. As specified in the "Notice to Tender" the unit price weights against other factors.

If the unit price in B. Q. contradicts with the total price, it's the unit price should be subjected to; if unit price figures contradict with description, description words should be subjected to.

From the sub-clause we can see that all the payments are actually calculated based on the measured quantity of work. Thus the Contract under such a calculation mode can be called "unit price contract after remeasurement".

The "Schedules" are defined as including a "Bill of Quantities", which is also called Price

Sheet in tendering documents. It's the base on which the tendering prices are calculated.

B. Q generally consists of several items and sub-items for users to look up, for instance, in real estate project, these items are grouped according to processes, including clearance of Site, excavation, concrete process, brickwork process, bitumen process, carpenter process, join pointing process, steel structure, drainage pipe, plaster process, water and electricity, painting, internal decoration and fence, etc.

A capable contractor can often find the gaps between the B. Q. and actual work, and eventually gain more than what has been stated in the Contract. While under such particular circumstances when the offered price is even lower than the cost, the work will remain no longer profitable, because the more you do, the more you lose.

Except as otherwise stated in the Contract, wherever any Permanent Works are to bemeasured from records, these shall be prepared by the Engineer. The Contractor shall, as and when requested, attend to examine and agree the records with the Engineer, and shall sign the same when agreed. If the Contractor does not attend, the recordsshall be accepted as accurate. If the Contractor examines and disagrees the records, and/or does not sign them as agreed, then the Contractor shall give notice to the Engineer of the respects in which the records are asserted to be inaccurate. After receiving this notice, the Engineer shall review the records and either confirm or vary them. If the Contractor does not so give notice to the Engineer within 14 days after being requested to examine the records, they shall be accepted as accurate.

Sometimes the Contractor may decline to provide all the particulars when their own interests will be infringed, and the Engineer's representatives on site are advised to make proper records of the site, which will turn to great significance and be of help in variation. For example, when a sort of variation material needs to be revaluated in a project, the Contractor proposes that 10% of consumption rate shall be included in the cost according to the industrial convention. While after the Engineer check the warehouse records, the actual consumption rate is found to be as low as 1% . The Contractor dissatisfies with the result and resort to arbitrations. The arbitration organization reexamine the case the determines that the consumption rate shall be neglected. The sie records help the Employer save as much as thousands of dollars.

12. 2   Methmethod of valuation

The method of measurement may comprise:

(1) Three basic methods including unit price, lump-sum, cost-plus.

(2) A publication which specifies principles of measurement and which is incorporated into the Bill of Quantities,

(3) For a contract which does not contain many or complex items of work, principles included in each of the item description in the Bill of Quantity. [2]

12.3 Evaluation

This sub-clause is comprised by three parts: first, under normal circumstances, Contract Price is agreed or determined by evaluating each item of work, applying the measurement agreed or determined in accordance with the above sub-clause 12.1 and 12.2 and the appropriate rate or price for the item. Second, if the measured quantity has changed too much comparing with the quantity stated in the B.Q., the rate or price need to be adjusted. Third, if the work is instructed under Clause 13, a new rate or price should also be considered.

Sub-paragraph (a) specifies four criteria which are applicable without reference to Clause 13, and a new rate shall only be appropriate if all four criteria are satisfied. The first two criteria relate to change in quantity, the third criterion relates to its effect on Cost, and the fourth criterion allows adjustment of some items to be precluded.

One of four criteria is that the Cost actually incurred divided by the measured quantity must be less than 99% or more than 101% of the what the Cost would have been divided by the quantity stated in the B.Q., while in practice, the Contractor and the Engineer's opinions may diverge as to the calculation of the Cost per unit quantity. What is advisable is that the Contractor shall present the reasons why he think the rate should be increased, and the Engineer shall give out proofs confirming why he think the rate should be reduced and put them on table to discuss. Before two parties come to an agreement, the Engineer shall determine a provisional rate or price for the purpose of Interim Payment Certificate. If two parties fail to agree on the final new rate or price, the problems can be solved according to disputes procedures under Clause 20.

12.4 Omission

The Contractor is entitled to compensation for the costs reasonably incurred in the expectation of carrying out work subsequently omitted under the Variation.

Case 1: If the Contractor has ordered formwork for work which was subsequently omitted by Variation, the Accepted Contract Amount would typically have included direct cost plus profit in respect of this formwork. The Contractor would then be entitled to recover cost and profit.

Case 2: when some work has been omitted, relevant payment will subsequently be deducted from the Contract, while the overheads occurred in headquarter office or during on-site work won't diminish, and this will incur cost to the Contractor. So the Contractor shall be able to claim back the sum of money by invoking this sub-clause.

中文参考

[1] 第 12 条依据的原则是,工程要根据第 12.2 款测量每项工作的数量,并根据 12.3 款使用适宜的单位费率或者是适宜的总额价格。GPPC14 提到可用适当的专用条件中的总价合同或成本加价合同代替第 12 条的可能性。

[2] 测量方法可包括:

（1）三种基本方法，单价、总计和成本加价法；

（2）规定测量原则并被纳入工程量表的出版物；

（3）对于不包含很多复杂工作内容的合同，包含在工程量表中的原则。

Note

在下列情况下，适应新的费率或价格：

（1）（ⅰ）如果此项工作实际测量的工程量比工程量表或其他报表中规定的工程量的变动大于 10%；

（ⅱ）工程量的变更与对该项工作规定的具体费率的乘积超过了接受的合同款额的 0.01%；

（ⅲ）由此工程量的变更直接造成该项工作每单位工程量费用的变动超过 1%；

（ⅳ）这项工作不是合同中规定的"固定费率项目"；

（2）（ⅰ）此工作是根据第 13 款【变更与调整】的指示进行的；

（ⅱ）合同中对此项工作未规定费率或价格；

（ⅲ）由于该项工作与合同中的任何工作没有类似的性质或不在类似的条件下进行，故没有一个规定的费率或价格适用。

Vocabulary

assert　坚称；断言；坚决表明

If someone asserts a fact or belief, they state it firmly.

derive　获得；取得；得到

If you derive something such as pleasure or benefit from a person or from something, you get it from them.

omission　省略的东西；删节的东西；遗漏的东西

An omission is something that has not been included or has not been done, either deliberately or accidentally.

measurement　（质量、价值或影响的）衡量，评估，估量

The measurement of the quality, value, or effect of something is the activity of deciding how great it is.

13　Variation and Adjustment

Variations can be initiated by any of three ways：

（1）The Variation may be instructed without prior agreement as to feasibility or price, which may be appropriate for urgent work.

（2）The Contractor may initiate his own proposals, which may be approved as a Variation, or he rnay be given other instructions which constitute a variation.

（3）A proposal may be requested, in an endeavor to reach prior agreement on its effect and thereby minimize dispute.[1]

13.1 Right to Vary

Variations may be initiated by the Engineer at any time prior to issuing the Taking-OverCertificate for the Works, either by an instruction or by a request for the Contractor to submit a proposal.

Having received an instruction to execute a Variation, the Contractor must comply with it unless he promptly gives the notice described in the second paragraph of this Sub-Clause. He may be unable to obtain the Goods, which are the Contractor's Equipment, Materials, Plant and Temporary Works required for the Variation. It's advised to add one more reason "be in shortage of labour" as a compound sentence to "cannot readily obtain the Goods", for these two reasons for which the Contractor can't execute Variations have similar effect and results.

This sub-clause states that "The Contactor shall execute and be bound by each Variation, unless the Contractor promptly gives notice to the Engineer stating the reason with supporting particulars. Upon receiving the notice, the Engineer shall cancel, confirm or vary the instruction". And we can further derive that if the Engineer insists on the instruction to Variation under this circumstance, the notice and particulars given by the Contractor will provide reliable proofs for him to claim for compensation or extension subsequently, showing that to carry out the Variation is rather difficult due to the reason stated above. Thus the Engineer shall take into allowance in his determinations of the "degree of difficulties" of the work.

Each new rate or price shall be derived from any relevant rates or prices in the Contract, with reasonable adjustments to take account of the matters described in sub-paragraph (a) and/or (b), as applicable. If no rates or prices are relevant for the derivation of a new rate or price, it shall be derived from the reasonable Cost of executing the work, together with reasonable profit, taking account of any other relevant matters.

Two contradicting situations may both take place when a new rate or price is considered to be derived from the Contract during the execution of the sub-clause.

One intendancy is to adopt a comparatively higher rate, which is referred by most of the Contractors. For example, when a variation is to be issued in a concrete engineering project, material of cement needs to be reevaluated beforehand. As to the request of the Contractor, the current market price of 512 yuan/t shall be applied rather than the tendering price of 484 yuan/t. The Engineer insists on adoption of tendering price. The engineering law and ICE contract affirm that first, it's unjustifiable to deny the rate and price in accordance with the original B. Q in variation measurement grounded with such reasons that they are uneconomical. Secondly, the contractor shall not take the advantage of the variation measurement to compensate their losses and such uneconomical mistakes in tendering shall be undertaken by the Contractor himself otherwise.

While the Engineer inclines to adopt new rate or price to replace the comparatively low price stated in the contract. Sometimes the Contractor will give a much higher quotation of certain materials that are 2 ~ 3 times comparing with the price specified in the B. Q, thus disputes may arise unavoidably during the execution of the project when the Engineer issue an instruction of variation by using such materials. Under such circumstances, adoption of a new rate or price to reevaluate is also against the intention of FIDIC contract.

13.2　Value Engineering

"Value Engineering" is a new concept in engineering economics, with its focus on how to optimize the function per unit of costs(功能/费用最优化), thus to maximize the output of capital, this sub-clause introduces in the use of this term. Since engineering projects involve large amount of capital, optimized design and execution schemes will result in huge profits. This clause is often invoked in the new-edition engineering contracts in recent years in order to stimulate the Contractor to propose improved methods that will benefit both parties.

Because the Contractor is the executant of the project and familiar with the actual situation of the project, he will often propose ideas to accelerate completion or reduce costs based on his rich experience. The Contractor may wish to propose changes in the following situations:

(1)The proposal may appear to be of benefit to the Contractor, in which case he may offer a reduction in the Contract Price in order to encourage the Employer's acceptance;

(2)The proposal may appear to be of benefit to the Employer, by improving the quality of the Works (by reducing the cost of maintenance or operation, or improving productivity or efficiency). This might involve an increase in the Cost, and thus in the Contract Price. [2]

CONS 13.2 concludes with sub-paragraphs covering the possibility that the value engineering proposal may involve a change in the Employer's (or Engineer's) design of the Permanent Works. Problems may sometimes arise in these situations usually because the Parties failed to agree aspects such as design liability. They are entitled to agree what they wish, but the sub-paragraphs define the position if they fail to reach and record their agreement.

13.3　Variation Procedure

This Sub-clause specifies the procedure when the Engineer requests the Contractor to submit proposal before he issues a Variation. Two points need to be reminded:

(1)The request should be in writing and use the word "request". Otherwise, there is a risk that a request may appear to be an instruction, and thus as a Variation, entitling the Contractor to payment for complying with it.

(2)The Contractor must proceed with the Works with "due expedition and without delay"(正当快速且不延误地)unless and until he receives a response or is instructed otherwise.

It states that "The Engineer shall, as soon as practicable after receiving such proposal, respond with approval, disapproval or comments".

Hereby three sorts of consequences after the Engineer review the proposal may happen:

(1)The Engineer comments on the proposal of the Contractor as being unreasonable and requires the Contractor to modify it.

(2)The Engineer thinks the proposal is reasonable but still shows disapproval due to affordable costs.

(3)The Engineer thinks the proposal is reasonable and incurred costs are acceptable, thus he shows approval and instructs it as a Variation to the Contractor. In this situation, the Engineer will grant the Contractor reimbursement of costs and extension time based on the proposal. [3]

※ **Discussion**: This sub-clause states that he Engineer can show reject the proposal, so can the Contractor claim for reimbursement costs for drafting the proposal?

It's advised to add one more sentence in this sub-clause that "the Employer shall compensate the Contractor costs for drafting the proposal".

13.4 Payment in Applicable Currencies

※ **Discussion**: How shall the payment after adjustment be paid as contrasted to that the normal contract payment should be paid according to the proportion mentioned above?

Please refer to this sub-clause.

First, when an adjustment is determined, the amount payable in each of the applicable currencies shall be specified. Second, two factors shall be taken into account. No. 1: the actual or expected currency proportional of the Cost of the Varied work. No. 2: the proportions of various currencies specified for payment of the Contract Price. [4]

This sub-clause doesn't specify who is going to determine the proportion of various currencies. While it can be derived that determination of the proportion shall follow the procedure of determining adjustment payment, which is "negotiation, approval and determination", so to speak, the Engineer will negotiate with the Contractor, or the Contractor will propose currency proportion asking for approval from the Engineer, or when two parties can't agree with each other, the Engineer will proceed to make determinations.

13.5 Provisional Sums

Provisional Sums are determined in different ways: they can be either prescribed in the tendering documents by the Employer and then added into the tendering price by the Contractor; or to be filled by the Contractor before they constitute part of the Contract Price. This depends upon decision strategy. Considering the percentage they account for, they won't exert much influence on the Contract Price.

At their sole judgment, the Contractor can decide on the amount of the Provisional Sums, higher when they make allowance for the likelihood of the happening of the work relates to the provisional sums, and lower when they consider the relevant work are less likely to happen, since this will help to reduce the tendering price and make it more competent.

Under CONS, Provisional Sums are often included in the Bill of Quantities for parts of the Works which are not required to be priced at the risk of the Contractor. For example, Provisional Sums may be appropriate for any Materials which the Engineer is to select, or for any uncertain parts of the Works. Such arrangements provide considerable flexibility, because the work may be executed by a nominated Subcontractor or by the Contractor and valued under Clause 12 or on a cost-plus basis.

Sometimes, work is mentioned without referring to the quantity, in such a case, the Contractor can increase the unit price, which will enable them to earn more if large amount of relevant work are executed, leaving no effect on quotation. House renovation and outdoor work in reconstruction projects fall into this category.

13.6 Daywork

Daywork, which is sometimes called "time-work", is typically necessary for minor or contingent work paid at Cost-plus basis.

The Daywork schedule to be priced by tenderers and included in the Contract should define:

(a) A time charge rate for each person or category (money per person per hour, for example).

(b) A time charge rate for each category of Contractor's Equipment (money per hour per unit, for example);

(c) The payment due for each category of Materials. This is usually on a basis similar to that described in Sub-Clause 13.5(b). However, for some Materials (for example, natural Materials and Materials manufactured on the Site), it may be appropriate to provide items for pricing on a money per unit quantity basis. [5]

FIDIC contract conditions are not applicable in all circumstances, however, and usually need some other widely recognized documents as technical support. Especially when it relates to the Daywork covered by Provisional Sums, FIDIC will refer to the "Schedules of Dayworks carried out Incidental to Contract work" edited by the Civil Engineering Contractors Association.

According to the schedules, the Contractor will charge extra overheads of 12.5% to 148% on the Works and Materials that regarded as Daywork, which may include insurances, tool charges and transportation fees, etc. Of which, a rate of 12.5% can be charged on staff transportation and 88% can charged on Daywork done by the Nominated Subcontractor. This percentage also provides reference for the Contractor to choose subcontractors when filling in the Appendix of Tender, allowing some adjustment to be made considering the extent of their influence on the tendering price.

When appropriate dealt with, daywork can turn out to be an opportunity to make extra income. For instance, in an oversea highway renovation project, $230,000 is set aside as Provisional Sums to repair the highway, while FIDIC Contact also states that Daywork is to be calculated on the basis of FCEC Schedules of Dayworks which results in as much as $700,000 of Daywork payment. This happens after the Engineer has tried their best to cut back the costs. Finally the Employer agrees to give the payment in prevent that disruption of the construction may cause the collapse of transportation to and from the capital.

13.7　Adjustment for Changes in Legislation

Changes include：

—in the Laws of the Country（including the introduction of new Laws and the repeal（废除）or modification（修改）of existing Laws）or

—in the judicial（司法）or official governmental interpretation of such Laws.

We all know that the Contractor make the quotations based on the laws of the country where the project locate, such as：Tax Law, Labour Law, Insurance Law, Customs Law, Environmental Protection Law, etc. The changes of these laws will unavoidably lead to changes of Costs and remain unforeseeable for the Contractor.

For example, in the Xiao langdi hydro-project, the modification of Chinese Labour law, that the working days of 5 and half were reduced to 5 days, entitled the Contractor to claims for enormous sum of money.

If the change delays the Contractor and increases his Cost, he is required to give notice under the second paragraph. If the change decrease the Contractor's Cost and the Employer considers himself to be entitled to a reduction in the Contract Price, the Employer is required to give notice under Sub-Claus 2.

13.8　Adjustments for Changes in Cost

Applying the payment formulae is a comparatively easy and more acceptable way to make profits, being of a more utilitarian role than making claims. The earnings are realized before the signing of contract instead of after that, thus can be applied to all the due payment after valuation. It has to be mentioned that the formula only applies to long working period project, which is normally more than 1 year.

Fluctuation Adjustment Formula：

$$P_n = a + b \times L_n/L_0 + c \times M_n/M_0 + d \times E_n/E_0 + \cdots$$

Of which,

The adjustment multiplier "P_n" is "to be applied to the estimated contract value". Note that P_n will usuall exceed "1" reflecting the escalation costs due to inflation and also possible be smaller than "1" reflecting the reduction of costs due to deflation.

Typically, the Employer will have defined the fixed（non-adjustable）coefficient "a" before the tender documents are issued to tenders, but may prefer each tenderer to define the other coefficient and all the sources of the cost indices in the table for each currency, so that they can fairly reflect：

—the proportion of Cost（for example, different tenderers may anticipate different percentage for labour and equipment）, and

A project contract allows for the price adjustment and adopts the Adjustment Formula.

After the analysis and calculation on the quotation, the proportions of different adjustment items accounting for the Contract Price are determined. Please refer to the table below about the reference price on the day that is 28 day prior to the latest date for submission of the Tender. The accomplished project amount in the 1st month is $2, 300, 000.

—the sources of the cost indices (each of which should relate to the currency of Cost, *which may also differ between tenderers*).

Aajustment items	Proportion of the Contract Price(I)	Reference price on the day that is 28day prior to the latest date for submission of the Tender(T_0)	Pubished reference price in I month(T)	T_i/T_0	$I(T_i/T_0)$
Unadjustable	0.30	N/A	N/A	1	0.30
Wage(dollar/day)	0.25	3	3.6	1.2	0.30
Steel(dollar/t)	0.12	520	580	1.115	0.134
Cement(dollar/t)	0.06	80	82	1.025	0.062
Fuel(dollar/litre)	0.08	0.4	0.48	1.2	0.096
Wood(dollar/cubic meter)	0.1	420	480	1.143	0.114
Other materials (according to price index)	0.09	100	120	1.2	0.108
In total					1.114

So, the adjusted project amount in this month is:

$P_i = P_0 \times I \times (T_i/T_0) = 2.3 \times 1.114 = 2.5622$ million dollars

Of which, the adjusted amount caused by price index is:

$P_i - P_0 = 2.5622 - 2.30 = 0.2622$ million dollars

For instance, in a railway renovation project with loans from World Bank, the Contract Price was 5.34 million US dollars, the working period was 32 months and later extended to be 38 months by the Employer. During the period when the project was executed, the Congress proclaimed to improve the lowest wage standard and 17,500 in local currency per month was increased to 30,000 in local currency per month. This largely contributed to the increase of labor coefficient, which almost doubled and also led to the escalation of labor costs. As a result, the adjusted amount reached as much as 1.4 million us dollars and was in excess of 26% of what had been stated in the Contract Price.

※ **Discussion**: Learning from the case above, what will you suggest to the Employer as measures of self-protection?

Adjustment formulae is an important way to protect the Contractor from being affected by the price fluctuation. It's advisable that the Employer shall be entitled to set limit to adjustment, for example, to state in Contract that 10% of changes are allowable, and the excessive part shall be t the risk of the Contractor. Whilst no such stipulations had been specified in this Contract, thus correspondingly the adjusted value increased with the escalation of costs indices, free from any limitation.

中文参考

[1] 变更可用三种方式任意提出：

(1)变更可在没有关于可行性或价格的事先协议情况下提出，这对于紧急情况是适用的；

(2)承包商可提出自己的建议，该建议可能被批准为变更，或它可能会被给予构成变更的其他指示；

(3)可以要求提出一份建议书，尽力就其影响达成事先协议，从而使争端减至最小。

[2] (1)建议书可能对承包商有好处，在此情况下，他可能提出降低合同价格以促使雇主接受；

(2)通过改进工程的质量（或通过减少维护和运行费用，或提高生产率或效率），建议书可能对雇主有好处。这样做可能使费用增加，并因此提高合同价格。

[3] (1)工程师认为承包商的建议书不合理，他可以给出自己的建议，要求承包商修改；

(2)如果工程师认为承包商的建议书合理，但是变更的代价太大，可能决定不变更；

(3)如果工程师认为承包商的建议书合理，而且变更的代价又可以被业主接受，则可以指示承包商进行变更工作。

[4] 考虑从两个因素：一是完成变更工作实际需要哪些货币，二是合同规定支付合同价格的货币比例。

[5] 要由投标人定价，并含在合同内的计日工作计划表应明确规定：

(1)每人或每类的计时费率（例如，每人每小时金额）；

(2)每类承包商设备的计时费率（例如，某项设备每小时金额）；

(3)每类材料的应付款，通常依据与第13.5款(a)项所述类似的原则。但对于某些材料（例如，天然材料和在现场加工的材料），规定按单位数量金额定价的物品，可能是适合的。

Note

1. 创收的三大支柱：

①索赔（Claims）；②工程变更令（Variation Order）；③调价公式（Fluctuation Adjustment Formula）。

2. 每项变更可包括：

(1)对合同中任何工作的工程量的改变（此类改变并不一定必然构成变更）；

(2)任何工作质量或其他特性上的变更；

(3)工程任何部分标高、位置和(或)尺寸上的改变；

(4)省略任何工作，除非它已被他人完成；

（5）永久工程所必需的任何附加工作、永久设备、材料或服务，包括任何联合竣工检验、钻孔和其他检验以及勘察工作；

（6）工程的实施顺序或时间安排的改变。

＊承包商不应对永久工程作任何更改或修改，除非工程师发出指示或同意变更。

3. 公式常用的形式如下：

$$P_n = a + b \cdot L_n/L_0 + c \cdot M_n/M_0 + d \cdot E_n/E_0 + \cdots$$

其中："P_n"是对第 n 期间内所完成工作以相应货币所估算的合同价值所采用的调整倍数，这个期间通常是一个月，除非投标函附录中另有规定；

"a"是规定的一个系数，代表合同支付中不调整的部分；

"b""c""d"相关数据调整表中规定的一个系数，代表与实施工程有关的每项费用因素的估算比例，此表中显示的费用因素可能是指资源，如劳务、设备和材料；

"L_n""E_n""M_n"…是第 n 期间时使用的现行费用指数或参照价格，以相关的支付货币表示，而且按照该期间（具体的支付证书的相关期限）最后一日之前第 49 天当天对于相关表中的费用因素适用的费用指数或参照价格确定；

"L_0""E_0""M_0"…是基本费用指数或参照价格，以相应的支付货币表示，按照在基准日期时相关表中的费用因素的费用指数或参照价格确定。

Vocabulary

borehole　（尤指为了寻找石油或水而在地上凿的）钻孔，井眼

A borehole is a deep round hole made by a special tool or machine, especially one that is made in the ground when searching for oil or water.

exploratory　（行动）探究的，探测的，探索性的

Exploratory actions are done in order to discover something or to learn the truth about something.

accelerate　（使）加快；（使）增速

If the process or rate of something accelerates or if something accelerates it, it gets faster and faster.

await　等候；等待

If you await someone or something, you wait for them.

proportion　比例

The proportion of one kind of person or thing in a group is the number of people or things of that kind compared to the total number of people or things in the group.

overheads　日常管理费用；杂项开支；一般经费

quotation　报价；开价

When someone gives you a quotation, they tell you how much they will charge to do a particular piece of work.

voucher　代金券；票券；收据

A voucher is a ticket or piece of paper that can be used instead of money to pay for something.

收据，凭单会计术语。会计人员根据审核无误后的原始凭证或汇总原始凭证，按照经济业务的内容加以归类，用来确定会计分录而填制的直接作为登记账簿依据的会计凭证。

substantiation　实体化；证实，证明；使实体化

adjustable　（位置或大小）可调整的

If something is adjustable, it can be changed to different positions or sizes.

indicative　指示的；象征的；暗示的

If one thing is indicative of another, it suggests what the other thing is likely to be.

tabulated　将…制成表格；以表格形式排列

To tabulate information means to arrange it in columns on a page so that it can be analysed.

render　致使；造成

You can use render with an adjective that describes a particular state to say that someone or something is changed into that state. For example, if someone or something makes a thing harmless, you can say that they render it harmless.

unbalance　使失衡；使紊乱；使失常

If something unbalances a relationship, system, or group, it disturbs or upsets it so that it is no longer successful or functioning properly.

14　Contract Price and Payment

14.1　The Contract Price

※ **Discussion**：The difference between the Accepted Contract Amount and the Contract Price?

The former is a provisional price which is submitted by the Contractor as quotation and determined after tendering evaluation and negotiations. And the latter is the total due payment paid to the Contractor. This shows the evolution in description wording on payment of the Works and avoids the uncertainties in using the word of "Contract Price" and the ambiguity of the concept which occur in previous editions. [1]

14.2　Advance Payment

This Sub-Clause specifies that total advance payment must be included in the Appendix to Tender and sets out the procedures to be followed in repaying the advances.

Whenever the Contractor is required to be paid prior to the Employer having received anything in return, the Employer will probably require some security for his outlay. This security is to be in the form of a guarantee, which is to be issued by an entity approved by the Employer. It is required to be in the form annexed to the Particular Conditions, or in another form approved by the Employer. The Particular Condition should therefore include details of the Employer's requirement regarding the entity, and the details of the specified form.

※ **Discussion**: The definition of the advance payment?

The Employer shall pay the Contractor a sum of money called advance payment when the Contractor submit bank guarantee of advance payment according to this sub-clause. It may be regarded as interest free loan for the Contractor to launch his work. The amount of advance payment, times of installments, payment schedule (when there's more than one payment), applicable currency and its proportion shall comply with what has been specified in the Appendix to Tender.

※ **Discussion**: Will repayment of advance payment affect extension of the guarantee?[2]

The guarantee is required to be valid until the advance payment has been repaid. And this Sub-Clause requires the guarantee to be extended if, 28 days before its expiry date, the advance has not been repaid in full. If the advance has not been repaid by the date 28 days before the guarantee expires, and the Contractor fails to extend it, this Sub-Clause entitled the Employer to call the guarantee. The period of 28 days is specified so as to allow the Employer a reasonable period within which to make the necessary arrangements for the call.

※ **Discussion**: How does the payment progress affect the use of the advance payment?

The repayment program needs careful consideration when put into work, since being haste or too much procrastination will both adversely affect the use of the advance payment. The specifications in this Sub-Clause are rather thoughtful and reasonable.

Here I'd like to recommend you a formula to calculate the repayment of advances.

$$R = \frac{A(C - aS)}{(b - a)S}$$

Of which:

R represents the accumulated repaid advances deducted from Interim Payment Certificates;

A represents total advance payment;

S represents the Accepted Contract Amount;

C represents the accumulated due payment shown in interim payment certificates, it's value depends upon the detailed specifications in the Contract, for example: is it before the deduction of retention money or after that (generally excludes retention money)? Is it before the adjustment or after that (generally before adjustments)? And the scope of C is: $aS < C < bS$;

a represents the percentage of the interim payments in all interim payments when their accumulated value has begun to exceed the 15% of the Accepted Contract Amount less Provisional Sums and deductions commence;

b represents the percentage of the accumulated interim payments accounting for the Accepted Contract Amount, when all the advance payments have been repaid. [3]

14.3   Application of Interim Certificate

This Sub-Clause consists of three parts: ① time to submit Monthly Statement; ② supporting documents submitted together with the Statement; ③ items included in the Statement.

It's only specified that the after the end of each month shall a Statement be submitted rather than to impose strict time limit on the submission of Statement. Because the Contractor will try their best to submit the statement as early as possible even without being urged, and the earlier they take action, the earlier they will receive the payment.

It's stated that the statement form needs to be approved by the Engineer, In practice, in order to avoid the form being rejected by the Engineer, the Contractor can choose the negotiate with the Engineer in advance and determine the form before it's submitted. When considering what form to approve, the Engineer should take account of the need to facilitate his rapid checking of the various amounts, and take account of the financial provisions in the Contract on which the amounts are to be based. He should allow the Contractor to utilize any computerized system with which the Contractor's staff are familiar, provided it produced clear and comprehensible Statement.

The " Contract Value" is value of the Works in accordance with the Contract, namely the applicable part of the Contract Price, in accordance with Sub-Clause 14. 1 (a). Under CONS, the calculation of contract value is based on the measurement of the quantities of the work executed up to the end of a month, in accordance with Sub-Clause 12. 3.

Each statement must be accompanied by supporting documents and these documents are required to include the progress report specified in Sub-Clause 4. 21 for the relevant period.

14. 4   Schedule of Payments

Interim payments typically are based upon monthly measurements of quantities of works, applying the rates and prices from a Bill of Quantities. However, a schedule of payments may sometimes be considered appropriate for a contract under CONS. If project progresses steadily, it's convenient to apply Schedule of Payment, while in fact, real work progress does not always keep pace with the plan (no matter it falls behind or goes ahead), thus Schedule of Payment may not be as effective as they are expected to be.

It's specified that the Engineer may revise installments if actual progress is found to be less than that on which this schedule of payment was based, but does not mention the other situation when the actual progress if more than that of the plan. It's understandable that in the opinion of the Employer, it's good enough for the execution of Works to comply with the original plan, and speeding-up of work pace is not encouraged due to its possible adverse effect on project quality. [4]

Except for in a privately-financed commercial project, for example BOT project, and quality of the work being ensured, the Employer won't press for completion of the work in advance. Based on experiences, this payment mode is not advised to apply on unit price contracts after remeasurement, but is acceptable for contracts on lump-sum basis.

A project needs a large amount of investment, and the Employer needs time to make budget and prepare for give payment, Schedule of Payment is the one to help them plan installments. And if there is no such schedule of payments, the last paragraph requires the Contractor to submit non-binding estimates every three months, which is actually the Contractor's quarterly cash flow plan.

14.5   Plant and Materials Intended for the Works

For civil engineering projects(工程建设项目), Materials and Plant account for a large percent of the Contract Price value, hereby forcing the Contractor to raise enough money to procure these Goods. In international trade, credit card is typically required for procurement of goods, and the Contractor needs to present bank credit card with equal amount to procurement contracts value when issuing orders. Sufficient deposit in bank account is required in order to prepare a credit card. In one word, the Contractor needs large amount of cash to procure Materials and Plant. Hence it's customary to pay for the Materials and Plan in advance.

This Sub-Clause specifies the payment mechanism for Materials and Plant under CONS.

We learn that there're two types of Materials and Plant listed in the Appendix to Tender and the listed Materials and Plant can acquire advance payment equal to 80% of their costs before they are installed or used in the Works. When their contact value has been included as part of the Permanent Works, the payment paid at advance will be deducted. This shows that the Materials and Plant are actually paid by two installments under CONS.

In large-scale mechanical equipment installation project, expenditure of Plant procurement is rather high, in order to relieve the Contractor from financing pressure, the Contract may specify that the Materials and Plane can be paid in installments, for example, the first installment paid when the Contractor issues orders by referring to the contract or invoice, the second paid when cargos have been shipped, the third paid when they have arrived at the Site, and the rest paid after they have been installed and tested.

※ **Discussion**: Pros and cons of the advance payment.

It's specified that the Contractor needs to open a bank guarantee in order to get advance payment, the bank guarantee is to be provided under sub-paragraph (b) by an entity, and in a form, approved by the Employer. This may be helpful to ensure the safety of the Employer's money, while on the whole it's more disadvantageous because it increases the "business costs". The Contractor needs to pay bank services fees and keep a large amount of money in his account, and rationally, all tenderers will include this in their tendering price, thus increase the cost of the Works. Submission of guarantee is mainly to prevent the Contractor to take advantage of goods procurement to do the Employer out of project payment. While in practice, it doesn't make sense at all.

14.6   Issue of Interim Payment Certificate

Under CONS, the Contractor received a copy of an Interim Payment Certificate which notifies him of the payment to which he is entitled, as fairly determined by the Engineer. This procedure may require less time than the 28 days mentioned in the first paragraph.

This sub clause stipulates the procedure and conditions for issuing of interim payment certificate: ①time limit for the Engineer to issue interim payment certificate; ②minimum amount of interim payment certificate；③conditions to distain certain payment；④rights of the Engineer to revise the payment.

This Sub-Clause concluded with a sentence confirming that certification or payment is not to be taken as indicating "acceptance, approval, consent or satisfaction". This sentence is required so as to discourage：

—the Employer from withholding an interim payment if he feels entitled to withhold acceptance, approval, consent or satisfaction；

—the Contractor from relying upon certificates or payment as evidence of acceptance, approval, consent or satisfaction in respect of paid work. [5]

It's specified that if only the Contractor's work doesn't comply with the Contract or he does not perform his obligations in accordance with the Contract, the Engineer is entitled to withhold the costs or value of the work. For example, when quality problems occur to the concreting, the Engineer as stated is to be entitled to withhold the progress payment. Such a statement does not mean that payment certificate shall be withheld but just the relevant amount of payment instead.

14.7 Payment

This Sub-Clause specifies the payment time.

※ **Discussion**：Time management technics：two 28-day verse one 56-day.

In previous edition, payment of the amount certified in each Interim Payment Certificate is phased into two periods and each period is as long as 28 days. Within the first 28 days, the Engineer will issue Payment Certificate, and the Employer is required to pay the Contractor within the following 28 days after receiving the Payment Certificate. The new specification in new edition provides more flexibility for the Employer, since no matter how soon the Engineer issue the payment certificate upon receiving the Statement, the Employer can wait until the 56th date to make payments.

In effect, the Employer usually prolong the waiting time in Particular Conditions, the extent of which depends upon the Contractor's financial strength. If the Contractor can't maintain the work at his own cost, thus cause the slow-down or even suspension of the work, this may entitle the Employer to claim for extension of working period.

14.8 Delayed Payment

Project capital running out will lead to project suspension or even termination. As stated, financing charges compounded monthly are to be calculated at the annual rate of three percentage pointes above the discount rate of the central bank in the country of the currency of payment. This is more of a punishment. If this rate is considered inappropriate when tendering documents are being prepared, a new rate may be defined in the Particular Conditions. The Contractor is entitled to these financing charges without being required to give notice and, under CONS, without a Payment

Certificate. However, it may be preferable for financing charges to be included in Payment Certificates under CONS, for accounting purpose.

In practice, the Contractor should know that in the contract, in addition to specify the obligation of the Employer to pay extra interest charges for delayed payment, the Contractor shall be also entitled with the right to suspend work or terminate contract. Because though the Employer can pay for fined interest, the failure of raising procurement money will affect the procurement of Plant and Materials and prolong the working period, consequences of which shall be at the risk of the Contractor.

14.9   Payment of Retention Money

※ **Discussion**: What is Retention Money?

The accumulated moneys (if specified in the Contract) which are deducted (扣减) and retained(保留) by the Employer from the payment otherwise due to the Contractor(属于承包商的), and which are only paid after completion.

※ **Discussion**: How about regulation on retain and release of the retention money?

Retention money is retained under Sub-Clause 14.3 (c), and is release in installments based upon the Taking-Over Certificates issued under Clause 10. It's specified in 14.3 that any amount to be deducted for retention, calculated by applying the percentage of retention stated in the Appendix to Tender to the total of the estimated contract value of the Works executed, the percentage is normally around 10%, until the amount so retained by the Employer reaches the limit of stated in the Appendix to Tender, which is about 5%.

In international projects, retention money is an important issue deserving special attention. For example, 5% may be reasonable profit of a project, and as stated the percentage of retention money is also about 5% of the contract price,therefore the contractor's revenue may be fully counterfeited if he fails to claim back the retention money.

Retention money is used to compensate the costs during the period of project maintenance, which incur if the Works doesn't comply with the specifications but the Contractor refuse or unable to rectify the shortcomings. It's held by the Employer as kind of economic guarantee.

Whether the retention money can be claimed back and how much can be claimed back depend on quality of the Works, attitude of the Employer, the persons who dun for debts, and the district or country where the project locates. For example, in such a place like Hongkong which has complete legislation system and standardized operation specifications, it's less likely to become a big headache for the Employer.

14.10　Statement of Completion

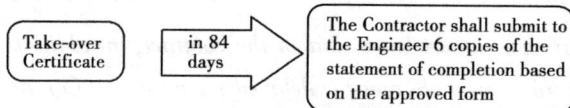

| Take-over Certificate | in 84 days | → | The Contractor shall submit to the Engineer 6 copies of the statement of completion based on the approved form |

This Sub-Clause specifies the basic procedure for the Employer to pay what remains due to the Contractor when the Works has been completed. In order to notify the Employer the due payment, the statement not only include the value of all work done in accordance with the Contractor up to the date, but also include any further sums which the Contractor considers to be due and an estimate of any other amounts which the Contractor considers will become due to him under the Contract, enabling the Employer to make according arrangements.

The Statement at completion is the basis of the cessation of liability, and encourages the early settlement of financial aspects.

14.11　Application for Final Payment Certificate

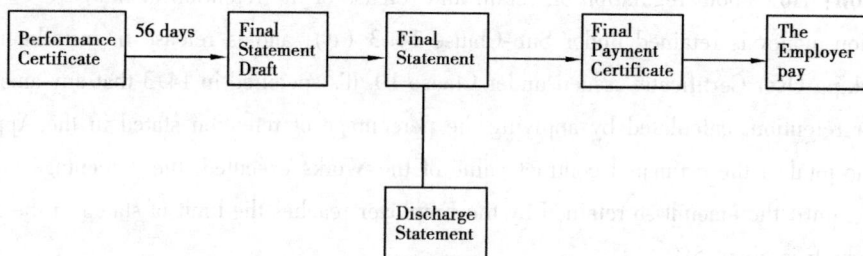

| Performance Certificate | 56 days → | Final Statement Draft | → | Final Statement | → | Final Payment Certificate | → | The Employer pay |

Final Statement → Discharge Statement

14.12　Discharge

When submitting the "Final Statement", after agreement or after resolution of all disputes under Sub-Clause 20.4 or 20.5, the Contractor confirms his agreement in this written discharge.

Sample Form of Discharge（结清证明的范例格式）

We—_____ hereby confirm, in the terms of Sub-Clause 14.12 of the Conditions of Contractor, that the total of the attached Final Statement, namely—_____ represents the full and final settlement of all moneys sue to us under or in connection with the Contract. This discharge shall only become effective when we have received the Performance Security and the outstanding balance of this total of the attached Final Statement.

※ **Discussion**：Which day shall be the effective day of the discharge certificate?

The last sentence is questioned in a book to construe FIIDC contract conditions, "This discharge may state that is becomes effective when the Contractor has received the Performance Security and the out-standing balance of this total in which event the discharge will be effective on such date." Literally, such a date should be the date when the Contractor has received the Performance Security and the out-standing balance. In effect, such a date should be the date when the Contractor receives the out-standing balance. We all know that the Employer shall return to the Contractor Performance Security within 21 days after he receives a copy of the Performance Certificate from the Engineer. While the out-standing balance is required to be paid within $(56 + 28 + 56)$ days after the Performance Certificate is issued, and may be further delayed if any disputes arise. Thus typically, return of the Performance Security will happen earlier than paying of out-standing balance. Ambiguity occurs when it's so stated.

14.13 Issue of Final Payment Certificate

After the Contractor has submitted the Final Statement and discharge, the Engineer then issues the Final Payment Certificate. The last paragraph provides for the possibility that the Contractor fails to apply for a Final Payment Certificate within the prescribed period, 56 days as stated in Sub-Clause 14.11. At the fist thought, this shall not happen since it's presumed that every Contractor wishes to receive the due payment as early as possible.

This possibility may be defined by the sentence in this Sub-Clause that there's balance due from the Contractor to the Employer, as the case may be, before the issue of the Final Payment Certificate. The Contractor will justifiably decline to apply for the Certificate when he realizes the situation.

In this event, the Engineer should request the Contractor to submit his application within 28 days. Unless it is received within 28 days, the Engineer is required to issue the Final Payment Certificate without further delay. Under Sub-Clause 1.3, certificates shall not be unreasonably withheld or delayed.

14.14 Cessation of Employer's Liability

※ **Discussion**: Contrasting to that the Contractor's contractual obligations are fulfilled by being awarded performance certificate, how to acknowledge the fulfillment of the Employer's contractual obligations?

This Sub-Clause implies the conclusions as follows:

(1) if the Engineer and the Contractor have agreed on the payment in the Final Statement, after the Employer pay the due payment to the Contractor stated in the Final Payment Certificate issued by the Engineer, the Employer's payment liability is deemed to be ceased.

(2) If two parties fail on agree on the payment in the Final Statement, after the Employer has paid the agreed part stated in the Engineer's provisional decision, and the payment confirmed after arbitration, the Employer's payment liability is deemed to be ceased.

Noted that the Contractor is required to submit:

—the notice in respect of each claim, within four weeks after he should have become aware of the relevant event or circumstance giving rise to the claim,

—the Statement at completion, stating the actual or estimated amount of each claim, within twelve weeks after the Taking-Over Certificate for the Works;

—particulars of each claim, within periods proposed and approved in accordance with the procedures described in Sub-Clause 20.1.

Make sure that none of the items stated above shall be neglected, since once neglected, even it can be made up for in the Final Statement, the Engineer may be reluctant to give approval (except for maters arising after the Taking-over Certificate for the Works). [5]

14.15 Currencies of Payment

FIDIC contract sometimes will require the Contractor to include in tendering documents with analysis on estimates of foreign currencies demand, tenderers is allowed to choose foreign currencies but no more than 3. Of which, analysis and explanation are required to be made on use of foreign currencies in quotation, such as:

(1) payment for employing foreign staff;

(2) imported materials, including both of Permanent Works and temporary Works;

(3) mechanical equipment of the Contractor;

(4) transportation fees in foreign countries, insurance fees and insurance service fees;

(5) incurred costs including overheads, contingencies, and profits in foreign countries.

By summarizing the above items, can we estimate proportions of foreign currencies.

中文参考

[1] 中标合同款额和合同价格。前者指承包商投标报价,经过评标和合同谈判后确定下来的一个暂时工程价格,而后者指的是实际的应付给承包商的最终工程款。

[2] 保函的延期,跟预付款有关吗?

[3] R 表示在期中支付证书中累计扣还的预付款总数;

A 表示预付款的总额度;

S 表示中标合同金额;

C 表示期中支付证书中累计的应付工程款总数,该数额的具体计算方法取决于合同的具体规定,如:是在扣除保留金之前或之后呢(一般不包括保留金)? 是调价之前还是之后呢(一般为调价之前)? C 的取值范围为:$aS < C < bS$;

a 表示期中支付总额累计达到整个中标合同金额开始扣还预付款的那个百分数;

b 表示当期中支付款累计额度等于中标合同金额的那个百分数,到此百分数,预付款必须扣还完毕。

[4] 如果实际进度比支付进度表依据的计划进度慢,工程师可以对支付计划表进行相应调整,但没有规定,如果承包商的实际进度快于计划进度时也相应调整支付计划表。对业主来说,如果承包商能按原计划进度实施工程,就已经不错了,他并不一定鼓励承包商的进度高于计划进度。

[5] 注意承包商要提交:

—在他应已察觉引起索赔的相关事件或情况后,在四周内提交关于每笔索赔的通知。

—在收到工程接受证书后十二周内,提交竣工报表,说明每笔索赔的实际或估计金额。

—按照第20.1款所述程序简易并经认可的期间内,递交每笔索赔的详细资料。

请注意以上款项不可以漏项,因为一旦漏项,即使在最终报表可以补上,工程师也不一定认可(接收证书签发后增加的工作除外)。

Note

1.以下的工程投标价构成表的案例,显示了几大部分费用的比例状况。其中材料费用占了大部分。

工程投标价构成内容	金额(美元)	比例(%)
一、人工费	1 932 000	11.23
二、材料费	8 774 705	51.00
三、施工机械费	799 475	4.65
其中:自由机械费	666 268	
当地租赁费	133 207	
四、分包费	1 509 090.9	8.77
其中:打桩工程	330 136	
仓库装修	59 726	
无线电工程	61 917	
临时道路	4 274	
市政工程	1 053 037.9	
五、直接费小计	13 015 270.9	
六、间接费合计	2 641 318	15.35
其中:投标开支费用	13 200	
保函手续费	12 710	
保险费	45 600	
税金	594 000	
经营业务费	520 333	
临时设施	70 000	
贷款利息	500 000	
施工管理	885 475	
七、上级管理费及代理费	688 204	4.00
八、风险和利润	860 255	5.00
九、工程总报价	17 205 048	100.00

2.预付款应在支付证书中按百分比扣减的方式偿还。条款中所规定的偿还速度只是建议,实践中仍然存在一定的问题,例如:

(1)此种扣减应开始于支付证书中所有被证明了的期中付款的总额(不包括预付款及保留金的扣减与偿还)超过接受的合同款额(减去暂定金额)的10%时。(由于在计算开始还款的10%时,是不包括预付款本身和保留金的扣发与偿还的款项。当预付款为中标合同金额的

10%时,承包商在偿还预付款之前实际上已经拿到 20% 中标合同金额。)

（2）按照预付款的货币的种类及其比例,分期从每份支付证书中的数额(不包括预付款及保留金的扣减与偿还)中扣除 25% ,直至还清全部预付款。(但是扣还速度似乎稍快了一些,如果按照本款规定,为每个期中支付证书额度的 25% ,当合同进行到一半时,业主就可以收回全部预付款。)

3. 保留金的目的是确保能在项目保修期间,用来弥补工程不合规范而承包商又拒绝或无力进行维修所发生的返工费用,也可以说是业主持有的一种经济保证。保留金能不能取回,以及能取回多少,要取决于项目的工程质量、业主态度和去索要的人的能力,以及项目所在地的国家和地区。比如说,在香港就应该没有问题,因为它的法制健全操作也比较规范。

4. 最终支付证书中应该包括:最终到期应支付的金额;在扣除业主以前已经支付的款额后,还应支付承包商的余额,但如果业主已经多支付了承包商,承包商应退回差额。

5. 雇主在他感到有权扣押、接受、批准、同意或满意时,不要扣发其中付款证书。承包商不要依赖证书或付款,作为对已付费工作的接受、批准、同意或满意的证据。

Coursework：

In a real estate project, the developer requires the deduction of advance payment shall commerce only after the completion of all foundation engineering, when the total of all certified interim payments (excluding the advance payment and deductions and repayments of retention) exceeds approximately thirty percent (30%) of the total investment.

Please try to analyze the potential risks under such requirements. (Hint： normally, faster presale commerce soon after the foundation engineering accomplished.)

Vocabulary

breakdown （关系的)破裂;(计划、讨论等的)失败,结束

The breakdown of something such as a relationship, plan, or discussion is its failure or ending.

mobilization 动员

installment 部分；分期付款

indicated 表明的；指示的

amortization 分期偿还；[会计]摊销

deterioration 恶化；变坏；退化；堕落

expiry （合同、最终期限、签证等的)期满,到期

The expiry of something such as a contract, deadline, or visa is the time that it comes to an end or stops being valid.

settlement （争议双方的)正式协议,和解

A settlement is an official agreement between two sides who were involved in a conflict or argument.

verify 证实；证明

If you verify something, you state or confirm that it is true.

discharge 清偿(债务)

If someone discharges a debt, they pay it.

be liable to 该受(罚)；应遵守…；有…的倾向；易于…

expressly   （命令）明白表示的,明确的

An express command or order is one that is clearly and deliberately stated.

reckless   轻率的;不计后果的;鲁莽的;无所顾忌的

If you say that someone is reckless, you mean that they act in a way which shows that they do not care about danger or the effect their behaviour will have on other people.

misconduct   （尤指专业人员的）渎职,不端行为,不当行为

Misconduct is bad or unacceptable behaviour, especially by a professional person.

15   *Termination by Employer*

15.1   Notice to Correct

Before the Employer believes that the Contractor's failure is sufficiently serious to merit termination under Sub-Clause 15.2,the Employer should consider

(a) whether termination appears to be the most appropriate course of action and;

(b) take legal advice, and issue a notice to;

(c) require the Contractor to make good the failure and to remedy it within a specified reasonable time.

If the Employer intends to reply on a notice under this Sub-Clause the notice should:

—state that it is given under this Sub-Clause;

—describe the nature of the Contractor's failure;

—specify a reasonable time within which the Contractor is to remedy the failure.

15.2   Termination by the Employer

A notice of termination that is subsequently decided to be unjustified would constitute a breach of contract by the Employer. It may also be prudent for the legal advice to prepare the notice of termination.

There're two type of causes for termination, ①the Contractor's incompliance with the Contract, ②crisis like bankrupt and insolvent happen to the Contractor.

In case of sub-paragraph (e) or (f), the Employer may by notice terminate the Contract immediately, otherwise, the Employer may, upon giving 14 days' notice to the Contractor, terminate the Contract and expel the Contractor from the Site.

If the termination is caused by the Contractor's incompliance, the Employer is entitled to distrain on the Contractor's items by a temporary decision, or even sell them in order to recover the payment owned by the Contractor to the Employer.

15.3   Valuation at Date of Termination

This Sub-Clause requires the Engineer to determine the value of work completed by the

Contractor, including first of all, the value of the Works completed by the Contractor, and the Permanent Works, Materials, Plant and other Temporary Works purchased by the Contractor for execution of the Works, as well as files and design documents the Contractor made for the Works, etc.

15.4 Payment after Termination

After termination, the Employer would probably have had to make other arrangements for the completion of the Works, including the rectification of any defects.

Interruption of the execution of Contract will lead to the exceeding of the real costs than the tendering price submitted by the first Contractor and prolong the construction period of the new Contractor than he planned, thus incur costs to the Employer. So the Employer may recover his losses, damages and extra costs incurred by termination of the Contract from the first Contractor. [1]

※ **Discussion**: How can the Employer recover his losses incurred by the termination of the Contract from the first Contractor?

    (a)The performance security;

    (b)The retention money retained;

    (c)He construction equipment on-site;

    (d)Retained contract payment.

15.5 Employer's Entitlement to Termination

※ **Discussion**: In cases when financial crisis happen to the Employer, it goes beyond the Contractor's capability to be carried on the project, compliance with the Contract will lead to more losses, etc., will the Employer be entitled to terminate the Contract in such circumstances?

Because the termination of Contract is caused by the Employer, thus it's the Employer who should undertake the consequences, which are mainly about losses and damages incurred to the Contractor. And the Contractor shall be paid in accordance with Sub-Clause 19.6 "Optional Termination, Payment and Release". Meanwhile, the Contractor should also perform his obligations to cease the work and withdraw from the Site, following the procedures in Sub-Clause of 16.3 "Cessation of Work and Removal of Contractor's Equipment".

中文参考

[1] 由于工程的连续性被打断,完成整个工程的费用一般会超过原承包商的投标价格,新承包商完成工程的工期也会迟于原定的竣工时间,这些无疑会给业主带来意外损失。所以业主应该从原承包商的工程款中扣除所遭受的损失和额外费用,以弥补他的损失。

Note

1. 如果承包商发生下述违约行为,则业主有权终止合同(15.2,11.4):

(1)承包商未能在收到中标函28天内向业主提交一份履约保证或者未能使履约保证持续有效;

(2)承包商未能根据合同履行任何义务,并且在工程师发出改正通知后,仍不履行合同;

（3）承包商放弃工程；

（4）承包商证明自己不愿继续按照合同履行义务；

（5）承包商无正当理由而未能遵守第 8 条有关工程开工、延误、暂停方面的合同规定；

（6）承包商无正当理由而未能在接到工程师通知的 28 天内执行下述工作：

①对工程师拒收的永久设备、材料或工艺，实施修复工作；

②将工程师认为不符合合同规定的永久设备或材料从现场移走并替换；

③将不符合合同规定的工程移走并重建；

④实施保护工程安全急需的工作。

（7）承包商未能经业主同意就将整个工程分包出去或转让合同；

（8）承包商处于破产或无力偿还债务或停业清理等类似的境地；

（9）承包商或者承包商的人员、代理商、分包商给予或提出给予任何人以贿赂等类似物品，以使他们作出与合同有关的行动；

（10）在缺陷通知期内，承包商未能在一合理时间内修补缺陷或损害，而这些修补工作应由承包商自费进行并且由于这些缺陷或损害业主无法享用全部工程或部分工程的利益，则业主可就此部分工程终止合同。

当上述情况发生后，业主、工程师、承包商进一步行动如下：

（1）终止合同。业主在向承包商发出通知 14 天后，可以终止合同，将承包商逐出现场。或者当上述（8）、（9）违约情况发生时，业主可立即终止合同，但业主选择终止合同，不应影响他根据合同应享有的权利。（15.2）

（2）承包商的义务。承包商在合同终止后应立即撤离现场，自费运走他的设备和临时工程，并留下业主要求的货物、承包商的文件等，此外，承包商还应遵守工程师为分包合同的转让和为保护生命、财产、工程而发出的指示。（15.2）

（3）工程的继续进行。业主可自己继续实施工程，也可安排其他实体完成工程，并且业主和这些实体有权使用任何货物、承包商的文件等。（15.2）

（4）终止时的估价及支付。

合同终止后，工程师应尽快确定工程、货物和承包商文件的价值以及根据合同承包商应得到的所有款项；业主应扣留向承包商支付的进一步款项直至他确定了工程施工、竣工、修补缺陷的费用、误期损害偿费和所有其他费用；在业主从承包商处收回终止合同的损失和超支费用后，业主应向承包商支付结存金额。

但如果承包商还有应付给业主的款额而未付，则业主有权出售承包商的设备和临时工程，余额归还承包商。（15.4，15.2）

Vocabulary

trustee   （财产）受托人，托管人

A trustee is someone with legal control of money or property that is kept or invested for another person, company, or organization.

liquidation   清偿；结算；清算；清除

insolvent   无清偿能力的；资不抵债的；破产的

A person or organization that is insolvent does not have enough money to pay their debts.

bribe   贿赂；向…行贿

A bribe is a sum of money or something valuable that one person offers or gives to another in order to persuade him or her to do something.

If one person bribes another, they give them a bribe.

gratuity 小费;赏钱

A gratuity is a gift of money to someone who has done something for you.

inducement 诱惑;引诱物

If someone is offered an inducement to do something, they are given or promised gifts or benefits in order to persuade them to do it.

16 *Suspension and Termination by Contractor*

16.1 Contractor's Entitlement to Suspend Work

Under CONS, the Employer is required to pay the amount actually certified by the Engineer, without deductions. From this, we can see that the premier obligation for the Employer is to make payment to the Contractor, thus once he default on his obligation to make payment, he shall be punished. This Sub-Clause specifies that the Contractor will be entitled with the following rights in such circumstances:

(1) Reduce the rate of work or suspend work.

(2) Obtain financing charges (interests, etc) under Sub-Clause 14.8 "Delayed Payment" and to termination under Sub-Clause 16.2 "Termination by Contractor".

(3) Obtain an extension of time for any such delay or payment of any such Cost plus reasonable profit.

(4) Terminated the Contract in accordance with 16.2 "Termination by Contractor". [1]

16.2 Termination by Contractor

※ **Discussion**: What measures shall be taken to ensure the Contractor's benefits when the Employer goes into bankrupt or insolvent?

Though many options are provide under this Sub-Clause, these rights are not properly guaranteed. In the Clause 14 of the Particular Conditions about "example provisions for Contractor Finance" that its has been pointed out that when the Contractor make arrangements for financing, the Employer shall deliver payment guarantee in the form annexed to the Particular Conditions to the Contractor. Even if the Employer provides payment guarantee, when the Employer goes into bankrupt or insolvent, whether the guarantee can be cashed still depends upon specific provisions in the local applicable laws. Thus we can conclude that one of the most important factors that the Contractor shall take into account in tendering is whether the Employer has reliable financing resource.

16.3 Cessation of Work and Removal of Contractor's Equipment

After termination, for the Employer's convenience or because of default, the Contractor is required to hand over the things for which the Employer has paid, and the parts of the Works executed on the Site. Whilst it may seem unrealistic to expect the Contractor to be willing to carry our much of the works described in Sub-Paragraph (a), the Contractor's compliance with these instructions may be required by the Country's safety laws.

16.4 Payment on Termination

The Contractor is entitled to receive the Performance Security, and to payment of an amount to be determined as described in Sub-Clause 19.6 and of the amount of any loss or damage which he suffered.

Sub-Clause 14.2 requires the Contractor to repay the advance payment immediately upon termination. The advance payment guarantee should be returned to the Contractor as soon as the advance payment has been repaid in full. If the Contractor fails to repay the advance payment, the Employer may call the advance payment guarantee.

中文参考

[1] 承包商享有 4 种权利：

(1) 放慢工作速度或者暂停工程；

(2) 享有延误工程款的融资费(利息等)；

(3) 索赔工期以及有关额外开支,加上相应利润；

(4) 根据第 16.2 款的规定,终止合同。

Note

1. 在合同条件原版后,附有业主支付保函标准格式。但是在涉及支付条款中(如第 14 条)并没有出现要求业主向承包商提交支付保函的规定,仅仅在专有条件第 14 条后有关"承包商融资范例条款"中提到,当承包商负责融资时,业主应按后附的支付保函格式项承包商提供支付保函。即使业主提供了支付保函,如果业主破产,保函是否能兑现还得看支付保函的使用法律的具体规定。因此,业主的项目资金来源是否可靠是承包商投标时应考虑的重要因素之一。

2. 如果业主发生下述违约行为,则承包商可以暂停工作或降低工作速度。

(1) 业主在接到承包商的请求 28 天之内未能提供合理的证据,向承包商表明他的资金安排或者在业主的资金安排发生实质变更时未能向承包商发出通知提供详细资料。(16.1)

(2) 业主在工程师收到报表及证明文件之日起 56 天内未向承包商支付期中支付证书中开具的款额或者在业主收到最终支付证书之日起 56 天内未向承包商支付该证书中开具的款额。(16.1)

对于业主的延误支付,承包商有权根据合同的规定获得延误期的利息支付,利率采用支付货币所在国中央银行的贴现率加上 3 个百分点进行计算。(14.8)

对于因业主的上述违约造成的承包商的工期延误和费用增加,承包商有权根据合同获得工期和费用的补偿。(16.1)

3. 如果发生下述违约行为,则承包商可以终止合同。(16.2)

（1）针对业主未能在合同规定的期限内向承包商证明其资金安排这一情况，承包商已向业主发出通知暂停工作，但在通知发出后 42 天之内，承包商仍未收到合理证明。

（2）工程师在收到报表和证明文件后 56 天之内未能颁发相应的支付证书。

（3）在合同规定的支付期限到期后 42 天之内，承包商仍未收到支付证书中开具的款额。

（4）业主基本上未执行合同规定的义务。

（5）业主没有按合同规定在承包商收到中标函后 28 天内与其签订合同协议书。

（6）业主没有征得承包商的事先同意，就将整个合同或部分合同或根据合同的应得利益转让出去。

（7）对于非承包商责任引起的工程暂停已持续 84 天以上，并且工程师在收到承包商的复工请求 28 天之内没有给予许可，而这部分工程又影响整个工程。

（8）业主破产或无力偿还债务或停业清理。

当上述违约行为发生后，承包商可在向业主发出通知 14 天后终止本合同。此外，如果上述（7）、（8）情况发生，承包商可立即通知业主终止合同。承包商选择终止合同不应影响根据合同他应享有的其他权利。（16.2）

在合同终止后，承包商应尽快停止一切进一步的工作，并移交已获可付款的文件、永久设备及材料，撤离现场上所有其他货物，随后离开现场。（16.3）

业主在合同终止后，应将履约保证退还承包商，支付已完工程、已订购的永久设备和材料的相应款额，并承担承包商的设备、临时工程、人员遣返回国的费用，此外还应向承包商赔偿因合同终止而产生的利润损失。（16.4）

Vocabulary

suspend　暂缓；推迟；暂停

If you suspend something, you delay it or stop it from happening for a while or until a decision is made about it.

prolong　延长；拉长；拖长

To prolong something means to make it last longer.

cease　停止，终止，结束

sustain　使持续；保持

If you sustain something, you continue it or maintain it for a period of time.

17　*Risk and Responsibilities*

The Contractor shall indemnify and hold harmless the Employer, the Employer's Personnel, and their respective agents, against and from all claims, damages, losses and expenses (including legal fees and expenses) in respect of:

The Employer shall indemnify and hold harmless the Contractor, the Contractor's Personnel, and their respective agents, against and from all claims, damages, losses and expenses (including legal fees and expenses) in respect of.

17.1　Indemnities

If something provides indemnity, it provides insurance or protection against damage or loss.

※ **Discussion**: How to distribute the liabilities arisen as to the personal injury and financial loss?

After the happening of such things, compensation can be claimed from insurance companies. While those that are not covered or not sufficiently covered by insurance will be born by the Party who shall be responsible for it.

Claims for personal injury are to be born by the Contractor, if they are attributable to his execution of the Works. The Employer bears the cost of claims for personal injury which are attributable to any act or negligence of the Employer or Employer's Personnel.

Under CONS, claims for property damage are to be born by the Contractor to the extent they are attributable to any act or negligence of the Contractor or Contractor's Personnel, and by the Employer to the extent that they are attributable to any act or negligence of the Employer or Employer's Personnel.

17.2　Contractor's Care of the Works

The Contractor shall take full responsibility for the care of the Works and Goods from the Commencement Date until the Taking-Over Certificate is issued (or is deemed to be issued under Sub-Clause 10.1 [Taking Over of the Works and Sections]) for theWorks, when responsibility for the care of the Works shall pass to the Employer.

※ **Discussion**: Which party shall be liable for the loss incurred during the custody period of the project?

If any loss or damage happens to the Works, Goods or Contractor's Documents during the period when the Contractor is responsible for their care, from any cause not listed in Sub-Clause 17.3 [Employer's Risks], the Contractor shall rectify the loss or damage at the Contractor's risk and cost, so that the Works, Goods and Contractor's Documents conform with the Contract. [1]

※ **Discussion**: Which party shall be liable for the loss incurred after the issue of the take-over certificate?

The Contractor is also responsible for the care of any work which he executes after the Taking-Over Certificate is issued. This work includes completing the outstanding work and remedying any defects. Besides, it's stated that the Contractor shall also be liable for any loss or damage which occurs after a Taking-Over Certificate has been issued and which arose from a precious event for which the Contractor was liable. It's so stated against the opportunist and to protect the benefit of the Employer.

17.3　Employer's Risks

International projects can be subjected to various risks, many unforeseeable. This Sub-IClause lists out the risks, consisting of 4 types: ①Political risks (1,2); ②Social risks (3); ③Contaminations and external impediment (4,5,8); ④Risks of Employer's act (6,7). [2]

And we can further conclude by referring to other clause that Employer shall bear "economic risks" (for example, Sub-Clause 13. 8 "Adjustment for Changes in Cost", Sub-Clause 14. 15 "Currencies of Payment", etc.) ; "legislative risks"(for example, Sub-Clause 13. 7 "Adjustment for Changes in Legislation", etc.)[3]

Strictly speaking, the risks that Employer and Contractor bear respectively are throughout the whole contract, and this Sub-Clause just concentrates on basic risks to be born by Employer. The main text do not use the phrase "Employer's risks", because the Employer is not wholly liable for all the consequences of the events listed in this Sub-Clause.

Some of these risks may also constitute Force Majeure (不可抗力) events under Clause 19, depending on their exceptional severity (严重程度) and adverse consequences(不好的后果).

※ **Discussion**: What is "Force Majeure"?

Refer to: Sub-Clause 1. 1. 6. 8 as meaning "not reasonably foreseeable by an experienced contractor by the date for submission of the Tender".

The question whether a natural event is Unforeseeable may be resolved by reference to the duration of the Time for Completion of the Works and to the statistical frequency of the event, based upon historic records. For example if the Time for Completion is three years, an experienced contractor is expected to foresee an event which occurs (on an average) once in every six years, but an event which occurs only once in every ten years might be regarded as Unforeseeable.

17. 4　Consequences of Employer's Risks

※ **Discussion**: How about the Contract's obligations?

Employer has to bear the consequences happened due to Employer's risks, this doesn't mean Contractor is exempted from any obligations. If Contractor wishes to rely upon this Sub-Clause, he must first give the notice described in its first paragraph. The notice should identify the Employer's risk and the resulting loss or damage to the Works, Goods and Contractor's Documents, the Contractor then is entitled to receive instructions on the extent to which he is required to rectify the loss or damages.

If compliance with these instructions causes the Contractor to suffer delay or incur Cost, he should give the further notice in order to obtain relief. And if the risks are only attributable to the Employer's act, then Contractor can add profits into his claim for reimbursement.

17. 5　Intellectual and Industrial Property Rights

This Sub-Clause provides appropriate protection to each Party in respect of any breaches pf copying or of other intellectual or industrial property right. If a third party make a claim in respect of any of the matters mentioned in this Sub-Clause, the Parties should each consider taking advice from a lawyer familiar with the applicable intellectual; property right law.

The Third Party mentioned in this Sub-Clause is the Party other than Employer and Contractor who raise the claims alleging infringement. If the Contractor is directly responsible for the infringement event, claimers may claim against Contractor; if it's the Employer who should be responsible for the event, then the Employer should go to conduct negotiations in lieu of the Contractor and ask the Contractor to assist. If the Employer refuses to conduct negotiation in lieu of the Contractor, the Contractor can accept the claims against him but at the cost of the Employer.

17.6   Limitation of Liability

When preparing Tenders, tenderers will wish to assess their potential liability to the Employer, and include in their prices some allowance for their risks. The basis of this Sub-Clause is to maintain a reasonable balance between the differing objectives of the Parties, each of whom will wish to limit his own liability whilst being entitled to receive full compensation for default by the other Party. The first paragraph applies to the maximum compensation liability of the Employer. Which is to say, if the Employer defaults on his obligation, the maximum compensation the Contractor is entitled to is equivalent to the amount of reimbursement cost claimed under the condition when Contract terminates due to default of the Employer plus the indemnities under 17.1.

The applicable law may limit the duration of its liability:

—Under some common law jurisdiction, a period of liability may not begin until the Employer ought reasonably to have been aware of the Contractor's defective work. [4]

—Under some civil law jurisdictions, the Contractor will be liable absolutely (i. e., without proof of default) for hidden defects for tem years from completion (which is called decennial liability). [5]

—If the Works include major items of Plant, it is usually appropriate for the Contract to limit the duration of the Contractor's liability for such Plant; for example, to a stated number of years after the completion date stated in the Taking-Over Certificate. [6]

中文参考

［1］由于第 17.3 款【雇主的风险】所列的雇主的风险所致,业主承担。如不是,则承包商应自担风险和费用弥补此类损失或修补损害,以使工程、货物或承包商的文件符合合同的要求。

［2］本款规定了业主的风险,可以分为 4 种:①政治风险;②社会风险;③污染及外力风险;④业主行为风险。

［3］我们还可以从其他条款中概括出业主负担的"经济风险"(如第 13.8 款"费用变更的调整",第 14.15 款"支付货币"等),"法律风险"(如第 13.7 款"立法变更的调整")。

［4］根据某些普通法管辖范围,知道雇主应已合理了解承包商有缺陷的工作时,责任期间才能开始。

［5］根据某些民法管辖范围,承包商对竣工十年后的隐蔽缺陷(即无须缺陷证据)绝对地负责(称为十年责任)。

［6］如果工程包括主要生产设备,合同限制承包商对此类生产设备的责任持续时间通常是合适的,例如,到接收证书说明的竣工日期后的一些年数。

Note

如果发生业主的风险,导致工程、物品或承包商的文件受到损害,承包商应立即通知工程师,并按工程师的要求予以修复和补救;

若承包商因此遭受损失,可以按索赔条款提出费用和工期索赔;

若是由于业主的行为风险(上款第6和7项)造成的,承包商还可以索赔利润。

Vocabulary

injury 伤害,损害;受伤处;伤害的行为

respective 分别的;各自的

Respective means relating or belonging separately to the individual people you have just mentioned.

wilful 故意的,有意的,成心的(尤指意在造成伤害)

If you describe actions or attitudes as wilful, you are critical of them because they are done or expressed deliberately, especially with the intention of causing someone harm.

attributable 可归因于…的,可归结于…的

If something is attributable to an event, situation, or person, it is likely that it was caused by that event, situation or person.

negligence 疏忽;失误;失职

If someone is guilty of negligence, they have failed to do something which they ought to do.

hostility 敌意;对抗;敌对行为

Hostility is unfriendly or aggressive behaviour towards people or ideas.

rebellion 谋反;叛乱;反叛

A rebellion is a violent organized action by a large group of people who are trying to change their country's political system.

insurrection 起义;造反;叛乱

An insurrection is violent action that is taken by a large group of people against the rulers of their country, usually in order to remove them from office.

usurped 夺取;篡夺;侵占

If you say that someone usurps a job, role, title, or position, they take it from someone when they have no right to do this.

riot 暴乱;骚动;暴动

When there is a riot, a crowd of people behave violently in a public place, for example they fight, throw stones, or damage buildings and vehicles.

commotion 喧闹;混乱;骚动

A commotion is a lot of noise, confusion, and excitement.

munitions 军需品;(尤指)军火

Munitions are military equipment and supplies, especially bombs, shells, and guns.

ionizing (使)电离,(使)成离子

sonic　声的；声音的

Sonic is used to describe things related to soundpreventative.

infringement　（对他人权利等的）侵犯，侵害

An infringement is an action or situation that interferes with your rights and the freedom you are entitled to.

allege　（未提出证据而）断言，指称，声称

If you allege that something bad is true, you say it but do not prove it.

18　Insurance

18.1　General Requirement for Insurances

Insurance is generally advisable to protect both Parties from the financial consequences of unexpected loss, damage or liability. The primary purpose of insurance is to ensure that the Contractor has the financial capability to execute the Works irrespective of fortuitous loss or damage. Where a risk is allocated to the Employer, the insurance should enable the Employer to pay for the rectification of damage caused by an Employer's risk. Additionally, if the Contractor fails to complete the Works, the insurance should enable the Employer to pay another contractor to rectify loss or damage to incomplete works. [1]

This Sub-Clause generally consists of: conditions to effect and maintain insurance, nature of insurance, the right of being notified of the Party other than the insuring Party, obligations of both Parties to comply with insurance policy, rectification of loss and damage after they fail to make insurance.

As stipulated in this Sub-Clause, insurance can be required to effect either by the Contractor or the Employer, which depends the specific requirements of the project, and to be clarified in the Particular Conditions or the Appendix to Tender. Typically, insurances are obtained by the Contractor from insurers. Sometimes, the Employer elects to obtain insurance for all the contracts for a particular project, with a view to achieving competitive terms due to economies of scale and reduced duplication of insurance.

The insuring Party shall be particularly reminded that during the execution of the Works, when certain conditions change and differ from the information provided to insurance company, the insurer shall be promptly notified and the original insurance shall be modified. If additional insurance items need to be added, application can be submitted to be confirmed by the endorsement of the insurer. If claims about insurance arise, insurer needs to be notified, and at the mean time, Site of the accidence needs to be preserved and accidence to be recorded, for the adjuster of the insurance company to give appraisals.

18.2　Insurance for Works and Contractor's Equipment

This Sub-Clause specifies the insurance of the Works, Goods and Contractor's Documents.

Unless the Particular Conditions state otherwise, these insurances are arranged by the Contractor, who may wish to consult insurance experts.

If insurance shall also cover loss or damage from the risks listed in the subparagraphs of Sub-Clause 17.3 (Employer's Risks), then the Contractor shall consider to calculate the premiums at commensally reasonable terms, which is enquired from the insurance company and regarded as fair and feasible, otherwise, insurances are nor required to cover this sort of Employer's risks.

For example, if the construction period is 3 years as stated in the Contract, and start from the 2nd year, premiums increase and remains no longer at commensally reasonable terms, which prevent the insurance from being continued. Under such circumstance, if the Employer approves omission, the premiums are actually paid for only 1year, and the other 2 years' premiums are unpaid. Thus at the mean time when the Employer approves omission, he can also be entitled to payment of an amount equivalent to the amount calculated at such commensally reasonable terms as the Contractor should expected to have paid for such cover and thereafter deduct the amount from the Contract Price.

18.3　Insurance against Injury to Persons and Damage to Property

This Sub-Clause specifies the details of the required insurance against liability to third parties, and the "third parties' property" includes physical property which are not covered under the 18.2. In practice, the third parties' insurance cover all items listed under this Sub-Clause, except for the definition of "the third parties" including not only people and property irrelevant to the projects but also the Employer's other property than those insured under 18.2, according to the conventions of the third parties' liability insurance in the business circle.

The loss and damage occurred to the third parties may be huge, and minimum insurance premium is advisedwith no limit on the amount of occurrences. For example, blasting for excavation of tunnels may affect the adjacent paralleling pipes. Such risks shall be covered by the third parties' insurance, no matter the pipelines belong to the Employer or some other third parties.

18.4　Insurance for Contractor's Personnel

This Sub-Clause specifies the Contractor shall effect and maintain insurance against liability arising from accidents and injury of the Contractor's employees. In practice, for the convenience of operation, it's also required each employer of personnel to effect this insurance in respect of his employees. The last sentence would be equally applicable to sub-contractors.

中文参考

[1] 保险的主要目的是:①确保承包商不管有什么偶然的损失或损害,能有财务能力去实施工程;②对划归雇主的风险,保险应使雇主能支付修正因雇主风险造成的损害;③如果承包商未能完成工程,保险应使雇主能支付另一承包商修补未完工程的损失或损害。

Note

1. 第三方责任险:第三方责任险由于保险人疏忽过失而给第三者造成财产损失或者人身伤害,保险公司对第三者财产进行赔偿或对第三者人身伤害进行给付的一种保险。

2. 承包商应为其雇用的任何人员的伤亡和疾病导致的赔偿责任办理保险,承包商的人员的保险单应保障业主和工程师,但该保险可不包括由业主或其人员的行为或渎职造成的损失和赔偿;该类保险应在雇员从事项目工作的全部时间内保持有效;分包商的人员的保险可由分包商办理,但承包商应保证分包商遵守本条的规定。

3. 工程和承包商设备、人身伤害和财产伤害的保险。

险种	含义	金额	有效期
工程(18.2)	承包商应为工程、生产设备、材料和承包商文件投保	保险金额应不低于全部复原的费用	从开工到颁发履约证书为止持续有效
承包商设备(18.2)	承包商应为其施工设备投保		从设备运往现场到不再需要为止持续有效
人身伤害和财产伤害的保险(18.3)(第三者责任险和业主人员的保险)	承包商应为可能由工程施工引起的任何人身和财产(工程、承包商的财产和人员除外)损失和伤害办理		
承包商人员的保险(18.4)	承包商应对雇用的任何人员的伤害、疾病或死亡引起的赔偿(包括法律费用)责任,办理保险。分包商负责其人员的保险		人员参加工程实施的整个期间

4. 投保金额 = 全部重置成本 + 相应利润额
投保覆盖时间 = 开工 + 验收证书签发 + 签发履约证书

Vocabulary

insuring party   保险方

rectification   纠正;修正;矫正

The rectification of something that is wrong is the act of changing it to make it correct or satisfactory.

precedence   优先;优先权

If one thing takes precedence over another, it is regarded as more important than the other thing.

premium   保险费;保险金

A premium is a sum of money that you pay regularly to an insurance company for an insurance policy.

debris   (被毁物的)残骸;碎片;垃圾

Debris is pieces from something that has been destroyed or pieces of rubbish or unwanted material that are spread around.

replacement   替代;替换;取代

If you refer to the replacement of one thing by another, you mean that the second thing takes the place of the first.

deductible   可扣除的

19 Force Majeure

19.1 Definition of Force Majeure

"Force Majeure" originates from the Civil Law System, which is analogous to the "Frustration" or "Impossibilities of Performance" of the Common Law System. FIDIC adopts the use of "Force Majeure" in its new edition because this term has been widely used in the international trade.

For an event or circumstance to constitute Force Majeure, six criteria need to be satisfied:

(1) it must be exceptional, so the event or circumstance is not merely "usual". [1]

(2) It must be beyond the control of the Party who has been affected by it and who will need to give due notice in order to be excused performance. For example, this may exclude most deliberate acts by his affected Party's personnel. [2]

(3) This affected Party could not reasonably have provided against it before the Contract was made. For example, this may exclude foreseeable events which had a reasonable likelihood of occurring during the Time for Completion and in respect of which the affected Party could "reasonably have been expected to have taken adequate preventative precautions". [3]

(4) This affected Party could not reasonably have avoided or overcome it. For example, this may exclude events or circumstances which may be avoided or overcome by making appropriate arrangements, with some extra cost, delay or inconvenience. [4]

(5) It must not have been substantially attributable to the other Party. This may exclude events or circumstances which would normally be a breach of the Contract by such other Party, entitling the affected Party to the relief due to breach of contract. [5]

(6) It prevents the affected Party from performing any of its obligations. This criterion is not incorporated into the above definition in Sub-Clause 19.1, but is stated as a precondition in Sub-Clause 19.2 and 19.4. [6]

The Contractor was conducted a mining and smelting project in a country of south Asia. At the inceptive stage of work, the survey subcontractor's worker went on strike and the project was suspended by one month. This resulted in a delay of the Contractor's design work and postponed the whole work. The subcontractor referred to the "Force Majeure" clause and requested for an extension of working period and an exemption of the delay liabilities. The Contractor also applied for extension of time as well as exemption of liabilities of delayed hand-over of the Works.

In international projects, strikes generally will be taken as an act of "Force Majeure" with exceptions, for example, the FIDIC 19. 1 excludes the strike by employees of the subcontractor from the list.

Which is to say, the strikes of the subcontractor's employees are neither beyond a Party's control, nor what such Party could not reasonably have provided against before entering into the Contract.

Suggestions: The Contractor shall

①specify the requirements on subcontractors in subcontract;

②clarify the conditions for define "Force Majeure";

③define the terminology of "Force Majeure" as clearly as possible.

19. 2   Notice of Force Majeure

In order to be able to rely upon this Clause to excuse a failure to perform an obligation, the affected Party is required to notify the other Party within fourteen days of becoming aware of the event or circumstance. Fourteen days may seem a generous period comparing with the well developed information technology and convenient communications methods, but it has to take allowance for the effects of Force Majeure events and their possibilities to suspend the communications. Thus it's apparently advantageous giving longer period of waiting time.

The notice must specify:

①the event or circumstance which is considered to constitute Force Majeure[7],

②its effect, namely will it prevent performance and of which obligations. These effects would typically not have to be listed in great detail, it being preferable to describe them in suitably broad terms. [8]

19. 3   Duty to Minimize Delay

The first paragraph states that the Parties should endeavor to overcome the adverse effects of the Force Majeure (which is required by the laws of most countries).

Good contract conditions shall impose constrain on the speculation act of either Party, especially under the current environment. This Sub-Clause is purposed to impose constraint on such speculation acts. In practice, more often that one Party under contract may dispose with an event passively with certain intention, aiming to make illegal profits, hence result in an undue loss.

The second paragraph states that the affected Party must give notice recording when the effect of the Force Majeure ceases.

19.4 Consequences of Force Majeure

We can see from this Sub-Clause that after the happening of Force Majeure events, risks are to be born by the Employer. If the events or circumstances are of the kind described in sub-paragraph (v) under Sub-Clause 19. 1-natural catastrophes, the Contractor in only entitled to extension of time to the extent that completion is delayed by the notified Force Majeure but not to reimbursement costs. That means after the happening of such natural events, the Contractor and the Employer shall respectively bear a part of the losses.

The Contractor's entitled to reimbursement of such Cost as is attributable to the prevention of performance by a notified Force Majeure:

①Which is of the kind described in sub-paragraphs (i) to (iv) of Sub-Clause 19. 1, namely a man-made event. [9]

②Which either occurs in the Country or is of the kind described in sub-paragraph (i) of Sub-Clause 19. 1, namely war, hostilities, invasion, or act of foreign enemies. [10]

19.5 Force Majeure Affecting Subcontractor

If any subcontractor is entitled to relief from force Majeure on terms additional or broader than those specified in this Clause, this successfully claim for longer extension period or more reimbursement costs that the Contractor is entitled to under this Clause, the excessive part shall be at the risk and cost of the Contractor.

This Sub-Clause is prudent in specifying so. In practice, subcontract typically contains more harsh items than contract instead.

19.6 Optional Termination, Payment and Release

Upon such termination, the Engineer shall determine the value of the work done and issue a Payment Certificate which shall include:

(1)the amounts payable for any work carried out for which a price is stated in the Contract; [11]

(2)the Cost of Plant and Materials ordered for the Works which have been delivered to the Contractor, or of which the Contractor is liable to accept delivery: this Plant and Materials shall become the property of (and be at the risk of) the Employer when paid for by the Employer, and the Contractor shall place the same at the Employer's disposal; [12]

(3) any other Cost or liability which in the circumstances was reasonably incurred by the Contractor in the expectation of completing the Works; [13]

(4)the Cost of removal of Temporary Works and Contractor's Equipment from the Site and the return of these items to the Contractor's works in his country (or to any other destination at no greater cost); [14]

(5)the Cost of repatriation of the Contractor's staff and labour employed wholly in connection with the Works at the date of termination. [15]

For payment upon termination, if the contract is terminated by the Employer because the Contractor defaults on his obligation, the Employer shall complete the surplus work by himself or by employing others and recover from the Contractor losses and damages incurred by the Employer and any extra costs of completing the work, and return the balance to the Contractor. For other situations, payment shall be paid following the procedures stipulated in this Sub-Clause.

19.7   Release from Performance under Law

This Sub-Clause actually deals with a special type of Force Majeure, under which circumstance, it's impossible to carry on the contract obligations and there's no hope for resumption of work.

This Sub-Clause describes two extreme situations. These situations arise if an event or circumstance outside the control of both parties occurs which:

①makes it impossible or lawful for a Party to fulfill its contractual obligations;

②under the applicable law, entitles the Parties to be released from further performance.

中文参考

［1］它必须是特殊的,所以时间或情况不仅仅是不寻常的。

［2］它必须是受到它影响的一方无法控制的,该方必须根据 19.2 款发出该发的通知,以取得对其行为的谅解。例如,这样可以排除受影响方人员的大多数故意行为。

［3］受影响方在签订合同时,不能合理防备它。例如,这样可排除在竣工时间期间内可能发生的可预见的事件,以及对之能"合理预期"受影响方应"已采取适当的预防措施"。

［4］受影响方不能合理避免或克服。例如,这样可排除通过对一些额外费用、延误和不方便,做出适当的安排,可以避免或克服的事件。

［5］必须是不主要归因于他方。例如,这样可排除通常是该他方违反合同,是受影响方由此有权得到责任免除的事件或情况。

［6］它阻碍受影响方履行起任何一个义务,此标准没有纳入上述第 19.1 款的定义中,但是在 19.2 款和 19.4 款中规定作为一项先决条件。

［7］认为构成不可抗力的时间或情况。

［8］它的影响,即它将会如何阻碍履约和关于哪项义务。这些影响通常不必详细列出,用使用的、概括的词语描述较好。

［9］属于第 19.1 款(i)到(iv)项所述的类型,即人为事件。

［10］发生在工程所在国,或属于第 19.1 款(i)项所述类型,即战争、敌对行动、入侵、外敌行为。

［11］已经完成的工作的款项。

［12］为工程定购的永久设备和材料款项。

［13］承包商在不可抗力情况下为完成工程而导致的任何合理开支。

［14］承包商将临时工程或施工设备运回自己国家存放的遣散费。

［15］合同终止时承包商在工程上的专职雇员的遣散费。

Note

从 19.2 款可以推知,如果一方由于发生不可抗力而不能执行它的义务,承包商应直接将此情况通知给业主。但按本款,承包商关于不可抗力的索赔需要向工程师提出,这会导致沟通方面的失败。因此建议在发生不可抗力时,承包商应直接通知工程师,同时抄送业主,或通知业主同时抄送工程师。

Vocabulary

hostilities   战争行动

You can refer to fighting between two countries or groups who are at war as hostilities.

invasion   武装入侵;侵略

If there is an invasion of a country, a foreign army enters it by force.

catastrophe   重大灾难;灾祸;横祸

A catastrophe is an unexpected event that causes great suffering or damage.

procrastinate   拖延;耽搁;延迟

If you procrastinate, you keep leaving things you should do until later, often because you do not want to do them.

contamination   污染;弄脏;毒害;玷污

volcanic   火山的;由火山引发的

Volcanic means coming from or created by volcanoes.

endeavor   尝试,试图;尽力,竭力

relief   宽慰;安心;欣慰;解脱

If you feel a sense of relief, you feel happy because something unpleasant has not happened or is no longer happening.

continuous   连续不断的;持续的;不中断的

A continuous process or event continues for a period of time without stopping.

20   *Claims, Disputes and Arbitration*

20.1   Contractor's Claims

This Sub-Clause prescribes the procedure to be followed by the Contractor if he considers himself to be entitled to an extension of time, to additional payment, or to both.

The first notice is the start of the detailed procedure. The Contractor must ensure that notices are given in due time, in order to protect his right under the Contractor, Failure to give notice in accordance with the first paragraph deprives the Contractor of his entitlement to an extension of time and compensation, as stated in the second paragraph.

On the whole, making claim is a difficult thing. Actually both of the Parties are entitled to claims and the Employer may make counter-claim or defensive claims against the claims the Contractor raised. The reimbursement costs the Contractor claimed is often offset by what the Employer counter claims for. Besides, too many claims will cause the Contractor adverse effect, i. e. going into the blacklist and being classified as the type of claim-conscious. This may deprive the Contractors of chances to win other projects in tendering thereafter. Thus it's necessary to weigh the advantages and disadvantages properly when making claim decisions.

During the claims, the Contractor often propounds Ripple Theory, which is also called Impact Effect. Because during the long process of the execution of the project, the Engineer may often give the Contractor instruction other than what's stated in the Contract, if the Contractor follows the instructions, the original plans and arrangements may be affected, the work procedures may be interrupted, which will lead to disorganization to some extent, hereby incur extra costs to the Contractor. When it's required to execute instructions different from the contract content, it's analogous to the surface of water is disturbed and ripple forms. Thus the Contractor is entitled to claim for reimbursement costs, which is also the theory basis for claim for additional payment for Variation, acceleration of completion, etc.

Groundings for raising a claim（索赔的依据构成合同的原始文件）：
①*instruction from the Engineer*（工程师的指示）
②*correspondence*（往来函件）
③*meeting minutes*（会议记录）
④*construction site record*（施工现场记录）
⑤*project financial information*（工程财务记录）
⑥*site climate information*（现场气候记录）
⑦*market information*（市场信息资料）
⑧*legislation and policies*（政策法令文件）

20.2   Appointment of the Dispute Adjudication Board

The Book is prepared so as to facilitate the use of any of three procedures. The three procedures are as follow：

—A "full-time" dispute adjudication board, which comprises one or three members who are appointed before the Contractor commences executing the Works, and who typically visit the Site on a regular basis thereafter. During their visit, the DAB would also be available to assist to Parties in avoiding a dispute, if they and the DAB all agree. [1]

—An "ad-hoc" dispute adjudication board, which comprises one or three members who are only appointed and when a particular dispute arises, and whose appointment typically expires when the DAB has issued its decision on that dispute. [2]

—Under cons, pre-arbitral decisions may be made by the Engineer, if he is an independent professional consulting engineer with the necessary experience and resource. [3]

As to the one member to be proposed by each Party, each Party should endeavor to nominate a truly independent expert with the ability and freedom to act impartially, develop a spirit of teamwork within the DAB, and make fair unanimous decisions. As to the third member, the Parties may consider it advantageous to appoint as chairman of a three-person DAB either a person who has spent parts of his or her career with each type of Party, or a lawyer with considerable practical experience in construction law.

20.3 Failure to Agree Dispute Adjudication Board

This Sub-Clause provides the solution if both Parties fail to agree upon the appointment of DAB members. The appointing entity (or official) named in the Appendix to Tender shall appoint the member of the DAB and the appointment shall be final and conclusive.

Under CONS, the appointing entity shall be the President of FIDIC or the person he entrusted. That is to say, when both Parties cannot agree upon the appointment of DAB member, FIDIC President or the person he entrusted can help them to appoint the member and shall be remunerated, and each party shall be responsible for paying one-half of the remuneration.

20.4 Obtaining Dispute Adjudication Board's Decision

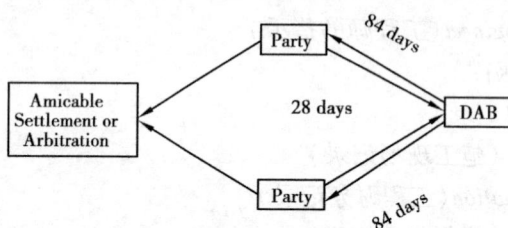

When disputes arise, both Parties should provide convenience to the DAB for it to make decisions including providing additional information, further access to the Site, the appropriate facilities, etc. Within 84 days after receiving such reference, the DAB shall give its decision. If either Party is dissatisfied with the DAB's decision, then either Party may, within 28 days after receiving the decision, give notice to the other Party of its dissatisfaction, otherwise the notice shall become final and binding upon both Parties.

20.5 Amicable Settlement

This Sub-Clause specifies that during the first 56 days after the notice of dissatisfaction has been issued, and by agreement thereafter, the Parties should attempt amicable settlement before they go into arbitration.

The DAB should not become involved in amicable settlement procedures, whether before a dispute arises or after a Party has notified dissatisfaction with the DAB's decision.

20.6 Arbitration

Though comparing with mediation and amicable settlement, arbitration is less encouraged, yet it's much more advantageous and preferable than litigation. Moreover, many disputes cannot be resolved through amicable settlement but depend upon arbitration.

Compared with litigation, arbitration is a civil procedure(民间程序) in which a sole arbitrator, or panel of three arbitrators, will decide the dispute and render an award which should be enforceable by due legal process. Nowadays, with the globalization of economy and trade, arbitration has become a common method to settle international disputes. And more and more international conventions have been ratified, providing operational feasibility for implementation of arbitration award.

The 1958 New York "Convention on the Recognition and Enforcement of Foreign Arbitral Awards" (承认及执行外国仲裁裁决公约) make enforcement of the adjudication easier in the any countries which have ratified this Convention, particularly if the adjudication has been certified by a recognized arbitral institution: for example, the International Chamber of Commerce "ICC" (国际商会). China became one of its signatories (缔约成员) in 1987. Generally speaking, arbitration provisions consist of three parts: arbitration institution, arbitration rules and arbitration place. In practice, these three will be stated in contract like the Particular Conditions. Arbitration institution has their own rules; this Sub-Clause recommends the ICC rules, which is widely adopted internationally. As an alternative choice, arbitration can be conducted under the arbitration rules issued by UNCITRAL, the United Nations Commission on International Trade Law (联合国国家贸易法委员会).

In a hydropower project in Africa, construction period agreed in the contract was less than three years and contract price of 25 million US dollars. During the execution of the works, the Contractor raised many claims due to various reasons, and the accumulated value reached as high as 20 million US dollars. The Engineer proceeded to make determination and commented a total compensation of additional payment of 12 million US dollars. This determination was accepted by the Employer while denied by the Contractor, who asked for a reimbursement of more 6 million US dollars in addition to that.

The Contractor resorted to the international Chamber of Commerce (ICC) for arbitration after the trial of mediation ended in vain. Both parties proposed an arbitrator, and relied on these two arbitrators to jointly appoint a chief arbitrator. The arbitration processed near to 3 years, almost as long as the stipulated construction period and up to 5 million US dollars was spent on arbitration fees. The final verdict proclaimed was in supportive of the Engineer's original determination, which is to say, a compensation of 12 million US dollars to the Contractor.

Conclusion and suggestion: mediation and amicable settlement is preferable for less costly, less troublesome, and sustained reputation.

20.7   Failure to Comply with Dispute Adjudication Board's Decision

If the DAB's decision has become final as well as binding, both Parties must give effect to it. If either Party fails to do so, the other Party may refer this failure to arbitration, without having to request a further DAB decision or to attempt amicable settlement again. [4]

20.8 Expiry of Dispute Adjudication Board's Appointment

There may be "no DAB in place" because the DAB's appointment had expired. If a dispute arises thereafter, either Party can initiate arbitration immediately, without having to reconvene a DAB for a decision and without attempting amicable settlement.

中文参考

［1］"常任"争端裁决委员会由一名或三名成员组成,在承包商实施工程前任命,此后通常定期视察现场,在这视察期间,如果当时各方和 DAB 均同意,DAB 也可协助他们避免发生争端。

［2］"特聘"争端裁决委员会由一名或三名成员组成,只在发生争端时任命,他们的任期通常在 DAB 对该争端发出其决定时期满。

［3］根据 CONS,如果工程师是具有必要经验和资源的独立专业咨询工程师,他可作出裁决前决定。

［4］除非法律允许,在 DAB 的决定根据合同已成为最终的并有约束力后,任何一方不能反对此决定。如 DAB 的决定已是最终的并有约束力的,当事双方一方未能执行,另一方可将此未能执行提交仲裁,不必要求进一步的 DAB 决定或尝试再次友好解决。

The claim procedure of the Contractor

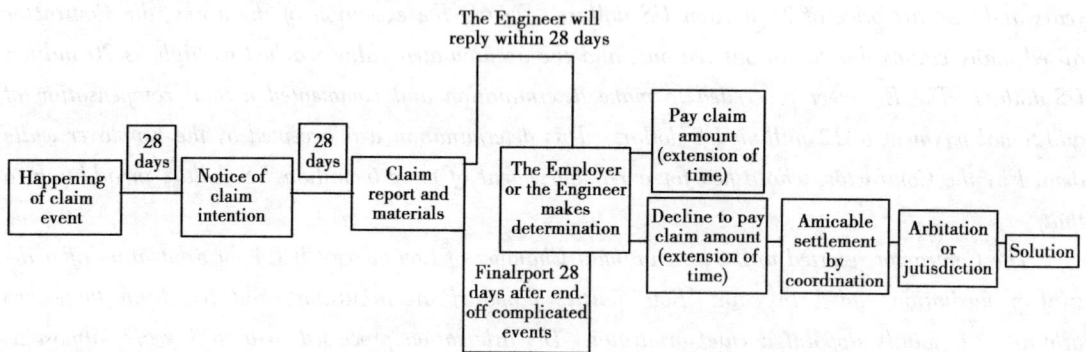

Vocabulary

contemporary　当代的;现代的

Contemporary things are modern and relate to the present time.

substantiate　证实;证明

To substantiate a statement or a story means to supply evidence which proves that it is true.

continuing　继续的,连续的,持续的

interval　(事件、日期之间的)间隔

An interval between two events or dates is the period of time between them.

adjudicator　裁判员;判决者,裁定者

remuneration　酬劳;薪酬

Someone's remuneration is the amount of money that they are paid for the work that they do.

conclusive　确定的;毫无疑问的;不容置疑的

Conclusive evidence shows that something is certainly true.

amicable　（关系）友好的,和睦的

When people have an amicable relationship, they are pleasant to each other and solve their problems without quarrelling.

arbitral　仲裁的

Chapter 7   The role of the Engineer

I   The duties and authority of an engineer is clearly stated in clause 3.1.

The Engineer shall have no authority to amend the Contract. The Engineer may exercise the authority attributable to the Engineer as specified in or necessarily to be implied from the Contract.

The Employer undertakes not to impose further constraints on the Engineer's authority, except as agreed with the Contractor. However, whenever the Engineer exercises a specified authority for which the Employer's approval is required, then (for the purposes of the Contract) the Employer shall be deemed to have given approval.

Except as otherwise stated in these Conditions:

(1) Whenever carrying out duties or exercising authority, specified in or implied by the Contract, the Engineer shall be deemed to act for the Employer;

(2) The Engineer has no authority to relieve either Party of any duties, obligations or responsibilities under the Contract;

(3) Any approval, check, certificate, consent, examination, inspection, instruction, notice, proposal, request, test, or similar act by the Engineer (including absenceof disapproval) shall not relieve the Contractor from any responsibility he has under the Contract, including responsibility for errors, omissions, discrepancies and non-compliances.

II   Duties that "should be exercised" by the Engineer are listed out in the following table

Table 1 Stipulated Duties and Authorities of the Engineer in FIDIC Contract Conditions

1.5 The Engineer shall issue any necessary clarification or instruction as to the priority of documents.

1.8 Care and Supply of Documents

Unless otherwise stated in the Contract, the Contractor shall supply to the Engineer six copies of each of the Contractor's Documents.

1.9 Delayed Drawings or Instructions

After receiving this further notice, the Engineer shall proceed in accordance with Sub-Clause 3.5 [Determinations] to agree or determine these matters.

4.4 The prior consent of the Engineer shall be obtained to other proposed.

Subcontractors and notice shall be given to the Engineer as to the commencement date of each

Subcontractor's work and of such work on the site.

8.1 The Engineer shall give the Contractor not less than 7 days' notice of the Commencement Date.

2.1 The Employer shall give the Contractor right of access to, and possession of, all parts of the Site.

8.4 Extension of time for completion

The Engineer shall review previous determinations and may increase, but shall not decrease, the total extension of time.

8.6 Rate of Progress

The Engineer may instruct the Contractor to submit, under Sub-Clause 8.3 [Programme], a revised programme and supporting report describing the revised methods.

3.3 Instructions of the Engineer

The Engineer may issue to the Contractor (at any time) instructions and additional or modified Drawings all in accordance with the Contract.

10.1 Taking Over of the Works and Section

The Contractor may apply by notice to the Engineer for a Taking-Over Certificate. (签发移交证书)

4.1 The Contractor shall, whenever required by the Engineer, submit details of the arrangements and methods which the Contractor proposes to adopt for the executionof the Works. (批准承包商图纸、计算书、技术说明书、手册)

11.1 The Contractor shall complete any work which is outstanding on the date stated in a Taking-Over Certificate, within such reasonable time as is instructed by the Engineer. (在通知缺陷期内完成修补)

4.12 If the Contractor encounters adverse physical conditions which he considers to have been Unforeseeable, the Contractor shall give notice to the Engineer as soon as practicable. (承包商遇到不利条件时协商决定延长工期)

11.4 Failure to Remedy Defects

The employer may require the engineer to agree or determine a reasonable reduction in the Contract Price in accordance with Sub-Clause 3.5 [Determinations]. (决定他人弥补缺陷的费用)

3.3 The Contractor shall comply with the instructions given by the Engineer or delegated Assistant, etc. (在施工过程中向承包商发出指示)

11.8 The Contractor shall, if required by the Engineer, search for the cause of any defect,under the direction of the Engineer. (指示承包商检查缺陷原因)

8.3 The Contractor shall submit a detailed time programme to the Engineer within 28 days after receiving the notice under Sub-Clause 8.1 [Commencement of Works]. (审查承包商施工计划)

13.1 Variations may be initiated by the Engineer at any time prior to issuing the Taking-Over Certificate for the Works. (指示变更)

8.3 The Contractor shall submit a revised programme to the Engineer in accordance with this Sub-Clause. (要求修改施工计划)

12.3 The Engineer shall proceed in accordance with Sub-Clause 3.5 [Determinations] to agree or determine the Contract Price by evaluating each item of work. (对变更估价)

14.4 The Engineer may proceed in accordance with Sub-Clause 3.5 [Determinations] to agree or determine revised instalments. (审查承包商流动资金使用计划)

12.3 The Engineershall determine a provisional rate or price for the purposes of Interim Payment Certificates. (确定变更单价)

4.3 The Contractor shall, prior to the Commencement Date, submit to the Engineer for consent the name and particulars of the person the Contractor proposes to appoint as Contractor's Representative. (批准承包商驻地代表)

20.1 The Engineer may monitor the record-keeping and/or instruct the Contractor to keep further contemporary records. (审查承包商索赔证据)

6.9 The Engineer may require the Contractor to remove (or cause to be removed) any person employed on the Site or Works, including the Contractor's Representative if applicable. (审查承包商现场工作人员工作,要求承包商撤换)

4.17 The Contractor shall not remove from the Site any major items of Contractor's Equipment without the consent of the Engineer. (控制承包商设备、材料、临时工程运离现场)

4.7 The Contractor shall set out the Works in relation to original points, lines and levels of reference specified in the Contract or notified by the Engineer. (检查放线工作)

12.1 Whenever the Engineer requires any part of the Works to be measured, reasonable notice shall be given to the Contractor's Representative. (计算工程量)

13.1 Variations may be initiated by the Engineer at any time prior to issuing the Taking-Over Certificate for the Works. (指示变更)

14.1 The Contractor shall submit to the Engineer, within 28 days after the Commencement Date, a proposed breakdown of each lump sum price in the Schedules. (审查总价项目的分解)

4.8 4.18 4.22 Enquire the Contractor to ensure the safety of the site. (要求承包商保证现场安全)

13.5 Each Provisional Sum shall only be used, in whole or in part, in accordance with the Engineer's instructions. (控制暂定金额的使用)

5.4 Before issuing a Payment Certificate, the Engineer may request the Contractor to supply reasonable evidence that the nominated Subcontractor has received all amounts. (审查承包商对分包商的付款)

17.4 The Contractor shall promptly give notice to the Engineer and shall rectify this loss or damage to the extent required by the Engineer. (要求承包商弥补特殊风险造成的损失损害)

14.3 The Contractor shall submit a Statement in six copies to the Engineer after the end of each month. (确定承包商月报表格式,审查月报表)

4.24 The Contractor shall, upon discovery of any such finding, promptly give notice to the Engineer. (指示承包商处理化石等)

14.6 Thereafter, the Engineer shall, within 28 days after receiving a Statement and supporting documents, issue to the Employer an Interim Payment Certificate. (签发付款证书)

4.16 The Contractor shall give the Engineer not less than 21 days' notice of the date on which any Plant or a major item of other Goods will be delivered to the Site. (决定运输过程中承包商的责任)

14.9 When the Taking-Over Certificate has been issued for the Works, the first half of the Retention Money shall be certified by the Engineer for payment to the Contractor. (签发退还保留金证明)

4.6 The Contractor shall, as specified in the Contract or as instructed by the Engineer, allow appropriate opportunities for carrying out work to. (要求承包商为他人提供方便)

14.6 The Engineer may in any Payment Certificate make any correction or modification that should properly be made to any previous Payment Certificate. (修改以前付款证书)

4.23 The Contractor shall confine his operations to the Site, and to any additional areas which may be obtained by the Contractor and agreed by the Engineer as workingareas. (检查竣工时现场清理)

14.10 Within 84 days after receiving the Taking-Over Certificate for the Works, the Contractor shall submit to the Engineer six copies of a Statement at completion. (审查承包商竣工财务报告)

6.10 The Contractor shall submit, to the Engineer, details showing the number of each class of Contractor's Personnel and of each type of Contractor's Equipment on the Site. (审查承包商劳务和施工设备报表)

14.1 Within 56 days after receiving the Performance Certificate, the Contractor shall submit, to the Engineer, six copies of a draft final statement. (审查承包商最后财务报告)

14.13 The Engineer shall issue, to the Employer, the Final Payment Certificate. (签发最后证书)

7.4 Testing

The Engineer may, under Clause 13 [Variations and Adjustments], vary the location or details of specified tests, or instruct the Contractor to carry out additional tests. (指示承包商进行合同未规定的检验和试验)

11.9 Performance Certificate

The Engineer shall issue the Performance Certificate within 28 days after the latest ofthe expiry dates of the Defects Notification Periods. (签发解除缺陷责任证书)

7.3 Inspection

The Contractor shall give notice to the Engineer whenever any work is ready and before it is covered up, put out of sight, or packaged for storage or transport. The Engineer shall then either carry out the examination, inspection, measurement or testing without unreasonable delay, or promptly give notice to the Contractor that the Engineer does not require to do so. (检查承包商施工作业)

15.3 Valuation at Date of Termination

As soon as practicable after a notice of termination under Sub-Clause 15.2 [Termination by Employer] has taken effect, the Engineer shall proceed in accordance with Sub-Clause 3.5 [Determinations] to agree or determine the value of the Works. (在合同终止时对工程估价)

7.5 Rejection

If, as a result of an examination, inspection, measurement or testing, any Plant, Materials or workmanship is found to be defective or otherwise not in accordance with the Contract, the Engineer may reject the Plant, Materials or workmanship by giving notice to the Contractor, with reasons. (拒绝材料和设备)

7.6 Remedial Work

Notwithstanding any previous test or certification, the Engineer may instruct the Contractor to：

(c) execute any work. (确定应进行的紧急补救工作)

3.2 Delegation by the Engineer

The Engineer may from time to time assign duties and delegate authority to assistants, and may also revoke such assignment or delegation. (委派独立检验单位)

17.4 Consequences of Employer's Risks

If and to the extent that any of the risks listed in Sub-Clause 17.3 above results in loss or damage to the Works, Goods or Contractor's Documents, the Contractor shall promptly give notice to the Engineer and shall rectify this loss or damage to the extent required by the Engineer. (确定特殊风险对工程的损害,附加费用)

7.6 Remedial Work

Notwithstanding any previous test or certification, the Engineer may instruct the Contractor to：

(a) remove from the Site (b) remove and re-execute any other work. (指示运走不合格材料、设备和工程)

17.4 Consequences of Employer's Risks

If the Contractor suffers delay and/or incurs Cost from rectifying this loss or damage, the Contractor shall give a further notice to the Engineer and shall be entitled subject to Sub-Clause 20.1 [Contractor's Claims]. (确定由特殊风险引起的费用增加)

8.8 Suspension of Work

The Engineer may at any time instruct the Contractor to suspend progress of part or all of the Works. The Engineer may also notify the cause for the suspension. (暂时停工)

20.1 Contractor's Claim

Within 42 days after receiving a claim or any further particulars supporting a previous claim, or within such other period as may be proposed by the Engineer and approved by the Contractor, the Engineer shall respond with approval, or with disapproval and detailed comments. He may also request any necessary further particulars, but shall nevertheless give his response on the principles of the claim within such time. (充当准仲裁人)

8.9 Consequences of Suspension

The Contractor shall give notice to the Engineer and shall be entitled subject to Sub-Clause 20.1 [Contractor's Claims] to：

(a) an extension of time for any such delay, if completion is or will be delayed, under Sub-Clause 8.4 [Extension of Time for Completion]；

(b) payment of any such Cost, which shall be included in the Contract Price. (决定对承包商

的补偿）

16 Suspension and Termination by Contractor

If the Contractor suffers delay and/or incurs Cost as a result of suspending work（or reducing the rate of work）in accordance with this Sub-Clause, the Contractor shall give notice to the Engineer and shall be entitled subject to Sub-Clause 20. 1［Contractor's Claims］to：

（a）an extension of time for any such delay, if completion is or will be delayed,under Sub-Clause 8. 4［Extension of Time for Completion］；

（b）payment of any such Cost plus reasonable profit, which shall be included in the Contract Price.（承包商中断工程时决定延期和追加费用）

8. 11 Prolonged Suspension

If the suspension under Sub-Clause 8. 8［Suspension of Work］has continued for more than 84 days, the Contractor may request the Engineer's permission to proceed.（发出复工命令）

13. 7 Adjustments for Changes in Legislation

If the Contractor suffers（or will suffer）delay and/or incurs（or will incur）additional Cost as a result of these changes in the Laws or in such interpretations, made after the Base Date, the Contractor shall give notice to the Engineer and shall be entitled subject to Sub-Clause 20. 1 ［Contractor's Claims］to：

（a）an extension of time for any such delay, if completion is or will be delayed,under Sub-Clause 8. 4［Extension of Time for Completion］；

（b）payment of any such Cost, which shall be included in the Contract Price.

13. 8 Adjustments for Changes in Cos

The cost indices or reference prices stated in the table of adjustment data shall be used. If their source is in doubt, it shall be determined by the Engineer.

Until such time as each current cost index is available, the Engineer shall determine aprovisional index for the issue of Interim Payment Certificates.（由于后继法规变化,确定费用变化）

Ⅲ　Limits of the exercises of the Engineer's duties exposed by the FIDIC Contract Conditions

（1）The Employer's agreement and approval are the prerequisite for the Engineer to exercise his duties and authority.（有些问题要征得业主同意和批准）

3. 1 Except as otherwise stated in these Conditions：

（a）whenever carrying out duties or exercising authority, specified in or implied by the Contract, the Engineer shall be deemed to act for the Employer；

（b）the Engineer has no authority to relieve either Party of any duties, obligations or responsibilities under the Contract；

（c）any approval, check, certificate, consent, examination, inspection, instruction, notice, proposal, request, test, or similar act by the Engineer（including absence of disapproval）shall not relieve the Contractor from any responsibility he has under the Contract, including responsibility for errors, omissions, discrepancies and non-compliances. (refer to 3.1)

(2)Before making determinations, the Engineer needs to negotiate with the Contractor. (有些问题要在决定之前同业主与承包商协商,见第 4.12, 7.4, 7.3, 7.6, 8.9, 8.4, 20.1, 11.4, 11, 12.3)

4.12 The Engineer may take account of any evidence of the physical conditions foreseen by the Contractor when submitting the Tender, which may be made available by the Contractor, but shall not be bound by any such evidence.

11.4 If the Contractor fails to remedy the defect or damage by this notified date and this remedial work was to be executed at the cost of the Contractor under Sub-Clause 11.2 [Cost of Remedying Defects], the Employer may (at his option):

(b)require the Engineer to agree or determine a reasonable reduction in the Contract Price in accordance with Sub-Clause 3.5 [Determinations].

(3)For each single unforeseeable event, the Employer and the Contractor shall be responsible for their own risks as stipulated in the Contract conditions and claim for compensations according to the procedures and rates prescribed. (对于几乎每一种可能发生的不测事件,都明确规定了业主与承包商各自的风险,以及一方可以向另一方提出索赔的条件。有一对一解决业主与承包商纠纷的具体规定。)

(4)The conditions leave no ambiguity and misunderstanding as to the specific claim requirement, speed of project progress, calculation of project installments. (按照详细具体的索赔条款,每一工程进展的速度,经测算已完的工程量需要支付的款项都有明确规定,不留含混之处。)

(5)Unless expressly stipulated in the contract, the Contractor shall not be responsible for the design of Plant. (除非合同明文规定,承包商不对永久工程的设计负责,其责任仅限于营造别人设计的工程。)

(6)Engineer's ethic standard. (工程师职业道德)

(7)20.6 Arbitration

The arbitrator(s) shall have full power to open up, review and revise any certificate, determination, instruction, opinion or valuation of the Engineer, and any decision of the DAB, relevant to the dispute. Nothing shall disqualify the Engineer from being called as a witness and giving evidence before the arbitrator(s) on any matter whatsoever relevant to the dispute. (国际仲裁是反对工程师决定的最后手段。)

(8)Market competition. (市场竞争)

Coursework

1. Thesis about 200 words, trying to describe the role of the engineer in the contract conditions.

2. Discuss the limits of authorized power by the contact to the Engineer.

Appendix 1　The contractor's contractual liabilities and rights

(1) The most important contractual obligations of the Contractor

①project type: B. Q. , specification and drawings (deliverable);

工程范围:工程量表、规范图纸(可交付成果);

②process type: design, construction, completion, maintenance;

项目过程范围:设计、施工、竣工、保修责任;

The Contractor shall provide all necessary superintendence, labor, materials, work equipment and other goods in order to fulfill the obligations as stated above, and delegate to the site according to the requirements of the Engineer his representative to supervise the whole process the project and any other personnel necessary to fulfill his contractual obligations.

应为完成上述责任提供所需要的工程(包括永久性的和临时性的)的监督、劳务、材料、工程设备以及其它物品。按工程师的要求向施工现场派遣授权的代表监督工程实施,提供完成他的合同责任所必需的各种人员。

③other obligations. (environment, insurance, performance guarantee, risk related, etc.)

The Contractor shall be abiding by the contract unless impermissible in law or otherwise unenforceable.

除法律上不允许或实际上不可能做到以外,承包商应严格按合同实施工程。

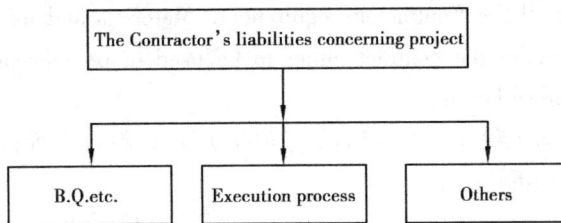

```
┌─────────────────────────────────────────────────┐
│ The Contractor's liabilities concerning project  │
└─────────────────────────────────────────────────┘
        │               │               │
        ▼               ▼               ▼
┌────────────┐  ┌────────────────┐  ┌────────────┐
│  B.Q.etc.  │  │Execution process│  │   Others   │
└────────────┘  └────────────────┘  └────────────┘
```

(2) Foundermental obligations

①make interpretations on all relevant data in the Employer's possession on sub-surface and hydrological conditions at the Site.

承包商对业主提供的水文和地表以下情况的资料解释负责。

②be responsible for environmental survey.

承包商对环境调查负责。

③to determine the construction scheme, and be responsible for the comprehensiveness, stability and safety of all relevant site works and the construction scheme.

承包商决定施工方法,并对所有现场作业和施工方法的完备、稳定和安全负全部责任。

④besides, the Contractor shall also be responsible for the accuracy and comprehensiveness of the costs and quotations stated in the Letter of Tender and the Bill of Quantities. He is deemed to have completely accepted the adaptability and sufficiency of the agreed contract price.

在上述基础上,承包商应对投标书以及工程量表中所作出的各项费用和报价的正确性和完备性负责。承包商被认为对双方约定的合同价款的适宜性和充分性已完全理解。

While as to the risks which shall be undertaken by the Contractor for the above obligations, the limit shall be within the practicable scope of time and costs.

但承包商对上述各方面所承担的风险程度,应限于在时间和费用方面实际可行的范围内。

The Contractor is not encouraged to conduct the things above with too much stakes. The risks he has to undertake shall be relevant to and also be covered by the time (from the obtaining of the Letter of Tender to the completion of tendering) and incurred costs he spent before the tendering. It's unrealistic for the Contractor to spend a large amount of expenditure to conduct detailed environmental survey (i. e. archeological exploration), let not to say, devised plan and implementation scheme.

考虑让承包商承担上述风险但不能让他冒险。他承担的风险的程度应与他在投标前所有的做标时间(从获得标书到投标截止)和可能的费用相关。承包商在合同签订前不可能花很多费用作十分详细的环境调查(如作地质勘探)、作精细的计划和实施方案。

(3) All the activities and behavior of the Contractor shall be abiding by the applicable laws and regulations, so as to ensure that the Employer will be exempted from all relevant liabilities.

承包商的一切工程活动和行为都应遵守所有适用的法律和各种规章制度,保证业主免于承担这方面的罚款和责任。

①the Contractor shall issue notice, pay taxes and incurred costs whatever in relevance to the implementation of the works and remedy of defects and enquire all necessary license.

对于实施、完成工程施工和修补缺陷工作中涉及的法律事项,承包商应负责发出通知、支付税款和费用,并获得所需要的许可。

②be responsible for all the Contractor's equipment. Materials and infringed equipment patent and other rights entitled under the contract either to be used or be relevant to the works, and all claims and jurisdictions arose herein.

负责工程所用的或与工程有关的任何承包商的设备、材料或工程设备侵犯专利和其它方权利而引起的一切索赔和诉讼。

③to undertake all tonnage dues of various materials and royalties, rents and other costs in relevant to the works.

承担工程用的各种材料的一切吨位费、矿区使用费、租金以及其它费用。

④to be responsible for all the formalities and costs in relevance to custom clearance, imp. & exp. permits, storage at the harbors of his own equipment, materials and other goods.

承包商负责他自己的设备、材料和其它物品的有关海关结关,进出口许可,港口储存等方面的手续和费用。

⑤to undertake all expenditures needed in order to obtain special or temporary accesses to and from the site, to provide at his afford the additional equipment used out of the site, the reconstruction or reinforcement of roads and bridges on the way to and from the site.

负担取得进出现场所需专用或临时道路通行权的一切费用和开支,自费提供他所需要的供施工使用的位于现场以外的附加设施,对通往现场,或位于通往现场道路上的桥梁加固或道路的改建负责。

⑥to keep the confidentialities of the works. Without the prior agreement of the Employer, the Contractor is not allowed to release any information related to the works, either by publishing commercial or technical dissertation or in other circumstances.

对工程有保密义务。没有业主事先同意,承包商不得在任何商业或技术论文或其他场合发表,或透露工程的任何细节。

(4)Unless otherwise stated in the Contract, two copies of the Contract and of each subsequent Drawing shall be supplied to the Contractor, who may make or request further copies at the cost of the Contractor.

承包商有权免费从业主处获得合同及每份后续图纸的两份复印件,如需要更多,则由承包商支付费用。(1.8)

Unless otherwise stated in the Contract, the Contractor shall supply to the Engineer six copies of each of the Contractor's Documents. The Contractor shall keep, on the Site, a copy of the Contract, publications named in the Specification, the Contractor's Documents (if any), the Drawings and Variations and other communications given under the Contract. The Employer's Personnel shall have the right of access to all these documents at all reasonable times.

承包商应向工程师提供6份承包商的所有文件的复印件,并在现场保留一份合同的复印件以供业主的人员使用。(1.8)

If a Party (the Contractor) becomes aware of an error or defect of a technical nature in a document which was prepared for use in executing the Works, the Party (the Contractor) shall promptly give notice to the other Party (the Employer) of such error or defect.

如果承包商在用于施工的文件中发现了技术错误或缺陷,应立即通知业主。(1.8)

As between the Parties, the Contractor shall retain the copyright and other intellectual property rights in the Contractor's Documents and other design documents made by (or on behalf of) the Contractor.

承包商对承包商的文件和其他由承包商编制的设计文件保留版权和其他知识产权。(1.10)

The Contractor may, at his cost, copy, use, and obtain communication of these documents for the purposes of the Contract. They shall not, without the Employer's consent, be copied, used or communicated to a third party by the Contractor, except as necessary for the purposes of the Contract.

承包商有权因合同之目的自费复印、使用、传输规范、图纸及业主编制的设计文件。但未经过业主同意,承包商不得因非合同目的为第三方复印、使用、传输上述文件。(1.11)

(5)The Contractor shall give notice to the Engineer and shall be entitled subject to Sub-Clause 20.1 [Contractor's Claims] to:

(a)an extension of time for any such delay, if completion is or will be delayed, under Sub-Clause 8.4 [Extension of Time for Completion];

(b)payment of any such Cost plus reasonable profit, which shall be included in the Contract Price.

承包商有权根据合同规定获得附加款项和(或)延长竣工时间两方面的索赔。(20.1,1.9,4.7等)

(6)If the Contractor suffers delay and/or incurs Cost as a result of a failure of the Engineer to issue the notified drawing or instruction within a time which is reasonable and is specified in the notice with supporting details, the Contractor shall give a further notice to the Engineer and shall be entitled subject to Sub-Clause 20.1［Contractor's Claims］to:

(a)an extension of time for any such delay, if completion is or will be delayed, under Sub-Clause 8.4［Extension of Time for Completion］;

(b)payment of any such Cost plus reasonable profit, which shall be included in the Contract Price.

如果由于非承包商的责任,工程师未能在合理时间内向承包商颁发图纸、指示,则承包商有权获得工期和费用补偿。(1.9)

(7)The Contractor shall disclose all such confidential and other information as the Engineer may reasonably require in order to verify the Contractor's compliance with the Contract.

承包商为证实自己遵守合同,应按工程师的要求透露其保密事项。(1.12)

(8)The Contractor shall give all notices, pay all taxes, duties and fees, and obtain all permits, licenses and approvals, as required by the Laws in relation to the execution and completion of the Works and the remedying of any defect.

对于实施、完成工程和修补缺陷工作中涉及的法律事项,承包商应负责发出通知、支付税款和费用,并获得所有许可。(1.13)

(9)If the Contractor constitutes (under applicable Laws) a joint venture, consortium or other unincorporated grouping of two or more person, these persons shall be deemed to be jointly and severally liable to the Employer for the performance of the Contract, the Contractor shall not alter its composition or legal status without the prior consent of the Employer.

当承包商是由两个或两个以上的当事人组成的联营体时,他们就合同的履行向业主承担共同与各自的责任,并且未经业主事先同意,不得改变其组成或法律地位。(1.14)

(10)The Contractor shall comply with the instructions given by the Engineer or delegated assistant, on any matter related to the Contract.

承包商仅应接受工程师或其助理的指示。(3.3)

(11)The Employer shall not replace the Engineer with a person against whom the Contractor raises reasonable objection by notice to the Employer, with supporting particulars.

如果承包商有充足理由反对业主更换工程师,则业主不得更换工程师。(3.4)

(12)The Contractor shall design (to the extent specified in the Contract), execute and complete the Works in accordance with the Contract and with the Engineer's instructions, and shall remedy any defects in the Works.

The Contractor shall provide the Plant and Contractor's Documents specified in the Contract, and all Contractor's Personnel, Goods, consumables and other things and services, whether of a temporary or permanent nature, required in and for this design, execution, completion and remedying of defects.

承包商应按照合同规定和工程师的指示对工程进行设计、施工、竣工和修补缺陷,并提供上述工作所需的永久设备、承包商的文件、承包商的人员、货物、消耗品等。(4.1)

The Contractor shall be responsible for the adequacy, stability and safety of all Site operations and of all methods of construction. Except to the extent specified in the Contract, the Contractor (i) shall be responsible for all Contractor's Documents, Temporary Works, and such design of each item of Plant and Materials as is required for the item to be in accordance with the Contract, and (ii) shall not otherwise be responsible for the design or specification of the Permanent Works.

承包商应就实施工程拟采用的方法和安排征得工程师的同意,并对所有现场作业和施工方法的完备性、稳定性负责。但对不由他负责的永久性工程的设计或规范不承担责任。(4.1)

If the Contract specifies that the Contractor shall design any part of the Permanent Works, then unless otherwise stated in the Particular Conditions: prior to the commencement of the Tests on Completion, the Contractor shall submit to the Engineer the "as-built" documents and operation and maintenance manuals in accordance with the Specification and in sufficient detail for the Employer to operate, maintain, dismantle, reassemble, adjust and repair this part of the Works.

对合同明文规定由承包商设计的部分永久性工程,承包商应按合同规定向工程师提交设计文件、竣工文件以及操作和维修手册。承包商对该部分工程负责。(4.1)

(13)The Contractor shall deliver the Performance Security to the Employer within 28 days after receiving the Letter of Acceptance, and shall send a copy to the Engineer. The Employer shall return the Performance Security to the Contractor within 21 days after receiving a copy of the Performance Certificate.

承包商在收到中标函后 28 天内,应按投标函附录中的规定,向业主提交一份履约保证。在承包商完成工程和竣工并修补缺陷前,履约保证应持续有效,并在履约证书颁发后 21 天退还承包商。(4.2)

(14)Unless the Contractor's Representative is named in the Contract, the Contractor shall, prior to the Commencement Date, submit to the Engineer for consent the name and particulars of the person the Contractor proposes to appoint as Contractor's Representative. The Contractor shall not, without the prior consent of the Engineer, revoke the appointment of the Contractor's Representative or appoint a replacement.

承包商代表的任命、撤换须征得工程师的事先同意。承包商代表的委托人的任命、撤换也须征得工程师的事先同意。(4.3)

Throughout the execution of the Works, and as long thereafter as is necessary to fulfill the Contractor's obligations, the Contractor shall provide all necessary superintendence to plan, arrange, direct, manage, inspect and test the work.

按工程师要求,承包商应提供对工程的必要监督人员。(6.8)

The Engineer may require the Contractor to remove (or cause to be removed) any person employed on the Site or Works, including the Contractor's Representative if applicable.

承包商应按工程师的要求,撤换工程师认为不合格的承包商的人员。(6.9)

The Contractor shall submit, to the Engineer, details showing the number of each class of Contractor's Personnel and of each type of Contractor's Equipment on the Site.

承包商每月应向工程师提交报告,说明在现场的承包商人员和设备情况。(6.10)

The Contractor shall at all times take all reasonable precautions to prevent any unlawful, riotous or disorderly conduct by or amongst the Contractor's Personnel, and to preserve peace and protection of persons and property on and near the Site.

承包商应采取各种预防措施,以防止其人员发生非法行为。(6.11)

(15)The Contractor shall not subcontract the whole of the Works.

承包商不得将整个工程分包出去。(4.4)

Unless otherwise stated in the Particular Conditions, the prior consent of the Engineer shall be obtained to other proposed:

Subcontractors:

①Material supplier;

②such subcontractor as being stated in the Contract. (4.4)

The Contractor shall be responsible for the acts or defaults of any Subcontractor, his agents or employees, as if they were the acts or defaults of the Contractor. (4.4)

除下述分包商以外,承包商的其余分包商的任命均须征得工程师的事先同意:

①材料供应商;

②合同中已注明的分包商。

承包商对分包商、分包商的代理人或雇员行为负全部责任。

(16)The Contractor shall set out the Works in relation to original points, lines and levels of reference specified in the Contract or notified by the Engineer. The Contractor shall be responsible for the correct positioning of all parts of the Works, and shall rectify any error in the positions, levels, dimensions or alignment of the Works.

承包商应根据合同规定的或工程师通知的参照项目对工程进行放线。承包商应对工程的正确定位负责,并矫正工程定位中的错误。

The Employer shall be responsible for any errors in these specified or notified items of reference, but the Contractor shall use reasonable efforts to verify their accuracy before they are used.

承包商不对参照项目的正确性负责,但他应在使用这些参照项目前付出努力去证实其准确性。(4.7)

(17)The Contractor shall:

①take care for the safety of all persons entitled to be on the Site;

②use reasonable efforts to keep the Site and Works clear of unnecessary obstruction so as to avoid danger to these persons;

③provide fencing, lighting, guarding and watching of the Works until completion and taking over under Clause 10 [Employer's Taking Over];

④provide any Temporary Works (including roadways, footways, guards and fences) which may be necessary, because of the execution of the Works, for the use and protection of the public and of owners and occupiers of adjacent land.

在整个合同实施过程中,承包商对现场人员安全、工程围护(围栏、照明、防护、看守)负责,并提供因工程实施而必需的临时工程(道路、人行道、防护及围栏)。(4.8)

(18)The Contractor shall institute a quality assurance system to demonstrate compliance with the requirements of the Contract.

承包商应按合同要求建立一套质量保证体系,并且遵守该体系不解除承包商的任何合同责任、义务。(4.9)

(19)The Contractor shall be responsible for interpreting all such data. To the extent which was practicable (taking account of cost and time), the Contractor shall be deemed to have obtained all necessary information as to risks, contingencies and other circumstances which may influence or affect the Tender or Works. To the same extent, the Contractor shall be deemed to have inspected and examined the Site, its surroundings, the above data and other available information, and to have been satisfied before submitting the Tender as to all relevant matters.

承包商对业主提供的水文和地表以下情况的资料的解释负责。承包商被认为在投标前已掌握了与工程有关的风险、意外事故及其他情况的全部资料,并且对现场及其周围环境等所有相关事宜感到满意。(4.10)

The Contractor shall be deemed to:

Have satisfied himself as to the correctness and sufficiency of the Accepted Contract Amount.

在此基础上,承包商被认为对接受的合同款额的适宜性和充分性已完全理解。(4.11)

(20)If the Contractor encounters adverse physical conditions which he considers to have been Unforeseeable, the Contractor shall give notice to the Engineer as soon as practicable. The Contractor shall continue executing the Works, using such proper and reasonable measures as are appropriate for the physical conditions. If and to the extent that the Contractor encounters physical conditions which are Unforeseeable, gives such a notice, and suffers delay and/or incurs Cost due to these conditions, the Contractor shall be entitled subject to Sub-Clause 20.1 [Contractor's Claims].

如果承包商遇到了在他看来是不可预见的外界条件,他应立即通知工程师,同时采取合理措施继续施工。如果经工程师确认此类条件确为不可预见的外界条件,则承包商有权获得工期和费用补偿。(4.12)

(21)The Contractor shall bear all costs and charges for special and/or temporary rights of-way which he may require, including those for access to the Site. The Contractor shall also obtain, at his risk and cost, any additional facilities outside the Site which he may require for the purposes of the Works.

承包商应自费获得他所需的道路通行权和现场以外的任何附加设施。(4.13)

(22)The Contractor shall be deemed to have been satisfied as to the suitability and availability of access routes to the Site. The Contractor shall use reasonable efforts to prevent any road or bridge from being damaged by the Contractor's traffic or by the Contractor's Personnel.

承包商应被认为对他选用的进场路线的适宜性和可用性满意,并维护这些道路、桥梁免受损坏负有责任。承包商应为使用这些路线取得有关部门的批准。(4.15)

(23)The Contractor shall give the Engineer not less than 21 days' notice of the date on which any Plant or a major item of other Goods will be delivered to the Site and the Contractor shall be responsible for packing, loading, transporting, receiving, unloading, storing and protecting all Goods and other things required for the Works.

承包商应在永久设备等主要货物运达现场前一合理时间通知工程师,并对工程所需所有货物从包装到保存的全过程负责。(4.16)

(24)The Contractor shall be responsible for all Contractors' Equipment. The Contractor shall not remove from the Site any major items of Contractor's Equipment without the consent of the Engineer.

承包商应对所有承包商的设备负责。所有承包商的设备一经运至现场,不经工程师同意不得移出现场,但运输工具除外。(4.17)

(25)The Contractor shall take all reasonable steps to protect the environment (both on and off the Site) and to limit damage and nuisance to people and property resulting from pollution, noise and other results of his operations.

The Contractor shall ensure that emissions, surface discharges and effluent from the Contractor's activities shall not exceed the values indicated in the Specification, and shall not exceed the values prescribed by applicable Laws.

承包商应采取合理措施保护现场内外的环境,限制其引起的污染、噪声等。承包商应保证他所产生的散发物、地面排水及排污不超过规范和法律中规定的较小值。(4.18)

(26)The Contractor shall be entitled to use for the purposes of the Works such supplies of electricity, water, gas and other services as may be available on the Site and of which details and prices are given in the Specification. The Contractor shall, at his risk and cost, provide any apparatus necessary for his use of these services and for measuring the quantities consumed.

为工程之目的,承包商有权享用现场供应的电、水、气及其他设施,但应向业主支付费用,并自费提供测量使用数量的仪器。(4.19)

(27)The Contractor shall be responsible for each item of Employer's Equipment whilst any of the Contractor's Personnel is operating it, driving it, directing it or in possession or control of it. The Contractor's obligations of inspection, care, custody and control shall not relieve the Employer of liability for any shortage, defect or default not apparent from a visual inspection.

当承包商使用业主的设备时,承包商应对业主的设备负责,并支付使用费用。承包商不对业主免费提供的材料的短缺、缺陷或损坏负责。(4.20)

(28)The Contractor shall submit a detailed time program to the Engineer within 28 days after receiving the notice under Sub-Clause 8.1 [Commencement of Works]. The Contractor shall also submit a revised program whenever the previous program is inconsistent with actual progress or with the Contractor's obligations. Unless otherwise stated in the Particular Conditions, monthly progress reports shall be prepared by the Contractor and submitted to the Engineer in six copies. If, at any time:

①actual progress is too slow to complete within the Time for Completion, and/or

②progress has fallen (or will fall) behind the current program under Sub-Clause 8.3 [Program], then the Engineer may instruct the Contractor to submit, under Sub-Clause 8.3

[Program], a revised program and supporting report describing the revised methods which the Contractor proposes to adopt in order to expedite progress and complete within the Time for Completion Goods, at the risk and cost of the Contractor.

承包商应在接到开工通知后 28 天内向工程师提交进度计划,承包商应按工程师的要求修改进度计划(如果有必要)。(8.3)

承包商每月应向工程师提交月进度报告的 6 份副本。(4.21)

如果实际进度落后于计划进度或竣工时间将被延误,则承包商应按工程师的要求采取赶工措施,并自付费用。(8.6)

(29)The Contractor shall keep Site clear during the execution of the Works. Upon the issue of a Taking-Over Certificate, the Contractor shall remove from the Site all Contractor's Equipment, surplus material, wreckage, rubbish and Temporary Works. However, the Contractor may retain on Site, during the Defects Notification Period, such Goods as are required for the Contractor to fulfill obligations under the Contract.

在工程实施期间,承包商应保持现场清洁。在工程接收证书颁发后,承包商应立即从现场清运走所有承包商的设备、剩余材料、残物、垃圾和临时工程。承包商可以在现场保留为履行缺陷通知期义务所需的货物。(4.23)

(30)All fossils, coins, articles of value or antiquity, and structures and other remains or items of geological or archaeological interest found on the Site shall be placed under the care and authority of the Employer. The Contractor shall take reasonable precautions to prevent Contractor's Personnel or other persons from removing or damaging any of these findings.

在工程现场发现的所有化石、硬币等遗迹或有价值的物品等应处于业主的看管和权力之下。一旦发现此类物品,承包商应立即通知工程师,并采取措施防止承包商的人员移动或损坏这些发现物。(4.24)

(31)The Contractor shall not be under any obligation to employ a nominated Subcontractor against whom the Contractor raises reasonable objection by notice to the Engineer as soon as practicable, with supporting particulars.

承包商没有义务雇用一名他已向工程师说明理由拒绝雇用的指定分包商。(5.2)

The Contractor shall pay to the nominated Subcontractor the amounts which the Engineer certifies to be due in accordance with the subcontract. Before issuing a Payment Certificate which includes an amount payable to a nominated Subcontractor, the Engineer may request the Contractor to supply reasonable evidence that the nominated Subcontractor has received all amounts due in accordance with previous Payment Certificates, less applicable deductions for retention or otherwise.

如果雇用指定分包商,则承包商应按合同规定向指定分包商支付工程款(5.3),并且在工程师颁发支付证书前,出示已向指定分包商付款的证明或拒绝付款、扣留付款的证据。(5.4)

(32)Except as otherwise stated in the Specification, the Contractor shall make arrangements for the engagement of all staff and labour, local or otherwise, and for their payment, housing, feeding and transport.

除规范另有规定外,承包商对其所有职员和劳工的雇用、报酬、住房、膳食和交通负责。(6.1)

The Contractor shall pay rates of wages, and observe conditions of labour, which are not lower than those established for the trade or industry where the work is carried out.

承包商采用的工资标准和劳动条件应不低于其所从事工作的地区同类工商业的现行标准。(6.2)

The Contractor shall comply with all the relevant labour Laws applicable to the Contractor's Personnel. The Contractor shall require his employees to obey all applicable Laws, including those concerning safety at work.

承包商应遵守所有适用于承包商的人员的劳动法,承包商的雇员应遵守所有适用的法律。(6.4)

No work shall be carried out on the Site on locally recognised days of rest, or outside the normal working hours stated in the Appendix to Tender.

承包商工作时间应符合合同的规定或取得工程师的同意。(6.5)

The Contractor shall not permit any of the Contractor's Personnel to maintain any temporary or permanent living quarters within the structures forming part of the Permanent Works.

承包商不得允许承包商的人员居住在永久工程内。(6.6)

The Contractor shall at all times take all reasonable precautions to maintain the health and safety of the Contractor's Personnel. The Contractor shall appoint an accident prevention officer at the Site, responsible for maintaining safety and protection against accidents.

承包商应采取合理的预防措施维护其人员的健康和安全,并在现场指派一名事故预防官员维持安全防止事故发生。(6.7)

(33) The Contractor shall submit the following samples of Materials, and relevant information, to the Engineer for consent prior to using the Materials in or for the Works.

承包商应按工程师的要求提供有关材料的样本。(7.2)

The Contractor shall give the Employer's Personnel full opportunity to carry out these activities, including providing access, facilities, permissions and safety equipment.

承包商应为业主的人员在一切合理时间内进入现场、自然材料的获得场所以及对永久设备和材料进行审查,提供一切机会,包括通道、设施、许可及安全装备。(7.3)

The Contractor shall provide all apparatus, assistance, documents and other information, electricity, equipment, fuel, consumables, instruments, labour, materials, and suitably qualified and experienced staff, as are necessary to carry out the specified tests efficiently. The Contractor shall agree, with the Engineer, the time and place for the specified testing of any Plant, Materials and other parts of the Works.

承包商应与工程师商定对永久设备、材料和工程进行检查的时间和地点,并为检验提供所需的物品和人员。(7.4)

The Contractor shall then promptly make good the defect and ensure that the rejected item complies with the Contract.

对于不符合合同规定被工程师拒收的永久设备、材料、工艺,承包商应立即使之符合合同的规定。(7.5)

The Engineer may instruct the Contractor to:

①remove from the Site and replace any Plant or Materials which is not in accordance with the Contract;

②remove and re-execute any other work which is not in accordance with the Contract.

承包商应执行工程师的指示,把工程师认为不符合合同规定的永久设备或材料从现场移走并替换;把不符合合同规定的工程移走并重建。(7.6)

(34) Unless otherwise stated in the Specification, the Contractor shall pay all royalties, rents and other payments for: natural Materials obtained from outside the Site.

除非规范中另有规定,否则承包商对相关材料应支付矿区使用费、租金或其他费用。(7.8)

(35) The Contractor shall commence the execution of the Works as soon as is reasonably practicable after the Commencement Date, and shall then proceed with the Works with due expedition and without delay.

承包商应在工程师通知的开工日期后尽快开始施工,随后应迅速且毫不拖延地进行施工。(8.1)

(36) The Engineer may at any time instruct the Contractor to suspend progress of part or all of the Works. During such suspension, the Contractor shall protect, store and secure such part or the Works against any deterioration, loss or damage.

承包商应按工程师的指示随时暂停部分或全部工程。暂停期间,承包商应保护、保管以及保障该部分或全部工程免遭任何损失。(8.8)

If the Contractor suffers delay and/or incurs Cost from complying with the Engineer's instructions under Sub-Clause 8. 8 [Suspension of Work] and/or from resuming the work, the Contractor shall give notice to the Engineer and shall be entitled subject to Sub-Clause 20. 1 [Contractor's Claims].

对于非承包商责任引起的暂停,承包商有权获得工期、费用补偿。(8.9)

The Contractor shall be entitled to payment of the value (as at the date of suspension) of Plant and/or Materials which have not been delivered to Site, if:

①the work on Plant or delivery of Plant and/or Materials has been suspended for more than 28 days;

②the Contractor has marked the Plant and/or Materials as the Employer's property in accordance with the Engineer's instructions.

暂停期间,如果有关永久设备、材料的工作暂停已超过28天,并且承包商已根据工程师的指示将其标记为业主的财产,则承包商有权获得此类永久设备、材料的支付。(8.10)

If the suspension under Sub-Clause 8. 8 [Suspension of Work] has continued for more than 84 days, the Contractor may request the Engineer's permission to proceed. If the Engineer does not give permission within 28 days after being requested to do so, the Contractor may, by giving notice to the Engineer, treat the suspension as an omission under Clause 13 [Variations and Adjustments] of the affected part of the Works. If the suspension affects the whole of the Works, the Contractor may give notice of termination under Sub-Clause 16. 2 [Termination by Contractor].

如果上述暂停已持续84天以上,承包商可要求工程师同意继续施工,如果工程师未在28天内给予复工许可,则承包商可将暂停的工程作为变更中的删减。如果暂停的工程影响整个

工程,则承包商可提出终止合同。(8.11)

(37)The Contractor shall take full responsibility for the care of the Works and Goods from the Commencement Date until the Taking-Over Certificate is issued. The Contractor shall be liable for any loss or damage caused by any actions performed by the Contractor after a Taking-Over Certificate has been issued. The Contractor shall also be liable for any loss or damage which occurs after a Taking-Over Certificate has been issued and which arose from a previous event for which the Contractor was liable.

从工程开工日期至工程接收证书颁发前,承包商对工程的照管负全部责任。在此期间,承包商对非业主风险所致的工程、货物和承包商文件的损失负责,并自费弥补此类损失。(17.2)

(38)The Contractor shall indemnify and hold the Employer harmless against and from any other claim which arises out of or in relation to (i) the manufacture, use, sale or import of any Goods, or (ii) any design for which the Contractor is responsible.

承包商应保护业主,使其免遭由于不应由业主负责的情况所引起的对知识产权和工业产权的侵权,并保障业主对遭受的侵权进行索赔。(17.5)

(39)Neither Party shall be liable to the other Party for loss of use of any Works, loss of profit, loss of any contract or for any indirect or consequential loss or damage which may be suffered by the other Party in connection with the Contract, other than under Sub-Clause 16.4 [Payment on Termination] and Sub-Clause 17.1 [Indemnities].

承包商不向业主负责赔偿业主可能遭受的与合同有关的任何工程的使用损失、利润损失、任何其他合同损失,但由于承包商的欺诈行为、故意违约或管理不善导致的责任除外。(17.6)

(40)①The insuring Party shall insure the Works, Plant, Materials and Contractor's Documents for not less than the full reinstatement cost including the costs of demolition, removal of debris and professional fees and profit.

②The insuring Party shall insure the Contractor's Equipment for not less than the full replacement value, including delivery to Site.

③The insuring Party shall insure against each Party's liability for any loss, damage, death or bodily injury which may occur to any physical property or to any person.

承包商应根据合同的规定,以合同双方联合名义投保下列险别:

①工程、永久设备、材料及承包商的文件保险;(18.2)

②承包商的设备保险;(18.2)

③第三方责任险。(18.3)

The Contractor shall effect and maintain insurance against liability for claims, damages, losses and expenses (including legal fees and expenses) arising from injury, sickness, disease or death of any person employed by the Contractor or any other of the Contractor's Personnel.

承包商还应投保承包商的人员保险(包括业主和工程师)。(18.4)

Wherever the Contractor is the insuring Party, each insurance shall be effected with insurers and in terms approved by the Employer.

承包商应按业主批准的承保人及条件办理保险。(18.1)

The relevant insuring Party shall, within the respective periods stated in the Appendix to Tender

(calculated from the Commencement Date) , submit to the other Party:

①evidence that the insurances described in this Clause have been effected;

②copies of the policies for the insurances described in Sub-Clause 18.2 [Insurance for Works and Contractor's Equipment] and Sub-Clause 18.3 [Insurance against Injury to Persons and Damage to Property].

承包商应在投标函附录中规定的期限内,向业主提交保险已生效的证明,并在支付每笔保险费后,将支付证明提交给业主,同时通知工程师。

If the insuring Party fails to effect and keep in force any of the insurances it is required to effect and maintain under the Contract, or fails to provide satisfactory evidence and copies of policies in accordance with this Sub-Clause, the other Party may (at its option and without prejudice to any other right or remedy) effect insurance for the relevant coverage and pay the premiums due. The insuring Party shall pay the amount of these premiums to the other Party, and the Contract Price shall be adjusted accordingly.

如果承包商未能按合同要求办理保险并使之保持有效,或者未能按合同要求提供令业主满意的证明和保险单副本,则业主可办理相应保险,但承包商应向业主支付保险费。(18.1)

Appendix 2   Claim provision list

I   Explicit claim provisions

Code	Sub-clause No.	Title of the sub-clause	Claim Package
1	1.9	Delayed Drawings or Instructions	C + P + T
2	2.1	Right of Access to the Site	C + P + T
3	3.3	Instructions of the Engineer	C + P + T
4	4.6	Co-operation	C + P + T
5	4.7	Setting Out	C + P + T
6	4.12	Unforeseeable Physical Conditions	C + T
7	4.24	Fossils	C + T
8	7.2	Samples	C + P
9	7.4	Testing	C + P + T
10	8.3	Programme	C + P + T
11	8.4	Extension of Time for Completion	T
12	8.5	Delays Caused by Authorities	T
13	8.8&8.9&8.11	Suspension of Work & Consequences of Suspension & Prolonged Suspension	C + T
14	9.2	Delayed Tests	C + P + T
15	10.2	Taking Over of Parts of the Works	C + P
16	10.3	Interference with Tests on Completion	C + P + T
17	11.2	Cost of Remedying Defects	C + P
18	11.6	Further Tests	C + P
19	11.8	Contractor to Search	C + P
20	12.4	Omissions	C
21	13.1	Right to Vary	C + P + T
22	13.2	Value Engineering	C

continued

Code	Sub-clause No.	Title of the sub-clause	Claim Package
23	13.5	Provisional Sums	C + P
24	13.7	Adjustments for Changes in Legislation	C + T
25	13.8	Adjustments for Changes in Cost	C
26	15.5	Employer's Entitlement to Termination	C + P
27	16.1	Contractor's Entitlement to Suspend Work	C + P + T
28	16.2&16.4	Termination by Contractor & Termination by Contractor	C + P
29	17.3&17.4	Employer's Risks & Consequences of Employer's Risks	C + P + T
30	17.5	Intellectual and Industrial Property Rights	C
31	18.1	General Requirements for Insurances	C
32	19.4	Consequences of Force Majeure	C + T
33	19.6	Optional Termination, Payment and Release	C
34	19.7	Release from Performance under the Law	C

II   Implicit Claim Provisions

Code	Sub-clause No.	Title of the sub-clause	Claim Package
1	1.3	Communications	C + P + T
2	1.5	Priority of Documents	C + T
3	1.8	Care and Supply of Documents	C + P + T
4	1.13	Compliance with Laws	C + P + T
5	2.3	Employer's Personnel	C + T
6	2.5	Employer's Claims	C
7	3.2	Delegation by the Engineer	C + P + T
8	4.2	Performance Security	C
9	4.10	Site Data	C + T
10	4.20	Employer's Equipment and Free-Issue Material	C + P + T
11	5.2	Objection to Nomination	C + T
12	7.3	Inspection	C + P + T
13	8.1	Commencement of Works	C + T

continued

Code	Sub-clause No.	Title of the sub-clause	Claim Package
14	8.12	Resumption of Work	C + P + T
15	12.1	Works to be Measured	C + P
16	12.3	Evaluation	C + P

Note: C-costs; P-profits; T-time.

Appendix 3   Counter-claim provision list

(1)4.2 Performance Security

The Employer shall not make a claim under the Performance Security, except for amounts to which the Employer is entitled under the Contract in the event of:

(a)failure by the Contractor to extend the validity of the Performance Security as described in the preceding paragraph, in which event the Employer may claim the full amount of the Performance Security.

第4.2 履约保函

(a)承包商未能按照上一段的说明,延长履约保证的有效期,此时雇主可对履约保证的全部金额进行索赔。

(2)4.14 Avoidance of Interference

The Contractor shall indemnify and hold the Employer harmless against and from alldamages, losses and expenses (including legal fees and expenses) resulting from any such unnecessary or improper interference.

4.14 避免干扰

承包商应保障并使雇主免于因上述不必要或不适当的干扰带来的后果而遭受的损害、损失和开支(包括法律费用和开支)。

(3)4.16 Transport of Goods

(c) The Contractor shall indemnify and hold the Employer harmless against and from all damages, losses and expenses (including legal fees and expenses) resulting from the transport of Goods, and shall negotiate and pay all claims arising from their transport.

4.16 货物的运输

(c)承包商应保障并使雇主免于因为货物运输的损坏而遭受损害、损失和开支(包括法律费用和开支),并应协商及支付由于运输所导致的索赔。

(4)5.4 Evidence of Payments

Then the Employer may (at his sole discretion) pay, direct to the nominated Subcontractor, part or all of such amounts previously certified (less applicabledeductions) as are due to the nominated Subcontractor and for which the Contractor has failed to submit the evidence described in sub-paragraphs (a) or (b) above. The Contractor shall then repay, to the Employer, the amount which the nominated Sub-contractor was directly paid by the Employer.

5.4 支付的证据

否则,雇主应(自行决定)直接向指定分包商支付部分或全部已被证实应支付给他的(适当地扣除保留金)并且承包商不能按照上述(a)、(b)段所述提供证据的那一项款额。承包商应向雇主偿还这笔由雇主直接支付给指定分包商的款额。

(5)7.5 Rejection

If the Engineer requires this Plant, Materials or workmanship to be retested, the testshall be repeated under the same terms and conditions. If the rejection and retestingcause the Employer to incur additional costs, the Contractor shall subject to Sub-Clause 2.5 [Employer's Claims] pay these costs to the Employer.

7.5 拒收

若工程师要求对此永久设备、材料或工艺再度进行检验,则检验应按相同条款和条件重新进行。如果此类拒收和再度检验致使雇主产生了附加费用,则承包商应按照第2.5款【雇主的索赔】的规定,向雇主支付这笔费用。

(6)7.6 Remedial Work

If the Contractor fails to comply with the instruction, the Employer shall be entitled to employ and pay other persons to carry out the work. Except to the extent that the Contractor would have been entitled to payment for the work, the Contractor shall subject to Sub-Clause 2.5 [Employer's Claims] pay to the Employer all costs arising from this failure.

7.6 补救工作

如果承包商未能遵守该指示,则雇主有权雇用其他人来实施工作,并予以支付。除非承包商有权获得此类工作的付款,否则他按照第2.5款【雇主的索赔】的规定,向雇主支付因其未完成工作而导致的费用。

(7)8.6 Rate of Progress

If these revised methods cause the Employer to incur additional costs, the Contractor shall subject to Sub-Clause 2.5 [Employer's Claims] pay these costs to the Employer, in addition to delay damages (if any) under Sub-Clause 8.7 below.

8.6 进展速度

如果这些修正方法导致雇主产生了附加费用,则除第8.7款中所述的误期损害赔偿费(如有时)外,承包商还应按第2.5款【雇主的索赔】的规定向雇主支付该笔附加费用。

(8)8.7 Delay Damages

If the Contractor fails to comply with Sub-Clause 8.2 [Time for Completion], the Contractor shall subject to Sub-Clause 2.5 [Employer's Claims] pay delay damages to the Employer for this default.

8.7 误期损害赔偿费

如果承包商未能遵守第8.2款【竣工时间】,承包商应依据第2.5款【雇主的索赔】为此违约向雇主支付误期损害赔偿费。

(9)9.2 Delayed Tests

If the Contractor fails to carry out the Tests on Completion within the period of 21 days, the Employer's Personnel may proceed with the Tests at the risk and cost of the Contractor.

9.2 延误的检验

若承包商未能在21天的期限内进行竣工检验,雇主的人员可着手进行此类检验,其风险和费用均由承包商承担。

（10）9.4 Failure to Pass Tests on Completion

（b）If the failure deprives the Employer of substantially the whole benefit of the Works or Section, reject the Works or Section (as the case may be), in which event the Employer shall have the same remedies as are provided in sub-paragraph (c) of Sub-Clause 11.4 〔Failure to Remedy Defects〕.

9.4 未能通过竣工试验

（b）如果由于该过失致使雇主基本上无法享用该工程或区段所带来的全部利益,拒收整个工程或区段（视情况而定）,在此情况下,雇主应获得与第 11.4 款【未能修补缺陷】(c)段中的规定相同的补偿。

（11）11.3 Extension of Defects Notification Period

The Employer shall be entitled subject to Sub-Clause 2.5 〔Employer's Claims〕to an extension of the Defects Notification Period for the Works or a Section if and to the extent that the Works, Section or a major item of Plant (as the case may be, and after taking over) cannot be used for the purposes for which they are intended by reason of a defect or damage. However, a Defects Notification Period shall not be extended by more than two years.

11.3 缺陷通知期的延长

如果且在一定程度上工程、区段或主要永久设备（视情况而定,并且在接收以后）由于缺陷或损害而不能按照预定的目的进行使用,则雇主有权依据第 2.5 款【雇主的索赔】要求延长工程或区段的缺陷通知期。但缺陷通知期的延长不得超过 2 年。

（12）11.4 Failure to Remedy Defects

If the Contractor fails to remedy the defect or damage by this notified date and this remedial work was to be executed at the cost of the Contractor under Sub-Clause 11.2 〔Cost of Remedying Defects〕, the Employer may (at his option):

（a）Carry out the work himself or by others, in a reasonable manner and at the Contractor's cost, but the Contractor shall have no responsibility for this work; and the Contractor shall subject to Sub-Clause 2.5 〔Employer's Claims〕 pay to the Employer the costs reasonably incurred by the Employer in remedying the defect or damage.

11.4 未能补救缺陷

如果承包商未能在某一合理时间内修补任何缺陷或损害,雇主（或雇主授权的他人）可确定一日期,规定在该日或该日之前修补缺陷或损害,并且应向承包商发出一合理的通知。如果承包商到该日期尚未修补好缺陷或损害,并且依据第 11.2 款【修补缺陷的费用】,这些修补工作应由承包商自费进行。

（13）11.11 Clearance of Site

If all these items have not been removed within 28 days after the Employ erreceives a copy of the Performance Certificate, the Employer may sell or otherwise dispose of any remaining items. The Employer shall be entitled to be paid the costs incurred in connection with, or attributable to, such sale or disposal and restoring the Site.

11.11 现场的清理

若在雇主接到履约证书副本后 28 天内上述物品还未被运走,则雇主可对此留下的任何物品予以出售或另作处理。雇主应有权获得为此类出售或处理及整理现场所发生的或有关的费用的支付。

(14)12.4 Omissions

Whenever the omission of any work forms part (or all) of a Variation, the value of which has not been agreed, if:

(a)the Contractor will incur (or has incurred) cost which, if the work had not been omitted, would have been deemed to be covered by a sum forming part of the Accepted Contract Amount.

12.4 省略

当对任何工作的省略构成部分(或全部)变更且对其价值未达成一致时,如果:

(a)承包商将招致(或已经招致)一笔费用,这笔费用应被视为是如果工作未被省略时,在构成部分接受的合同款额的一笔金额中所包含的。

(15)15.4 Payment after Termination

After a notice of termination under Sub-Clause 15.2 [Termination by Employer] has taken effect, the Employer may:

(a)proceed in accordance with Sub-Clause 2.5 [Employer's Claims];

(b)withhold further payments to the Contractor until the costs of execution, completion and remedying of any defects, damages for delay in completion (if any), and all other costs incurred by the Employer, have been established;

(c)recover from the Contractor any losses and damages incurred by the Employer and any extra costs of completing the Works, after allowing for any sum due to the Contractor under Sub-Clause.

15.4 终止后的支付

在根据第 15.2 款【雇主提出终止】发出的终止通知生效后,雇主可以:

(a)按照第 2.5 款【雇主的索赔】的要求执行;

(b)扣留向承包商支付的进一步款项,直至雇主确定了施工、竣工和修补任何工程缺陷的费用、误期损害赔偿费(如有时),以及雇主花费的所有其他费用;

(c)在考虑根据第 15.3 款【终止日期时的估价】应支付承包商的任何金额后,自承包商处收回雇主由此招致的任何损失以及为完成工程所导致的超支费用。在收回此类损失和超支费用后,雇主应向承包商支付任何结存金额。

(16)17.1 Indemnities

The Contractor shall indemnify and hold harmless the Employer, the Employer's Personnel, and their respective agents, against and from all claims, damages, losses and expenses (including legal fees and expenses) in respect of.

17.1 保障

承包商应保障和保护雇主、雇主的人员以及他们各自的代理人免遭与下述有关的一切索赔、损害、损失和开支(包括法律费用和开支)。

(17)18.1 General Requirements for Insurances

Payments by one Party to the other Party shall be subject to Sub-Clause 2.5 [Employer's

Claims] or Sub-Clause 20. 1 [Contractor's Claims], as applicable.

18.1 有关保险的总体要求

一方向另一方进行的支付必须遵循第 2.5 款【雇主的索赔】或第 20.1 款【承包商的索赔】（如适用）的规定。

(18)18.2 Insurance for Works and Contractor's Equipment

Unless otherwise stated in the Particular Conditions, insurances under this Sub-Clause:

(c) shall cover all loss and damage from any cause not listed in Sub-Clause 17. 3 [Employer's Risks].

18.2 工程和承包商的设备的保险

除非专用条件中另有规定,否则本款规定保险:

(c)应补偿除第 17.3 款【雇主的风险】所列雇主的风险之外的任何原因所导致的所有损失和损害。

Appendix 4　Definitions listed alphabetically

Appendix 5　Typical sequence of principal events during contracts for construction

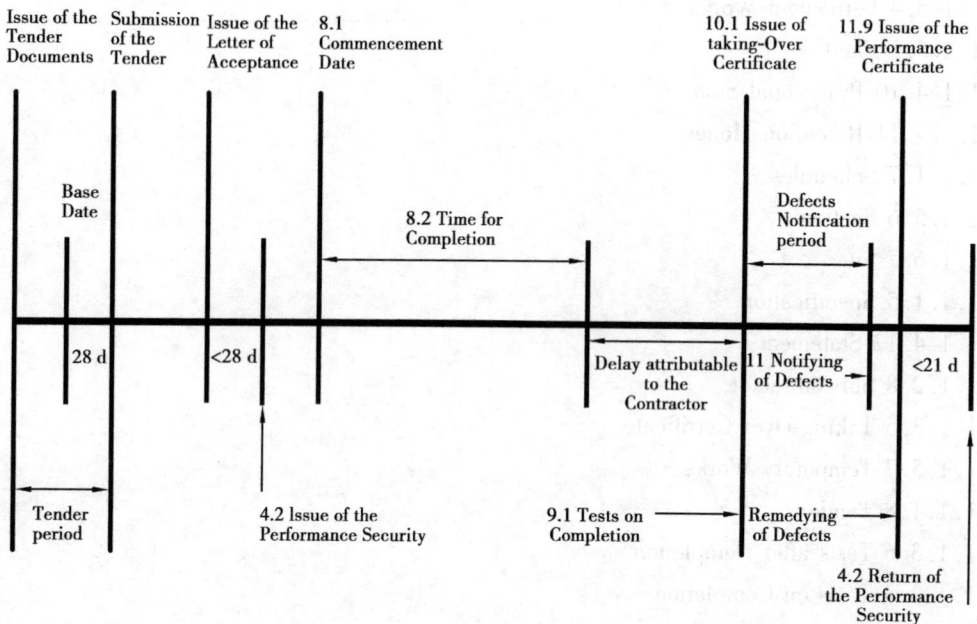

Typical sequence of Principal Events during Contracts for Construction

(1) The Time for Completion is to be stated (in the Appendix to Tender) as a number of days, to which is added any extensions of time under Sub-Clause 8. 4.

(2) In order to indicate the sequence of events, the above diagram is based upon the example of the Contractor failing to comply with Sub-Clause 8. 2.

(3) The Defects Notification Period is to be stated (in the Appendix to Tender) as a number of days, to which is added any extensions under Sub-Clause 11. 3.

14.3 Contractor
submits Statement
to the Engineer

14.6 Engineer
issues Interim
Payment Certificate

14.7 Employer makes
the payment to the
Contractor

Each of the
monthly(or
otherwise)
interim
payments

<56 d

<28 d

The final
payment

Engineer verifies
statement, Contractor
submits information

<28 d

<56 d

14.11 Contracror submits
draft final statement to the
Engineer

14.11 Contractor submits
Final Statement and the
14.12 discharge

14.13 Engineer issues
Final Payment
Certificate

14.7 Employer
makes payment

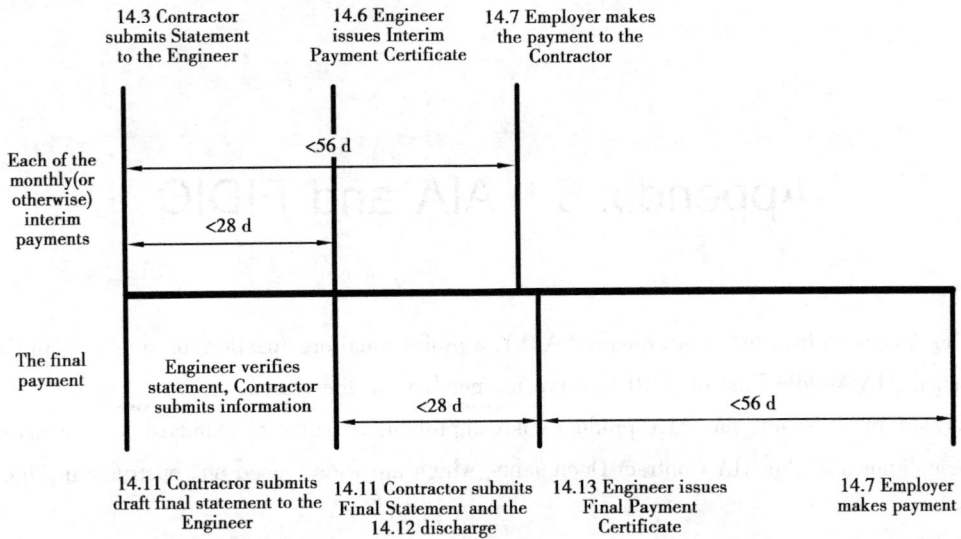

Typical sequence of Payment Events envisaged in Clause 14

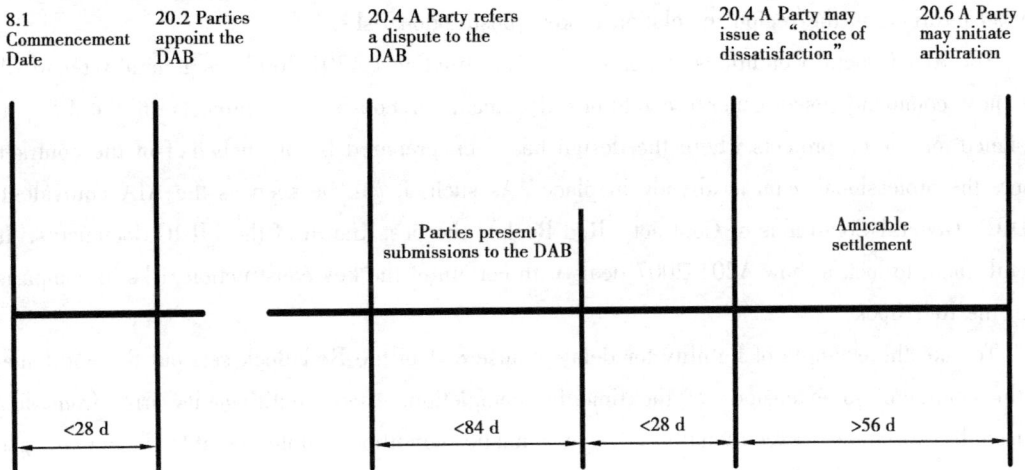

8.1
Commencement
Date

20.2 Parties
appoint the
DAB

20.4 A Party refers
a dispute to the
DAB

20.4 A Party may
issue a "notice of
dissatisfaction"

20.6 A Party
may initiate
arbitration

Parties present
submissions to the DAB

Amicable
settlement

<28 d

<84 d

<28 d

>56 d

Typical sequence of Dispute Events envisaged in Clause 20

Appendix 6   AIA and FIDIC

The American Institute of Architects (AIA), a professional organization for architects in the US, established AIA Middle East in 2010 to serve its members in the region.

As part of its remit, the AIA produces a comprehensive suite of standard form construction documents known as the AIA Contract Documents, which are widely used on construction projects in the US.

Despite their common usage in the US, the AIA Contract Documents are less well known in other international markets, particularly where the standard forms produced by the International Federation of Consulting Engineers (FIDIC) are in wide use. In order to promote their own documents, AIA members would have to show employers that the AIA forms are in line with current market positions in the region in relation to key construction risks.

The AIA General Conditions of Contract for Construction (A201-2007) is generally regarded as the most commonly used general conditions document on construction projects in the US. It is designed for use on projects where the design has been prepared by or on behalf of the contractor, where the professional team is already in place. As such, it can be seen as the AIA equivalent to FIDIC's General Conditions of Contract (Red Book), the best known of the FIDIC documents. It is useful, then, to look at how A201-2007 deals with certain of the key construction risks in comparison with the Red Book.

To take the example of liability for delay, clause 8.4 of the Red Book sets out the entitlements of the contractor to extensions of the time for completion. These entitlements arise from delays caused by variations, exceptionally adverse climatic conditions, unforeseeable labour or goods shortages caused by epidemic or government action and employer-caused delay. There are other entitlements enumerated throughout the remainder of the contract, including delays caused by failure to be granted access to the site and the occurrence of unforeseeable physical conditions.

Article 8.3.1 of A201-2007, on the other hand, sets out some arguably wider grounds for entitlement, including acts or neglect by the owner (as A201-2007 identifies the employer) and the architect (the contract administrator), causes beyond the contractor's control and other causes the architect determines justify delay. Employers used to the Red Book position may find these entitlements overly broad and seek to restrict them by way of amendment to the standard form.

A further point of difference emerges in the claims procedure. The claims procedure set out at clause 20.1 of the Red Book is generally considered to be onerous on the contractor. Notice of a claim must be given within 28 days of the date the contractor became, or should have become, aware of the relevant event. A further detailed claim must be made within 42 days of the same date. The submission of notice within 28 days is expressly set out as a condition precedent to entitlement under the claim. Depending on the applicable provisions of the governing law, this could lead to the contractor losing any entitlement to relief.

Article 15. 1 of A201-2007 sets out an arguably more "contractor-friendly" position; claims are required to be initiated within 21 days after the later of the date the event occurs or the date the contractor recognises it. The time limit is, therefore, based on the contractor's actual knowledge, rather than when it should have had such knowledge as in FIDIC. This requirement is not set out expressly as a condition precedent to a claim. In addition, Article 15. 1. 5. 1 states that, where an event has a continuing effect, only one claim is required. In such circumstances, the contractor under Clause 8 of the Red Book is required to submit monthly interim claims and a final claim within 28 days of the event ceasing.

参考文献

［1］田威. FIDIC 合同条件应用实务［M］. 2 版. 北京：中国建筑工业出版社，2009.

［2］陈新元. 工程项目管理：FIDIC 施工合同条件与应用案例［M］. 北京：中国水利水电出版社，2009.

［3］尼尔 G. 巴尼. FIDIC 系列工程合同范本——编制原理与应用指南［M］. 北京：中国建筑工业出版社，2009.

［4］国际咨询工程师联合会，中国工程咨询协会. 菲迪克（FIDIC）合同指南［M］. 北京：机械工业出版社，2003.

［5］张水波，何伯森. FIDIC 新版合同条件导读与解析［M］. 北京：中国建筑工业出版社，2008.

［6］王瑞玲，宋春叶.《FIDIC 施工合同条款》案例库的应用性研究［J］. 重庆科技学院学报，2011（16）：166-168.

［7］蒋仕琼，史银志. FIDIC 合同条件下公路施工承包商索赔案例分析［J］. 经管天地，2011（18）：35-37.

［8］王宏亮. FIDIC 合同条件下的一个三方合同问题的案例［J］. 四川水利发电，2005（2）：40-43.

［9］程建，张辉建，胡明. FIDIC 合同下的国际工程索赔管理——非洲某公路项目索赔案例实证分析［J］. 国际经济合作，2007（9）：59-62.

［10］王守清. 国际工程项目风险管理案例分析［J］. 施工企业管理，2006（234）：20-22.

［11］常乐，陆惠民. 基于 FIDIC99 的工程案例研究［J］. 山西建筑，2005（5）：37-39.

［12］夏论仁. 国际工程合同管理中灵活变通性思维案例分析［J］. 云南水利发电，2011，27（2）：121-123.

［13］陈志平，黄大乐. 国际项目合同变更索赔案例分析［J］. 华南港工，2007（4）：29-31.

［14］李卫东. 某指定分包工程合同管理及索赔案例浅析［J］. 福建建设科技，2008（1）：58-61.

［15］宋高丽. 透过案例看固定总价合同纠纷［J］. 建筑经济，2008（52）：47-49.

［16］韩周强，刘胜明，杨俊杰. 投标世行贷款项目应注意的细节及其建议——某世界银行贷款项目案例分析［J］. 建筑经济，2005（1）：27-30.

［17］A P Cotton, M Sohail, R E Scott. Towards improved labour standards for construction of minor works in low income countries［J］. Engineering, Construction and Architectural Management, 2005,12（6）：89-91.

［18］Blake David. Dispute resolution boards［J］. Contract Journal, 2007.

［19］Suryawanshi C S. Construction Claims their Basis Grounds［J］. Indian Highways Journal, 2009.

［20］Zhanglin Guo, Hua Zhang. Study of Natural Disasters Contract Conditions Based on the FIDIC Criteria［J］. Applied Mechanics and Materials, 2012(238):558-561.

［21］Zhen Wen, Qilan Zhou. Some Suggestions for China Construction Project Investment Control Present Situation Based on FIDIC Contract［J］. Applied Mechanics and Materials, 2012(209-211):1294-1297.

［22］Zhou Yihong, Tan Wei. Study on Construction Claim for International Project Based on Contract Status Analysis［J］. Applied Mechanics and Materials, 2012 (174-177): 3356-3359.